WISDOM BOWLS

Dedicated to all those who love.

7/16/05

To Mary Ann —

With love and Blessings

dear lady!

Fondly,

Meredith

ALSO BY MEREDITH YOUNG-SOWERS

Agartha: A Journey to the Stars (original & tenth anniversary editions)

Language of the Soul (workbook)

You Can Heal: Sound as Medicine (audio)

Spiritual Crisis

Angelic Messenger Cards

Teachings from the Angelic Messenger Cards

Heal Your Life and Honor Your Soul's Intention

■

For information about The Stillpoint School of Advanced Energy Healing and for workshops by the author, write or call:

The Stillpoint Institute
22 Stillpoint Lane
P.O. Box 640
Walpole, NH 03608, USA
603-756-9281 or 1-800-847-4014
or visit: *www.stillpoint.org* or
www.wisdombowls.com

WISDOM
BOWLS

Overcoming Fear and Coming Home
To Your Authentic Self

MEREDITH YOUNG-SOWERS

introduction by CAROLINE MYSS

STILLPOINT PUBLISHING

STILLPOINT PUBLISHING

*Building a society that honors
each person, the Earth, and the Sacred in all life.*

Most Stillpoint books & products are available at special discounts when purchased in bulk quantities
for educational, fund-raising, and service-oriented initiatives.
For more information, call 1-603-756-9281 or write to Stillpoint Special Markets,
22 Stillpoint Lane, PO Box 640, Walpole, New Hampshire 03608, USA.

Published by Stillpoint Publishing
Walpole, New Hampshire, USA

Original Book Art by Cameron Sesto
Cover and Text Design by Kathryn Sky-Peck
Cover Photograph by Eileen Woolbert

Library of Congress Cataloging in Publication Data

Young-Sowers, Meredith L. (Meredith Lady), 1944-
Wisdom bowls : overcoming fear and coming home to your authentic self
/ Meredith Young-Sowers ; introduction by Caroline Myss.
p. cm.
ISBN 1-883478-24-3 (alk. paper)
1. Conduct of life. 2. Spiritual life. I. Title.
BF637.C5 Y68 2002
158.1--dc21
2002009315

PRINTED IN THE UNITED STATES OF AMERICA
9 8 7 6 5 4 3 2 1

This book is printed on acid-free recycled paper
to ease our human impact on the Earth's precious resources.

*The information and practices in this book are based on the personal and professional experiences and research of
the author. They are not intended as a substitute for consulting with your physician or other healthcare provider.
All matters pertaining to your health should be supervised by a licensed healthcare professional.*

CONTENTS

INTRODUCTION

by Caroline M. Myss

FUNNY HOW LIFE IS at times. When I started to read Meredith's manuscript in my kitchen one evening, I noticed that within a few minutes I had fallen under its spell, which is to say, that I felt calm inside. A soothing energy radiates from the thoughts and poetry in this book, which examines the metaphor of bowls as containers of wisdom. I had never thought of bowls as a symbolic expression, much less had I ever considered the deeper significance of the powerful visualization of healing the cracks in one's interior energy bowls as a healing meditation. That was just the beginning of the enthralling insights that Meredith presents in her book.

In a rich and engaging fashion, she describes the seven qualities of the "authentic self:" wisdom, vision, joy, love, power, intimacy, and abundance. To be sure, each of those qualities has countless manifestations in our lives because they are the essential energies of life. They animate the experiences and relationships in our lives, giving them meaning and purpose. They are themselves containers of our memories. When you think of "joy," you recall something joyful that happened to you. When you think of "intimacy," you remind yourself of someone dear to you. These seven qualities make up our energetic spinal cord; in this book, learning to capture and work with these energies is beautifully described.

Continuing to read through the pages of this manuscript while seated at my kitchen counter, I noticed the bowl I keep on the counter. It's one of those "catch-all" bowls, a sterling silver piece of art that should probably be on display somewhere rather than buried beneath the stuff of everyday life. I decided to conduct an experiment, a type of active guided meditative journey, based on one of Meredith's teachings in her book, by rummaging through the contents of the silver bowl.

In my experiment, keeping those seven spiritual qualities in mind, I emptied my "catch-all" bowl seeking the symbolic meaning of its contents. My first thought was that I had just covered my counter with clutter that represented "fragments" of my life. Indeed, this bowl was a container of my fragments. Every day I tossed something in it or took something out of it without a thought of its having any real meaning or significance. In this exercise, however, the bowl symbolically represented my inner self, and its contents represented the fragments of my being. I now searched for the seven qualities among the fragments from the bowl.

I thought of Wisdom and chose the matchbook out of the clutter, because to me it represented inner Light. I thought of the image of the light at the end of the tunnel, the power of one light seen in the midst of the darkest hour, and the wisdom that emerges from within when you can once sense the Light of God. And naturally, I thought of the many times I desperately needed to find that Light in my own life.

For Vision, I chose a paper clip. It represented holding together bits and pieces, which is how I best articulate the experience of Vision—the gathering of pieces in order to see the whole.

Joy was easy. I selected a love note from my niece that read, "I love you, Auntie Carol." This was an effortless choice, because I felt an incredible warmth ignite within me while holding this love note once taped to my refrigerator door as a welcome-home surprise for me. Yep, I thought, this note and that precious girl are pure joy to me.

Love was my next quest. Admittedly, my niece qualified for this category as well (and in my heart I included her in this one), but I had to find something else that represented Love for me. And there it was—an invitation to a Baptism for the daughter of a friend of mine. Life and love belong hand in hand.

By the time I looked for something that symbolically represented Power, I was deep into the exercise. In fact, I was captivated with the image that I was excavating the fragments of my own self. These were pieces of my own life that I had tossed into a bowl—a symbolic interior space—without a second thought. In every way, they were carriers of my energy, my psyche, my life, representing people I love, places I had been, dates I needed to keep, times scheduled for appointments, restaurants for possible dinners, notes to myself, and notes from loved ones. In fact, if I had tossed out the contents of the bowl without looking through it, a great part of my life would have been made more complicated. "Meredith," I thought to myself, "you clever woman, you have found an extraordinary image of life and spirit with your Wisdom Bowls. Well done!"

But on to Power. Finally, I spotted the item that represented inner power to me, a pen. Writing, for me, has been my way to interact with the substance of life called Power. Whether I consider power in its most base and physical sense, or as personal and spiritual empowerment, it is the written word that holds the greatest "power" for me. My greatest sources of inspiration have been the words of others. Communicating as an author has given me my greatest satisfaction.

A restaurant advertisement represented Intimacy to me because I love sharing intimate moments and conversations with friends and family over meals. As for Abundance, I chose the bowl itself, because it represented the holder of all of the pieces of my life. And I have a life that is abundant in love, and in so much more.

At the end of this exercise, I realized that I had completed a rather extraordinary dialogue with myself. I had reached into my "interior bowl" via this silver bowl on my counter and its everyday contents, and I had pulled out fragments of my psyche and spirit that needed to be appreciated for what they represented. I recognized that symbolically this bowl contained quite a bit of my life, from people I love to unfinished business to future dates and commitments, all sitting in this bowl, and all of it living within me.

Just for fun, I observed the crystal bowl on my dining room table and noted, quite by contrast, that this bowl symbolized high energy for me, which is why I never put any odds and ends in it. Crystal speaks of the Universe to me, of God, of pure Light, Power, Joy, Intimacy, Love, Abundance, and Vision—all the energies of life. I would never have even considered such associations with that gorgeous bowl on my dining room table before, but now when I look at it, I see all those qualities of life. I love the image that radiates from the bowl on my table. But I love the image that radiates from the Wisdom Bowls I carry within my energy being.

After I completed this marvelous exercise (which I recommend highly), I re-read entire sections of Meredith's book, intrigued all the more by her directions to readers on how to understand the meaning of their lives and the healing process using the symbolic image of Wisdom Bowls. Meredith's ability to share her insights and articulate her knowledge, gained from many years as a practitioner of healing and a teacher of wisdom, is warmly and intimately communicated throughout this text. Within the first few pages, you know that you are reading the life knowledge of someone who lives in harmony with the words she writes.

On a personal note: when Meredith and I met twenty years ago, little did we know—little does any one know—what the future would hold. As I read her recollection of our early years together, working like crazy to get our publishing company off the ground, I felt waves of nostalgia come over me. How could twenty years have passed so quickly? We had such incredible ambition to be successful as publishers and to explore what we could do in the field of healing. I have to admit that her interest in healing was far more intense than mine ever was. From Day One, she had a passion to engage with others in the role of a healer.

Meredith went on to establish the Stillpoint School of Advanced Energy Healing. Her work now reaches numerous people to whom she brings her unique knowledge and skill of healing. The work she shares in *Wisdom Bowls: Overcoming Fear and Coming Home to Your Authentic Self* is a blessed addition to the healing knowledge coming forth from the heavens at this time. I encourage you to let her wisdom guide you through the pages of this remarkable book.

—CAROLINE M. MYSS
Author of *Sacred Contracts* and *Anatomy of the Spirit*

PREFACE

A FIVE-YEAR-OLD BOY STEPPED onto a crowded downtown subway train with his mother. He held fiercely to the chrome pole in the center of the car as the subway doors hissed shut and the train lurched forward. Losing his footing for a moment, he fell against a woman standing next to him. Looking up the long distance from his eyes to the older woman's face, he saw that she was very angry. He tried to explain that he was sorry, but she would have none of it. He stopped talking and just smiled up at her. He smiled because he didn't know what else to do and because he sensed that she wasn't really mad at him because he had stepped on her foot, she was angry because no one cared about her. The woman looked down into the child's bright brown eyes and, for just a second, was transported back to a happier time in life when her hazel eyes sparkled as his did. But she was no longer that woman. Life had left her behind, and no one cared. The little boy continued to smile at her, silently slipping his small, warm hand into hers. The world shifted.

Love is the only healing remedy that we use each day, often without realizing its power. We use love in many different circumstances, yet we never use up our supply of love, because love continues to regenerate within us. We trust physicians, therapists, and health practitioners who exhibit loving concern over our welfare. Their treatments delivered in a caring manner are more effective than those delivered in a more impersonal style.

Love is more than a sentiment. It is Creation unfolding before our eyes, to show us who we are. We are made of the energy of love. Love has

properties, just like the bowl that sits on your kitchen table. Love's properties emanate from our souls as wisdom, vision, joy, compassion, power,
intimacy, and abundance. These properties of love are the spiritual
resources that we draw upon in challenging times. At first, we look to
others for love: parents, friends, partners, children, and co-workers.
Eventually, we discover that love comes from inside us—from our
authentic selves, our souls.

Let's consider that bowl that sits on your kitchen table. It, too, has
properties. It can be filled or empty. It may contain fruits, candy, or odds
and ends. It can be any shape, color, or size, and can be filled with possessions we cherish or with sachets of sweet-smelling herbs. A bowl con-
tains little things we're not ready to throw away, or that we want to hide
in a safe place.

In Caroline Myss's Introduction to this book, she describes sitting at
her own kitchen table and looking through the familiar, everyday items
contained in a bowl on her counter. As she examines the items carelessly
thrown into her bowl, she remembers the experiences and relationships
in her life that they represent. When you read *Wisdom Bowls*, you'll also
recall high points of your life that relate to bowls. But the bowls you'll be
thinking about won't be any of those sitting in front of you on the
kitchen table; rather, they will be those that are inside you—invisible
parts of your authentic selves. Bowls are the perfect metaphors to help us
see how filled or empty our lives feel.

Our inner bowls are part of our energy fields—envelopes of energy
or life essence that surround our bodies. Called Chi or Prana in the East,
this force moves invisibly through and around us, keeping us healthy
and aware of our unique potential. As we uncover the mysteries of our
individual inner bowls, we find out how much energy each bowl holds,
when this useful energy is blocked or dissipated, and what that loss
could mean for our healing.

The ideas and stories in *Wisdom Bowls* came from spiritual insight,
hands-on work with clients, and twenty years of counseling and teaching

clients, workshop participants, and students. Much of what I've written in *Wisdom Bowls* is based on the healing model that I've developed and teach at the *Stillpoint School of Advanced Energy Healing*. The *Healer-Mentor Model of Energy Healing* works amazingly well, both at an emotional and spiritual diagnostic level and as a basis for healing with such practices as Loving Touch™. The Stillpoint healing model can be used as a complement to all traditional and non-traditional healing therapies. Yet it has a unique twist, relating to the two-directional flow of energy.

The energy that flows through our energy fields tells us two stories. The first story, one we may have learned in a course on yoga or an orientation to meditation, is that energy flows from the base of the spine to the crown of the head. This story comes from our roots in the history of our tribes and moves us slowly up through the major energy Chakras or centers, from the First Chakra to the Seventh. This story is valuable because it gives us insight into the ways we have developed, psychologically and emotionally. It helps us to understand our religious orientation that, like the flow of energy, encourages us toward a relationship with the Creator symbolized by the Seventh Chakra.

The second story is a foil for the first story. It tells us that our roots are in the Seventh Chakra, the center that symbolizes the Creator. We are made of Divine Love, so we are intended to rediscover and remember our connection with the Creator. From this connection, all other relationships unfold with great clarity and energy. This second story comes from following the flow of energy from the crown of the head to the base of the spine, from the Seventh to the First Chakra, instead of vice versa.

Putting these two stories together, we can see that the two energy flows form the pattern of a teardrop. They show us who we were and who we are becoming in our search for connection to Divinity. In order to answer the call for a peaceful planet and a harmonious global family, we need to direct our lives with greater confidence and wisdom. The will power we need is limited when it comes from our personalities alone.

But when our wills are aligned with Divine Will, we become the authentic human beings that we are meant to be.

The Creator, the Source of Love, lives within us. This healing love is our authentic selves. In this book, I purposely call God by the various names by which He/She is known to us around the world, names like The One, Source, God, Yahweh, The Creator, Allah, Great Spirit, The Absolute, and The Almighty. What we call The One doesn't matter. What does matter is that we have a relationship with the Source that is within us and around us.

Wisdom Bowls is a book without end, and I hope you'll refer to it over and over as you "mend your bowls" and heal your bodies when they need attention. Use the blank pages at the end of each chapter to sketch your bowls, write your prayers, or journal your discoveries as you read the book and do the Wisdom Bowl practices. It's time to discover the hidden treasure of your authentic selves and to realize the gifts you've brought into this life. Whatever old miseries still loom before you, learn what blessings lie behind these challenges, and reclaim your authentic essence.

No one can tell us that we're special. We have to feel it for ourselves. By taking this voyage together, we enter a fascinating journey of sacred awakening, and we unfold the goodness that lies in each of our hearts. Come with me, and let's discover how truly amazing you are!

The journey isn't to do more,
it is to be more.

—MEREDITH L. YOUNG-SOWERS
Walpole, New Hampshire
June 2002

CAmeron Sesto

BOWLS
AS METAPHORS

The Divine Invitation

Find your center.
Swirl deeper and deeper into your Divine heart.
Let no human criticism put you off your path.
Let no struggle tempt your earthly urges
with a solace
unfounded in God's grace.
You are God's own child, not fool's gold.
Mother and Father of the Universe, arise,
for future generations await your attention to what is worthier
than the chaff from today's windy tempests of flight and anguish.
Sleep in gratitude and awaken in compassion
for you have come to serve, and life awaits you.
Drop your heavy bags and remove the burdens that sadden your eyes.
The all-knowing Light of Lights sees and acknowledges you.
How, then, can you turn your back on this Divine Invitation?

— Meredith Young-Sowers

CHAPTER ONE

BOWLS AS METAPHORS

You are authentic, not because you've changed yourself,
but because you've become yourself.

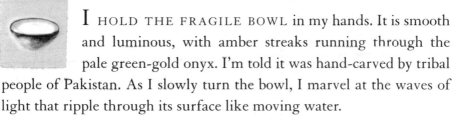 I HOLD THE FRAGILE BOWL in my hands. It is smooth and luminous, with amber streaks running through the pale green-gold onyx. I'm told it was hand-carved by tribal people of Pakistan. As I slowly turn the bowl, I marvel at the waves of light that ripple through its surface like moving water.

Johanna, an importer of extraordinary art from India, Pakistan, and Tibet, has brought me a gift on the occasion of our final healing session. Apologizing that the bowl is considered a "second" because of the cracks, she tells me that this piece speaks to her in a special way and that she wants me to have it.

As I look at Johanna I realize her hair is the same soft golden color of the onyx bowl and that the deep fracture lines and cracks speak volumes about her sense of her life. She is dying, and it is difficult. She has lost her husband, and she has two teenage daughters who are so afraid at the prospect of her leaving that they are filled with rage. She is being sued by a former employee and thinks she may lose her home. She doesn't want to leave life, because she feels her life is unfinished; nothing is settled to her satisfaction. And perhaps most significantly, she tells me she doesn't feel strong enough spiritually to die. I sit for a moment with this thought, wondering if anyone ever feels up to the task of dying when it's their time.

When I look at Johanna's bowl, I see the visual representation of the halting journey of our lives. We are the smooth shimmering stone one minute, one day; just as quickly we break apart into confusion and self-judgment when we think of, or others point out, our mistakes. Growing is the result of living, and the process inevitably produces cracks. Our first pair of jeans as a pre-teen cease to fit as our bodies round into womanhood. Our first car is probably not the one we'd choose now, twenty years past that mark. The feelings and impressions about ourselves and the world change as we do. Life looks different when we're ten, thirty, sixty, or eighty. Patching, mending, gluing, fixing, re-attaching, and re-balancing are the processes we go through without realizing we're trying to repair sorrow and disappointment in our lives.

It's hard to look at who we are today and find it good; yet this is our opportunity. The inevitable cracks from our difficulties can become our badges of adventures taken and risks accepted rather than bandages hiding our wounds. Our veneer as personality is softened as we seek clarity and renewed self-confidence from struggle; our edges become rounded, our fears subdued, our passions polished and awakened. We're meant to outgrow our old confinements, which limit feelings and beliefs about ourselves and others.

As I sit with Johanna, I realize that she's seeking approval that she's still alive and whole inside even though she's preparing to leave her physical body. We talk about the bowl she's brought me and the ways it represents her life. The golden color, I suggest, metaphorically, is the color of our own inner goldenness. I know she wants to find safety in her heart even though her life is changing so rapidly. We begin to talk slowly and gently of the cracks in her life and the meaning of these painful, changing dynamics. By the time she leaves my office, we've talked, prayed, and held love between us as an invisible witness to a greater Creative Universal Process that is unfolding. She's calmer and, I hope, in some small way, better prepared for the great adventure that awaits her.

The cracks in our own life bowls represent unresolved pain, rage, remorse, and anguish—a bevy of seemingly unwelcome companions. Slowly, with an effort toward true self-nurturing, the cracks turn into guideposts that offer us a way to see our lives as the continual process of growing and learning that they are. When we've tried in every way we know to uncover the "why did this happen to me" piece of our life puzzles, we want to know why things came down the way they did, leaving us so undone.

Healing is what happens when we view our past lives as the creative ground from which a clearer understanding of our futures emerges. What happened doesn't matter nearly so much as how we now interpret past events, impressions about our worthiness, and hope for new beginnings. We are on a journey to shift from our mental selves into our emotional selves and ultimately into our spiritual selves. Anything short of living in this dynamic, interior, creative landscape will prove totally unsatisfactory—dry, flat, and lifeless.

Do mistakes we've made in the past mean misery in the future? Does loss of love or health or monetary resources last year portend the same next year? The future is made of more than our past experiences. It also depends on the adjustments we are willing to make to head ourselves in new directions sensitive to what we've learned. It is, in part, what I call "Grace," the deep creative river that runs through us. Past events, clarity about necessary changes, and Grace to trust the process produce a very different future.

Our Inner Source inspires our natural creative energy of love—passionate, extraordinary, illuminating, insightful, and clarifying Love. When we choose to engage this deep and powerful internal energy of love, we prosper. When life opens yawning chasms of disappointment, loss, and sorrow, it's not as punishment but as the fodder for our spiritual unfolding, gathering the power of love within us and for us.

The cracks in Johanna's bowl spoke to her sorrows. They also formed the ribs or channels of new energy, creating a different picture of wisdom and courage. The bowl held together and was beautiful because of the cracks rather than in spite of them. They allowed Johanna to see that her tenacity to grow her life as best she could made her bowl pleasing to the Creator.

Our work is not so much about going to a job as it is about the acceptance of our lives as art in process. We can't touch, control, or fully comprehend this becoming with our minds alone. We must go deeper to the place from which our creativity flows. This is the place of our authentic and true selves, the loving place that heals all wounds.

Healing is similar to creating a work of art. When we "throw" a bowl on a potter's wheel, sculpt a figure from a piece of marble, paint a landscape, dance to thundering African drums, or write a book, we move in harmony with a greater, creative life rhythm. As artists, we begin with the raw material and then chisel, paint, draw, mold until we've given life to the original material. Healing is the same. We chisel away what we no longer choose to accept, molding ourselves in the likeness of those wise and loving mentors we trust, infusing ourselves anew with passion and vibrancy. We forgive the failures and broken places that inevitably result from pushing too hard for too long in unproductive ways and in meaningless directions. We grow to trust the process of creation, although when we start, we never know how the finished work will look. Just as in our lives, we uncover and rediscover the original intention for our existence.

Bowls speak to our deepest nature. As women, our ability to bear children ties us to our lineage. Men produce sperm from small sacs or 'bowls" through which a child can be conceived. Bowls tie us to the Earth, as do shapes in nature—small eddies and pauses in stream beds, a polar bear's den, or a hummingbird's nest. We grind, blend, and mix our food in bowls. We bake and eat our food in bowls. We throw, craft, and paint bowls for celebration and feasting. We hold and carry our water in bowls. Bowls come in a universal shape—two halves of a whole, the yin and the yang, the male and the female. A bowl is a universal image of offering, opening, allowing, and holding. A bowl speaks to us as no other shape can.

I find something of myself in the contours of many favorite bowls; my grandmother's prized centerpiece—dropped by my daughter's young hands and mended with loving care—shows me the beauty of a shape, a life, that has been put back together. My bread bowl, worn by years of repeated strokes while turning dough, offers the feeling of mellowing and wearing away the surface patina of my life to see a deeper, truer self. My first pottery bowl thrown on a wheel, looking more like a dog dish than a piece of art and weighing in like a cast-iron pot, taught me to cut through self-criticism and enjoy being a beginner. The tiny white Zen bowl with the wide black stripe, made by a sister writer whose work I admire, sits patiently on my kitchen windowsill. It reminds me to find the gift in the small, everyday, insignificant tasks of life: washing the evening dishes, feeding the cat, watering my plants, or talking long distance to my grandchildren.

Bowls become our companions. Each represents a new way to discover the beauty of our hidden, broken, and growing places. Bowls are the metaphors for our lives as we seek to feel fulfilled and complete.

Bowls Are Universal

Every shape in the universe is repeated over and over both inside our bodies and in the larger celestial bodies. Not surprisingly, bowl shapes we see in Nature are repeated in our bodies and hold our true and lasting creative energy. This deeply nourishing energy is Love in its many forms: love for and of God, for our family and friends, for ourselves, for our Earth and our Global Family. This Love flows abundantly from the Creator's Love, the Divine Light from which we all sprang. We have a continuously nourishing supply of Divine Creative Essence or Love. We receive this energy even when we're feeling sad, lonely, and totally disconnected.

We may not, as yet, have explored the connection between our inner, subtle layers of energy and the world around us. It's easy to think that what goes on inside us is totally different from what happens around us. We see life come and go, flowers bloom and die. We trade in our cars. We watch our children grow up and leave to go about their own business. We watch and help the best we can as our parents leave the earth. What does it all mean? How are we to proceed? What sense can we make of our lives and our opportunities? Where do we start?

We start at the beginning, and we continue to come back to the beginning, which is where we can center in our true creativity, our loving nature. We can think of this essence as the God within us, as our creative genius, our souls or authentic selves. It doesn't matter how we think of our inner vibrancy, just that we do think of it.

As an artist, I imagine our essence as Divine Light. I can easily picture this Light filtering into and through my body and my feelings. I can sense it when it's in my conversation with my children, husband, colleagues, and friends, and when it's in my writing. I can also feel when it's missing.

This inner light is our very core, our truest and most lasting resource, intended to illuminate our natural gifts and skills. As we learn to shine this Light into our hearts, we find the means to breathe through our disconnections from love. We become better at shining our Light into the lives of others—those we know and those for whom we can only pray.

Although energy is invisible to the physical eye, we can sense the flow of energy through our bodies and our environment. We know, for example, when we are with someone who drains our sense of personal power. We know what it is like to enter a room that is filled with vital, loving energy.

Energy, meaning prana, chi, or life-force energy, moves through the invisible field of energy, called the human energy system, in and around us. Our energy field is the invisible envelope of energy that surrounds

our physical bodies. This nourishing energy flows through a special network of energy lines that weave through and around us. Of these, the
strongest flow of energy moves down through our energy centers or
energy bowls. We have seven of these energy bowls, each endowed with
a special quality of love. The seven spiritual qualities are: Wisdom,
Vision, Joy, Love, Power, Intimacy, and Abundance. They are the special
qualities of our authentic nature—the part of us that we brought into
this life, the part that helps us live with inspiration and wisdom.

Picture a baby developing in a woman's womb. The baby has a tangible, physical body, and it moves around in warm water—amniotic
fluid—that cushions, nourishes, and supports the baby. We move within
our invisible bubbles of energy in similar ways.

Your energy field holds many subtle levels of energy that reflect your
consciousness and your physical body's state of health. Your attitudes,
beliefs, thoughts, feelings, and assumptions all influence these inner layers of energy. The way you cherish yourself and others is also evident in
your spiritual energy—the way you rest in and receive the power of Love.

The more you know about your subtle levels of energy, the greater
your opportunity to take actions that prevent or lessen illnesses and mit-
igate the impact of life's struggles. Imagery is a powerful tool for understanding what is going on inside us, emotionally and physically, that
otherwise would be difficult to discover. Images are non-threatening.
They give us an accurate picture of our imbalances as well as our
strengths. Ordinarily, we don't take the time to bring these into our conscious awareness so that we can see their impact on our daily lives. We
become sick or "sick at heart" from the outside in. In other words, it is
our reaction to life and people that erodes and weakens the energy available to us. We create health and happiness by freeing up our spiritual
resources. We stay centered and move toward our goals by engaging
and enhancing the seven qualities of Divine Love that are core to
expressing our authentic selves.

Healing from the Inside Out

We're always surprised at how clear we can be about the source of our suffering. Once we understand whom we blame for our anguish, the all-important step for healing is to find what aspect of our authentic selves was growing beneath the pain. This final step in the healing process is where all the power lies. Until we realize that suffering is inevitable in our less-than-perfect world and in less-than-perfect relationships, we're unable to accept our own responsibility for the quality of our lives. We do have the right to have a good life, to direct our own actions, and to believe in our goodness and happiness. Who gives us this permission to be in charge of being happy? Our own authentic selves!

The only way to break out of the old loop of misery is to find a different ending to the story of our suffering. I remember that when my children were teenagers, a publisher of young people's books produced a series of adventure stories that allowed readers to choose from three different endings. Imagine that you're in the same situation. Which ending do you want? Which are you creating for the story of your life?

I've often found it difficult to hold my own counsel. For many years, I struggled with wanting someone else to tell me what decision I should make, always wanting the "right" way. While I knew that I was supposed to have all the answers inside me, I didn't feel that I could trust myself not to make irrevocable mistakes. Looking back, I realize now that I felt insecure and unsure because I was afraid of being abandoned by those I loved.

Most of us experience feeling abandoned at times in our lives. At the root of this feeling is the suffering from our past that holds our precious life-force energy in abeyance, making it unavailable to us. We feel fatigued, mildly depressed, confused, and afraid to make a decision. We are stalled in picking up the threads of our life paths.

Bringing ourselves fully into our present lives and living with authentic power comes from taking back our need to have someone else take care of us, be responsible for us, and tend to our wants. As children, we needed parents to play this role, and many times they let us down and perhaps even brutalized us emotionally and physically. We carry this lack of trust as cellular memories in the tissues of our bodies. A previous partnership, friendship, or close working relationship can also leave us fractured and afraid to love again. But eventually we realize that our perspective, and not the actual situation, is what has made us hurt so deeply, though the situation may have been extremely painful.

Two people can have the same experience, after which one feels depleted and undone for life while the other is able to move on. Our way of evaluating a situation is based largely on how much we trust ourselves and are in communication with our authentic natures, our spiritual selves. It is this aspect of ourselves that allows us to experience greater resiliency, self-nurturing, and forgiveness of the events that have hurt us.

We forget that we have powerful spiritual resources to draw on. Our lapse of memory is like having a lottery ticket in our pocket and going hungry because we've forgotten that we hid the ticket in a safe place. So, too, do we all possess a genuine sense of inner authority and compassion for ourselves, an understanding of what we need, and the qualities that can heal our pain rather than re-stimulate it.

When I was twenty, my father told me he was leaving my mother. He had the bad judgment to announce this fact to me just before we walked down the aisle on my wedding day. Not long after, my father divorced my mother, married another woman, and moved away. This dissolution of my original biological family happened very quickly. And because I was busy with my own life and career, I thought there would still be time to have a relationship with my father, if only a changed one, in the years ahead.

We always think there will be time to sort things out, but sometimes there isn't. I saw my father only one more time. It was on a day when he'd had so much to drink that I worried for his safety in driving. Later he wrote to tell me of his deep dissatisfaction with our relationship and that I clearly wasn't accepting him and his new wife. I'd tried in every way possible to tell him and show him just the opposite. I wanted him in my life under any circumstances. I heard from him just one more time, after my son was born. Somehow, he'd heard he had a grandson, and he sent a gift. He told me in the note not to try contacting him, but at twenty-six, I was certain this new correspondence meant a fresh start. My letter to him came back marked, "Addressee unknown." And I never heard from him again.

For years I didn't think about him, and then I thought about him all the time. I had such a deep heaviness in my heart that sometimes I could hardly breathe. I had wanted the protection that only a father can offer a daughter who has yet to find her own firm footing. I had wanted to walk with him in the woods, arm in arm, and feel his strength and wisdom in my life. I'd wanted my children to know him, to laugh and cry with him. I missed his presence in my life even though our relationship had never been a close one. I missed him in ways I'd never imagined possible. He had deserted me.

As my spiritual life deepened, I was able to see how I had compensated for losing my father by finding others to play the role of "father as protector." Still, I didn't know how to compensate for the emptiness I felt. Just when I thought I had healed the loss, something unexpected happened that would again open that old, excruciating pain in my heart.

To try healing my pain, I began to use internal dialoguing, spirit-to-spirit. This dialogue became the core of the Mending Your Bowls healing practice and opened up a world of understanding, acceptance, and forgiveness in me and many of my clients and students. I talked to my father, person-to-person, as if he were sitting in front of me. I let him know how angry I was, how much he had hurt me, and that his leaving the Earth without needing to find me left me feeling scarred. Then I put my hand over my heart and moved to a different inner space that was filled with love for my own pain and his. From this quiet center I asked him to tell me what was in his heart. His real self, his authentic nature said, "I always loved you and was so proud of you. I didn't know how to tell you I loved you when I had such regret over the choices I'd made in my life. Each year I lost more of myself until there was nothing left. Can you forgive me?"

The gift in this challenge was that, finally, I felt I'd had a father who really loved me. And that has made all the difference.

The Blessings in Our Challenges

It takes a great deal of courage to consider that blessings live beneath the difficult challenges we face. While a challenge doesn't "feel good," it "does good" as it allows us to create new possibilities for our lives and put behind us what we can no longer change. We're learning all the while that we're suffering, but we don't usually stop to find the blessing inside us that is the antidote for our pain. Our spiritual growth continues while we are going through our hard times. Even when we feel ignored, abandoned, and abused, our souls are awakening to unconditional love. Finding the blessings in our challenges opens our lives to love, which ultimately translates into forgiveness, hopefulness, and gratitude.

Changing cracks in our bowls to guideposts for our lives comes from shifting our perception. The reason we feel resentful, uneasy, or diminished is not necessarily because of a particular circumstance but more likely because of our reaction to it. As a result of our history, we believe that we are destined to unhappiness or failure. We think we are so imperfect, so flawed, that we'll never find love or success in life. These assumptions are what crush us.

Of course they are untrue, but they hold our attention emotionally. It is easier to feel fear than grace. Suffering lives in our attachment to the things we believe will make us happy. As we learn to release our attachments to the changing material world around us, the things we thought would make us happy, such as people's opinions of us and their responses to our efforts, fade as we find a more meaningful connection to our authentic selves. Healing and empowerment come from shifting our external attachment to an inner connection with our authentic selves.

Healing Your Life by Mending Your Bowl

Intuitively, we know a great deal about ourselves. On an inner level, we realize our genuine gifts and strengths as well as our problems—the growing edges or the places that snag us. Using the Mending Your Bowl—Healing Your Life practice, many people find slow but steady relief from such emotional issues as lack of self-worth and continuous worry, issues that influence physical illnesses like cancer, diabetes, chronic fatigue, vision loss, and heart trouble. Whenever you juxtapose the energy of Love with any suffering, love always prevails. Our job is to allow love to win.

I have used the Bowl Practice below with many clients and students. It is a simple but powerful tool for the healing of pain and grief lodged in our bodies from old wounds and sorrows. Use this bowl exercise to reclaim the parts of your authentic self that have been hidden or frayed by your life's journey. You may find some surprises in the process, but inevitably, if you stay with it, you will find a jewel buried beneath the sadness. That is the gift given to you by your life journey, a gift that deepens and sweetens your sorrow. It is the gift of Grace.

Here is a brief description of each of the six stages of this practice. Please read the more detailed description of this exercise in the Appendix: Mending Your Bowl—Healing Your Life, A Step-by Step Process. You'll receive a much greater benefit if you actually draw your own bowls, using either the blank pages at the end of each chapter or a separate journal book. Focus on one spiritual quality at a time. Start with the quality that is most intriguing to you, and give yourself enough time to uncover the source of your suffering and the blessing in your challenge.

- ♦ **Create a picture** *of an imaginary bowl in your mind. Each bowl represents one of the seven aspects of your authentic self: Wisdom, Vision, Joy, Love, Power, Intimacy, or Abundance.*

- **Discover the cracks**, *broken places, chips, or holes in your bowl.* **Make the connection** *to the experiences or relationships that are the source of your suffering.*

- **Speak the truth about your loss, the grief** *it has caused you, and the person you hold most directly responsible. Imagine him or her seated across from you.*

- **Uncover your grace,** *asking for loving feedback from that person's authentic self, and* **find the blessing in the challenge** *by identifying the part of your authentic self that you are reclaiming.*

- **Mend your bowl,** *transforming the cracks and flaws in your bowl into brilliant emblems of your courage, inner power, and healing.*

- **Heal your life** *as you remember, every time the familiar pain returns, to reaffirm the aspect of your genuine and authentic self that you've identified and invited home to your heart.*

As you complete this healing process, realize that you may need to undertake some version of these six steps over and over again, addressing the same issue. Be patient. You didn't find yourself in this pain in just a few days. You'll need time and effort to move in a new direction. But Mending Your Bowl—Healing Your Life creates a genuine and lasting healing because instead of remembering your sorrow, you will now remember what you learned and the part of yourself that you have regained in the process.

The blessing in your suffering reveals the part of yourself that you had disowned, a part that now you are willing to let shine in your life. You may have felt heavily criticized as a child, and that has remained your life challenge. Your blessing may be feeling worthy of trusting yourself, making your own choices, and looking inside for approval rather than to other people.

Another example is the person who has always felt invisible to others, passed over, and never taken seriously. The blessing might be your willingness to approve of yourself, even when you make mistakes, knowing that the only way to learn is to try.

Every time you return to one of your bowl images in your prayers, meditations, or quiet times, affirm your mended bowl and the blessing that you've accepted and now welcome. The more you reinforce the healing instead of the original pain, the more smoothly your healing will proceed.

Each imperfection in your bowl shows you that life is a series of struggles that either destroy your joy and zest for living or awaken deeper understanding, a more compassionate heart, a stronger sense of conviction, and a truer desire to serve others. Each sorrow, rather than being a mark of failure, represents a tribute to success. You will slowly, over a lifetime, put the pieces of your true self together and see who you are—nothing short of an Embodiment of Love. All manner of joy and success follow that discovery.

Seven Qualities of Your Authentic Self

The exploration of our authentic nature leads to an amazing discovery. Rather than being the dim and unenlightened persons we may think we are, we find instead that deep inside we are as brilliant as the sun, no matter what tragedy has befallen us. We can have joy and love and power as we realize what has blocked those aspects of Love. We are opening our hearts to loving in ways that we may never have done before. There is no perfect time to find the answers to deep questions. The right time is whenever and wherever we begin our journeys toward an authentic reconnection with our true Selves.

The qualities of our authentic selves are the inner qualities of Divine

Love that we possess as the gift of life. As we let go of fear and allow these energies to fully nurture our bodies, minds, and spirits, we are able to make wise choices and live more fulfilling lives. The seven spiritual qualities of our authentic selves are:

■ *Wisdom*

Divine Love encourages us to know that all life is interconnected and precious. We are only one part, but a very important and essential part, of the whole universal plan. The voice of Wisdom, our Wise Counselor, asks us to recognize that we are capable of great things and not to be discouraged, deluded, or deceived into feeling insignificant. Opportunities to be wise come to us through the ordinary events of each day. Through the energy of Wisdom we heal the emotional suffering that comes from feeling betrayed by God and distanced from a Loving Source. Wisdom also serves us by strengthening the functioning of our brains, our spinal cords, and the various nerves in our body.

■ *Vision*

Divine Love is leading us toward the discovery and implementation of our chosen life paths. Vision, through the voices of our Vision Keepers, encourages us to learn from our families of origin so that we may move forward in implementing our unique vision in the world. We are encouraged to find spiritual community with individuals who share our spiritual values and help us stay on track in a changing world. Vision tells us to believe in ourselves and release opinions that others hold of us. Vision says: look inside, trust your path, and make your own contribution. Vision energy helps us to heal endocrine disorders or imbalances, such as an over- or under-active thyroid, adrenal depletion, and such pancreas imbalances as diabetes. Vision offers a way to deepen our spiritual guidance and develop a personal relationship with The Creator.

■ *Joy*

Divine Love offers us a way to deepen our experience of happiness into joy. The voice of Joy is our Peace Maker, who helps us to find our own authentic voices. Joy shows us how to be peaceful in a powerful way so that we may create non-violence in our families and in our world. We are helped to be congruent, aligned with our beliefs, attitudes, opinions, feelings, and actions. Joy gives us ways to be in harmony with the friends and family we love, moving these relationships from war to peace and joy. Peace Maker energy strengthens our sinuses and lungs, offering a way to breathe out deep suffering in preparation for receiving the energy of love from our hearts.

■ *Love*

Divine Love offers us Compassion for our healing and emotional growth. Love energy is directed toward enhancing our sense of self-worth and in creating a more empowered relationship with our partners. The voice of Love is our Compassionate Healer, who helps us to deepen our love for those around us and to nurture and care about others in the world. Love furthers our capacity to develop a "spiritual warrior" attitude in order to serve as advocate for those in need. It helps relieve suffering and strengthens our immune system's response to such conditions as rheumatoid arthritis, AIDS, chemical sensitivities, and infections. Our Love energy strengthens individual lymph nodes and the many disease-fighting cells that keep us healthy. Love energy also helps our heart muscles to be steady and strong, and it enhances the flow of blood in our arteries, veins, and capillaries.

■ *Power*

Divine Love brings together our natural gifts, talents, and creative brilliance with our self-confidence and desire to cooperate with others.

The result of this merger helps us to move into our most useful, meaningful, and effective career choices for our lives. The voice of Power is our Empowered Creator, which allows us to overcome feelings of competitiveness and the fear of being abandoned in order to develop what works best for all concerned. The Energy of Power is essential for effective digestion and elimination, for muscle strength and resiliency, and for the flexibility of tendons and ligaments. Power helps us to relax and receive the gifts and benefits from our efforts each day.

■ *Intimacy*

Divine Love heals our fragmented lives. Intimacy brings us a new picture of our past, one that is filled with learning rather than only suffering. The Energy of Intimacy opens us to attracting future opportunities. The voice of Intimacy is our Life Steward, who cares about the Earth and seeks to help us learn from the harmony of Nature. Intimacy energy holds together the positive part of our personalities and the negative side, showing us that we must learn to live as a fully integrated system. Intimacy has pioneering qualities, showing us that we are leading the way for others to follow, balancing the feminine and masculine in our reproductive systems. Strong Intimacy energy gives us the ability to create wholeness and overcome such diseases as breast, ovarian, and uterine cancers, along with such conditions as miscarriages and herpes. This powerful energy influences the healing of prostate cancer and infertility problems, and it helps to heal urinary and kidney problems, showing us that we need to trust our own choices to release the clutter of other people's opinions.

■ *Abundance*

Divine Love guides us to recognize that our greatest well-being and rewards come from serving others. Abundance energy enhances our ability to stay steady in our desire to serve others while serving our own spiritual growth. The voice of Abundance is our Abundant Servant, who allows us to shift from the feeling of "duty" in helping others to "compassion" in serving. Abundance energy is important in strengthening our bones and joints and is especially useful in healing osteoporosis and various kinds of arthritis.

Our Direct Connection to Love

I don't believe God sends us punishment, but sometimes—unknowingly—we find ourselves in difficult situations that require us to turn to God for resolution. Resolution means not outside absolution—although sometimes that can help tremendously—but internal empowerment, as we realize that each of us is sailing on the waters of life in our individual boats. Our boats may come very close to others, but we alone hold responsibility for our life's success. Success means not material advantage alone but what we've learned and the contributions we've made.

Each of us has our own direct link to the Creator and the dynamic streams of creative energy in the Universe. We are fully capable of having a good life no matter our background or the ways we've been diminished or hurt. We are learning to take appropriate steps to strengthen ourselves so that we can be the Creator's hands and feet. We each are all that any of us has.

By being aware of our direct connection to Divine Love, we can navigate successfully through our lives. As we discover more aspects of our authentic selves, we find the ways to enhance our work in the world, to bring closure to old wounds, to benefit from deeply loving relationships, and to forge honest and true paths for our children and their children to follow.

Whenever you juxtapose the energy of Love

with any suffering, love always prevails.

Our job is to allow love to win.

CAmeron Sesto

WISDOM

The Essence of Creation

All life comes from the same place,
breathing into the empty spaces of living and dying.
Sister trees unite atop their skyward view
of lofty branches smiling at the sky.
Brother waters tumble together, losing their way in the riverbeds of stone,
mud, and grit.
Peoples of all nations spill over the countrysides
like the colored squares of an old woman's quilt.
Indivisible lives flowing this way and that
intent upon living the day as if it alone mattered.
Rise up and into the breadth of your humanity,
for life, real full explosive life, awaits your raised hand and head.
Join in the intimacy of genuine renewal
and seek the roots of the family from which you sprang.
The Essence of Creation…
Enfolded in deepest wisdom…this is You as Creator.

— Meredith Young-Sowers

CHAPTER TWO

WISDOM

Kinship is between any two people, among all people,
and with the Creative Essence that holds all life in love.

 IT WAS SUNDAY MORNING, and I was carrying an armload of firewood into the house. I remember the exact moment and the specific place I stopped when I made the discovery because my feet refused to take another step. I stood still, as if any motion would interrupt the flow of words that were taking shape—the language to consider an old loss from a new perspective.

Guidance is what comes to us as legitimate insight, often unexpectedly, from the deep river that flows through us—the river of the collective consciousness, the collective goodness of all life. I think of this river as God, the Divine Absolute, the Loving Creator who provides the insight to heal old pains. I had assumed that my unanswered questions must have no answers, imagining that my deepest pain would never find a resolution. I felt as if I'd allowed an essential need to know what happened to the bond between my friend and me to be cast away, tossed to the winds.

Many times our understanding of the way to heal an old wound lies in our turning over a new leaf in our hearts. We have to wait many years before we're ready for the answer to our real question, which is how to mend what's broken rather than assigning fault for a painful loss.

We need to grow into friendships. In the beginning, we may not understand our attraction to special friends, but over time, we find ourselves gathered into their lives as they are into ours. Our shared experiences root more deeply in our hearts than we anticipated. We write our graduate theses together, canoe together, and drink cappuccinos at the local coffee shop side by side. We may shop at the mall together every Wednesday and find solace and comfort, fun and delight in the companionship. It surprises us because we didn't realize how much we enjoy the company of women.

For years, I felt competitive with other women. I wasn't interested in being the "weaker sex." I wanted to be in charge, although I could never find the inner authority to support my outer authority. Many of us learn our distrust of other women from our mothers, who taught us how to create the safe harbor of hearth and home. They sent us on a course to capture a man, a job, and a life-style, snatching the prize that others wanted. This borrowed approach to success and authority brings only unhappiness. How grateful I am for the changes in my world that brought women to me and me to women as mentors, allies, wise women, and sister healers.

Sometimes, a potentially long-term friendship—a sisterhood relationship—comes to us before we're ready, emotionally or spiritually, to be with it. Instead of facing the wind together, we cut our teeth on each other's growing edges. We hurt each other and ourselves trying to find our way together, only realizing the relationship's significance when we contemplate the smoldering remains of its undoing.

The Sunday morning of my startling discovery, I'd been revisiting the sadness I felt at the loss of one very special, long-term friendship that had self-destructed years earlier. This was no ordinary friendship. I started Stillpoint Publishing with this special woman friend, along with my first husband. We worked hard for many years to get this enterprise off the ground—a time of effort, outrageous fun, and meaningful spiritual discovery. Although we seemed as different as any two women could be, we shared a journey to the sacred that was at the core of both our lives.

On this particular Sunday morning, years after we'd gone our separate ways, I found myself ruminating over past events. There was no new ground to cover, no fresh thoughts, just the old accusations and self-pity. But, as if someone suddenly opened my heart and poured in a healing remedy, I made a discovery. It wasn't necessary for my friend to love me in order for me to love her. What an amazing thought!

As if my love for my friend had been waiting for permission to be rekindled, I felt the winds of change sweep over me. I knew that I had received a piece of wisdom that would take years for me to appreciate fully. In an instant, with my feet planted firmly in the sandy gravel of my driveway, I felt a rush of overwhelming love for my friend. She was once again my precious sister. I felt her lifeblood, as if it were my own, flowing through my body, and her joy as if it were my own. Whatever unresolved issues and sorrows remained in my mind, they no longer lived in my heart. I was stunned.

That experience has been a profound teacher. My inner Wise Counselor was saying to me, "Look, you're not separate at all. It only seems that way. You're as close to your friend in your heart as you ever were. Enjoy all that nourishes your love, for these feelings also support bonds of caring and tenderness in every other heart. You're all connected! As you honor your kinship with others, you accept the blessing of their kinship with you."

How many times we experience similar scenarios! Feeling left behind or shut out of someone's life, we get ourselves into a stir, filled with righteous indignation. Yet our hearts continue to hurt. In order to mend our hearts, we must return to our bonds of kinship. Kinship is a loving relationship held in the heart. Nothing destroys unconditional love, which is what genuine kinship embodies. We can heal our broken kinship bonds when we accept the sacred wisdom that we are all one.

When we set aside differences, competitions, and judgments and allow our genuine human bonds to fill us with love instead of anger and pain, we become kin. Instead of thinking about the voice of reason, we can adopt the voice of wisdom, which says, "Feel the connection you have with everything that draws a breath at this same moment that you do."

Not long after this realization I had a chance to put my understanding into practice. I didn't know it, but my friend had returned to my town for a visit. I was having lunch in a small local luncheonette when she walked in the door. My shock at seeing her was clearly matched by the look of disbelief on her face. She was with mutual friends who stopped to chat at our table before moving on to their own. The strain between us was palpable. Strangely, I felt enormously peaceful. When I was ready to go, I walked over to her table and said goodbye. She got up to walk me to the door. She felt frozen—a million miles away from any emotional connection to me. As we came to the door, I remember putting my arms around her and whispering, "I'll always love you." I didn't think it mattered in the least to her, but I knew it mattered deeply to me. I felt free, at last.

As irony would have it, she was persuaded to call me, and we spent several hours together before she left town. As we talked, the pain didn't just magically disappear, but beneath the pain, when I looked into her face, I knew that although our friendship had gone underground, it wasn't dead. I only hoped that we'd be able to walk safely through the field of landmines as we tried to rebuild our relationship. Maybe it was "karma," the bonds that can carry over from previous lifetimes; but whatever it was, when we said goodbye this time, both our faces were streaked with tears, and my hug was returned with genuine feeling.

Never underestimate the power of love to heal. Being willing to love someone even if that love doesn't set things right moves us to an entirely new inner space. Love frees us from the pain and anger that hold us captive.

God in the voices of our Wise Counselors reveals our kinship with all life when we feel alone and left behind. My prayers nowadays include a willingness to be kin with anyone who needs bonds similar to mine.

Wise Counselor Friends

Many people play the role of Wise Counselor in our lives. A Wise Counselor is a person, a mentor or spiritual teacher in disguise, who willingly guides, supports, comforts, inspires, and directs our lives when we need it most. Wise Counselors appear at just the time we're in greatest despair, asking questions like, "How could a loving God create such pain in my life?" or "What does God want from me?" Or, "How can I feel safe in this world when I don't know where to go or who can help?"

A Wise Counselor appears whether we're praying for help or just in need of guidance and lacking the realization that we can ask for it. A Wise Counselor can be an ordinary person saying something extraordinary, one who buoys us up when we have no energy, confidence, hope, or inspiration left. Wise Counselors say, "Let me help you," and they do. The grandmother who strokes her granddaughter's hair, saying, "Life doesn't need to be so hard if you just find love inside" is an example. So is the teacher who, seeing a student struggling with a writing assignment, hands her a piece of her own writing, saying, "Use my words until you find your own."

A Wise Counselor's words touch our spirits. Their caring comes from a generous nature and their insights from personal experience. They are more interested in our growth than our emotional comfort. They see what we need and help us in just the right way. Wise Counselors are precious to us because we know we can trust their guidance.

Wise Counselors can be our own authentic selves or people we've loved and trusted for years. They can appear out of nowhere with a word, thought, or solution for the exact situation we face. As so often happens, when we come to a difficult crossroads in our lives, a time when no one path seems clear, we may see no way out of our dilemma. In these times, the mysterious force of Divine Love seems to sense that we're in a "teachable moment," and if we're paying attention, we are thrown a lifeline.

Listening to Our Inner Wise Counselors

Just as we learn from a physical teacher, we can learn from our own inner teachers. Our inner Wise Counselors embody many of the same qualities as our Wise Counselor friends and mentors.

God plays many roles in our lives. The Essence of the Absolute is both the microcosm of energy that lives within us and the energy envelope that enfolds us, driving all of creation in the Universe and beyond. The Wise Counselor is the voice of wisdom that we all possess and can call on to choose the most appropriate and satisfying choices for our lives.

There is an inherent wisdom to life, a layer of knowing that lies hidden beneath our daily goings and comings. This wisdom helps us understand that we are an essential aspect of a Universal Kinship. It follows that if we are kin with all forms of life on Earth, we are also kin with The Almighty. Knowing that we are a part of God's creation helps us feel safe in a world that is anything but safe. We can feel safe in the world because we are the progeny of Divine Love.

How does Divine Love show up in our lives? It shows up as the ability to change and choose how we will live; as the opportunity to release old worn-out clothes and be re-born in a new set; and it's in restoring balance to the Earth so it can provide us with a beautiful home. Love—unconditional love—isn't just a sentiment. It's an opportunity for a better life.

Life emerged and knew how to develop. This innate knowing that is the mystery within our world is also a mystery within us. We are innately wise simply because we were born. We are part of the bigger plan simply because we are alive. We have consciousness, the ability to perceive, to reason, and to search for meaning in our lives because we are here on Earth.

While we don't know many of the particulars of this great mystery of Divine Wisdom, we can surmise that, as it is above, so it must be below. The principles that guide creation and dissolution of life also guide our everyday affairs. Three important aspects of Divine Wisdom that we, too, embody are: first, change happens when we're watching; second, we can share resources because we are more than the sum of our parts; and third, we self-correct imbalance to return to balance.

■ *Change Happens When We're Watching*

Wisdom allows us ever-changing choices in our relationships, offering us many opportunities to create new and different outcomes for our lives. Quantum physics illustrates this point. Physicists have discovered to their dismay that there is no end to the search for a universal molecular building-block. All they have found is a series of relationships that change according to who is the observer, thus suggesting that when we think about something, the material form we are thinking about changes in response to our attention. Matter is responsive to shifts in consciousness. Our thoughts shape the world around us, no matter whether they originate from fear or from love. The world reacts to us according to the way we perceive it. If we see love, we receive love. If we see hate, we receive hate. If we are only confused, we receive more confusion.

I saw an example of this in my relationship with a man who once worked for me. For a while, I thought he was doing a very good job. Then I began to see that he wasn't doing things the way I wanted them done, and I began to find fault with him. His performance became worse and worse, until finally, I had to fire him. The same pattern began to repeat with his replacement. When I resisted the temptation to let my concern about his performance snowball into a mountain of negative attention, I had an amazing realization. Managing my thoughts to maintain a positive attitude about him, I asked my authentic self to help me to understand the man's more perfect fit in our company. As a result of my shift from a critical to a supportive attitude, his performance improved dramatically. In fact, he went on to make major, positive contributions to Stillpoint.

Where we put our attention creates our reality. By having faith in a benevolent universe, we draw that reality to us.

■ *Sharing Because We Are More than the Sum of Our Parts*

We know that we are more than the sum of our parts. We are more than a hand, an arm, a foot, or a leg, but we can work these limbs together to play ball, make love, and feed ourselves. When the foot, the arm, and the stomach work together, they share resources. Each part of the body is wise enough to know that it is only one part of a big picture. Each is important, but together they make up the total body. When it's time to digest our lunch, for example, the digestive system takes top priority, and the flow of blood favors the processing of our food. But if we suddenly need to rush to our cars to respond to an emergency, our digestion slows and our hearts, mental acuity, breathing, and muscles together create a different priority. They can do that because they share resources.

Wisdom helps us to know that in order to live successfully we need other people and the Earth. Many people create the products and foods we eat. Our jobs require the cooperation of many different people and departments in order to produce finished products. It is the same with our bodies and souls; our minds are connected to our bodies, which are connected to our spirits, souls, or authentic selves.

Sometimes we forget that we have additional resources at our disposal. When we receive disheartening news, for example, we may stew about what was said and what we should do about it. We ask our minds to solve the problem. Our minds are capable only of emotional reactivity. They stick to the script requiring us or others to be inadequate. Our personalities are the wrong place to look for wise resolutions. Our authentic selves, however, have the appropriate perspective to help us see that no one is wrong; that the people we assumed were our adversaries, like us, want outcomes that lead to happiness and prosperity. Our Wise Counselors direct us to share the Divine Resources.

■ Self-Correcting to Return to Balance

Balance is a core component of the wisdom of our bodies. We marvel at the ways the physical body is programmed to bring us back to health, often with little or no assistance. We see this same rebalancing impulse in Nature. Rivers filter out pollutants; streambeds and eddies wash waters clean. We see life's wisdom in the balance of plants and animals that allow us to survive. Over a lifetime, our hearts beat continuously, contracting and expanding without rest. Our planet knows how to revolve at the speed necessary to maintain its position relative to the sun and the moon, and the Universe knows how to hold all its moving parts, systems, and forces in a dynamic balance where everything knows its place in the cosmic dance.

As we struggle to make sense of the reasons things happen to us, and as we seek to stay out of harm's way, we are wise to trust that we remain in a steady state. When we stop pushing to reach our objectives, we allow ourselves to move from imbalance—leaning precariously toward what we want—to the balance point.

When we wish for a certain outcome that isn't coming, we are wise to become quiet and return to our centers. In this place, we can review the wisdom of our efforts to make something happen. We may decide that what we really want is to start a business, but, in reviewing our financial situations and the lack of potential customers in a depressed economy, we might be wise to postpone launching the company at this time. Lacking wisdom, our personality selves say, "Oh, go ahead. God will bail you out because you're a good person trying to do a good thing." But our God-selves tell us: "Now is not the best time." God is like a good financial advisor. He gives us his best thinking and then puts the situation back in our hands so that we may decide whether or not we trust our inner voices!

Wisdom Subdues Fear

Over the years, while working with people in various phases of healing, I'm often dumfounded by the spiritual power available to us that we never touch. We tend to think of spiritual power as pertaining to God only. But our minds and bodies are expressions of our spiritual energy, too. We're all made of the spiritual energy of Divine Love. There is nothing else. Appreciating kinship speaks directly to the meaning of one life compared to every other. All is one. We are connected to all life and the Creator. We are all the energy of Divine Love.

Our spiritual resources permeate all aspects of our thinking, feeling, and bodily responses. It is only an illusion that the physical body is separate from other aspects of consciousness. Our bodies are the densest expression of our spirit, but we are all spiritual energy—the energy of Divine Love. As we consider the way we're put together, we see that paying attention to our physical needs—the needs of our bodies—is our First Healing Response. Our Second Healing Response asks us to re-activate the aspect of our authentic selves that is Divine Love in action.

Our First Healing Response involves the use of medicines and remedies to help the body return to balance. It includes various types of psychotherapies, psychiatric evaluations, and pharmaceutical treatments that we use to understand and manage the mind and emotions. But all too often we forget about the Second Healing Response, which provides energy to the first healing response. The Second Healing Response asks us to identify the aspects of our spirits that have been dimmed.

Imagine a person who hurts his back from too much exertion. His first healing response might be to take an aspirin to relieve the pain. Often we stop any treatment after taking a remedy to relieve the physical body's discomfort. Our Second Healing Response is necessary to re-engage the aspect of our authentic selves that has lost its vibrancy. In the case of our friend's back pain, the Wisdom component of his authentic self has been diminished. While back pain can involve muscles, it also involves nerves, the integrity of the brain, and the entire nervous system. To restore his diminished Wisdom energy, our friend could put one or both hands over his heart and ask his Wise Counselor what he needed to learn from the back pain, where he'd lost his way and failed to act from his own highest Wisdom. The heart center is the Universal home for receiving Divine Love and Compassion. He could create a healing prayer, which is the most direct remedy for nervous system problems. In this way, he could address not only the immediate needs of his physical body but also his spiritual needs, which will activate the more lasting healing response.

In listening to our sorrows and emotional problems, we discover a means to deepen our responses from anger, rejection, and remorse into love and forgiveness. In the case of our friend with back pain, the issues he could address with his Wise Counselor might deal with ways to draw wisdom more directly into his daily thinking and actions.

With Wise Counselor energy, we learn to detach from the accusations of others and become our own loving parents and mentors. Wise Counselor encourages us to know that "The Source" sees our value and helps us to make our unique contributions in life, and thus to make the most of opportunities we might otherwise miss. Wise Counselor demands our best efforts and allows us to love others even when they seem deeply flawed and unworthy of our love, and he/she restores our faith in the power of love to heal.

As we deepen our appreciation of the natural creative flow of life, we discover that the nervous system is directly related to the Wisdom aspect of our authentic selves.

Marsha's Story

Marsha came to me, asking, "How will I get better? What is the way through this problem? How must I think about myself and my situation, now that I'm not well?" Marsha had just been diagnosed with multiple sclerosis. She was having trouble putting her life back together so that she could have some hope of a worthwhile future. She had come to see me, she said, to explore new ways to heal. She had three small children, a loving but high-maintenance partnership, and a successful career as a guidance counselor in a good school.

When I completed my intuitive energy evaluation of Marsha before speaking with her, I realized that she had been devastated by the diagnosis, and she was still reeling from fear. She was worried that she would be unable to live with this progressive illness while caring for her family and maintaining a sense of personal dignity. I saw clearly that Marsha didn't trust God, and she didn't believe that there was a benevolent Universe. This lack of connection to the largest of all safety nets, The Creator, put her at immediate risk of a nervous system imbalance. I sensed that she had a much deeper loss and distrust of authority that we would need to explore when I spoke with her. She needed to find a belief in a different kind of Divine Presence and to allow this love to fashion a new sense of inner authority and support.

When she called for her phone appointment, I sensed that she was middle-aged and small in stature, and that her busy life was packed with activity, every minute of every day. The more afraid she felt, the faster she ran from an illness whose emotional and spiritual origins she didn't grasp.

As she talked, I could imagine her intense, questioning eyes and soft, ready smile. I thought, "Here is a woman many people have leaned on for support." But in her voice was an unspoken comment, a story she'd probably never shared. I hoped this would be the time she'd feel safe enough to tell me about it.

Together we began considering the nature of the Divine Plan and how she imagined her place in the bigger picture. I knew her distrust of authority had tainted her relationship with the Creator of Love. She told me, "I don't trust God because he let me down when as a little girl I prayed for my mother to love me. If God couldn't make that happen," she confided in me, "then how can I possibly trust my husband's love for me?"

"Or," I added, "your own love for you."

"Yes," she agreed quietly.

In multiple sclerosis (MS), the myelin sheath that encapsulates our fragile nerves begins to erode and disintegrate. The energy diagnosis behind MS usually reveals a person who feels a total lack of support and safety while recovering from a loss that feels irreplaceable. In Marsha's case it was the loss of a meaningful relationship with her mother that triggered an even larger loss, a loving relationship with The Creator.

Marsha lost her mother when she was young. Her mother hadn't died until recently, but long before that, Marsha lost the closeness to the Mom she needed. She was never clear what happened; all she knew was that she'd lost a needed pillar of support during her tumultuous teenage years.

Even though we give lip service to the belief that we're all connected, we may never have had a loving bond with the one person with whom we needed it most. When that person dies, we feel even greater anger and pain because we now assume that the person is beyond our reach and that it is no longer possible to heal. We believe that we can never again get the love we need. While the thread of connection may seem to be gone, it is never actually lost. It's like looking at a spider's single silk thread on a sunny day. For a moment, in the glint of the sun, it seems to disappear. But Divine Love never drops a single thread from our hearts to another's or from another's to ours.

The health of our physical nervous system is governed by the issue of trust in the unity of all things, a trust that bring us into a loving kinship with the Creator. This acceptance of Divine Kinship is essential in order for us to recognize that we are supported when we feel most adrift. Multiple sclerosis represents the destruction of our safety, our protection from irreconcilable loss. It was clear that Marsha needed to rebuild trust in authority figures that she felt had abandoned her. She would benefit from spending time moving through her sorrow, instead of avoiding it, by working with the Mending Your Bowl—Healing Your Life practice. I knew we could make a good beginning in our first session together.

As we talked about her sense of The Creator, she confirmed that not only did she not have a belief in God, but also she had married a man who was an ardent Christian. She felt disempowered in her relationship with her husband because she felt she was living a lie. She had never been able to tell him her true feelings because she believed they were misguided.

Misguided or not, what we believe is what influences the essential flows of energy within us. Safety in our belief about God is what allows us to experience our Wise Counselor energy—feeling loved because we are a part of a Divine Breath.

It was essential for Marsha to see that her mother had loved her even though she hadn't demonstrated that to Marsha's satisfaction. As Marsha began to feel safe in the love of her authentic self, she would be able to forgive her mother and her husband. Through the Loss, Grief, and Grace process, she would find the blessings in her situation and come to see that it was her divine nature and not her personality that was in charge of her healing. She had the resources for making wiser choices for herself, holding wiser thoughts, and hearing wiser words in her heart. All these changes would make a difference in the progression of the MS; and, most significantly, Marsha would feel loved.

To begin the healing process, I asked Marsha to close her eyes, soften her breathing, and move into her heart. I asked her to imagine a bowl that held the energy of her wisdom, the wise choices for her life. I told her that the bowl represented her sense of connection through love to authority figures, including her mother and father and to The Creator. "This bowl," I said, "is your Wisdom Bowl, located in the energy envelope that surrounds your body. Imagine it near the crown of your head." She immediately responded that her Wisdom bowl was slender and tall like an Egyptian water urn. She said it was beautiful from the outside, with many elaborate engravings in gold. When I asked her to tell me what the inside looked like, she hesitated and said it was too dark to see down into the center.

I continued slowly, telling her that this Wisdom Bowl sounded very beautiful on the outside, but she might want to widen the bowl a little or adjust it in some way so it could hold more energy and she could see inside. "I'm making the bowl lower and opening up the sides so I can see inside," she responded. In dismay, she added, "The inside isn't gold. It's just old, rusted iron."

I asked her, "What does the rusted iron suggest to you?"

"That I'm not worth loving," she replied.

I asked her why that was, and she replied, "Because my mother never loved me, and so I must not be worth loving."

Continuing the practice, I asked Marsha to imagine her mother seated across from her. "Tell your mother what you've just told me," I said. At first her voice trembled as she began to address her deceased mother. Slowly, her words built in intensity until they spilled out in a torrent of anguish. Quietly, I continued, "Now, Marsha, move from those feelings in your personality to your authentic self—that part of you where love lives and your authentic self is in charge. Ask your mother the question you really need her to answer."

Without hesitation, she responded, "I need to know why you never loved me!"

I said, "Listen to what your mother has to say to you from her own inner place of love—her authentic self." Marsha began to share her mother's dialogue, words of comfort and relief for finding a way to tell her daughter of her sorrow at never being able to convey the love she felt for her. "So what is the jewel, the blessing in this terrible challenge?"

Marsha thought for a few minutes and finally said, "That I'm worth loving."

"Now," I continued, "imagine the inside of the bowl that had been iron. Describe it to me now that you're aware of feeling connected to love and to your mother."

She said, "I'm waving a magic wand over the bowl, and the inside is turning into brilliant gold with the same beautiful etchings that are on the outside."

As we returned to our original discussion, we talked about how changing the bowl's image would help the flow of energy to her nervous system and help her re-balance from the MS. She seemed deeply changed, more serene, less anxious. She was taken with the understanding that she had powerful inner resources that she had never imagined before.

Marsha recognized that the image of rusted iron expressed her lack of trust in herself, in her mother as an authority figure, and in God, the ultimate authority figure. She felt inadequate because she had never allowed herself to accept that her mother really loved her. As she changed the image of her bowl, she felt that she was healing the old pains. She agreed to continue working with the premise that she was "golden on the inside" and that her mother loved her even though she hadn't told this to her until this healing. Now, for the first time in her life, Marsha knew that she was enough.

What a lovely woman, I thought as I hung up the telephone. She shared with me the intimate story of personal trauma. Disease—the gift that keeps on taking—often removes the covers on our authentic selves, while love—the gift that keeps on giving—restores that balance. Healing begins with knowing that we are Divine Creations, with all the safety, all the love and closeness we need in order to act with wisdom in our lives. I was anxious to see how the Bowl practice, along with other practices I suggested, would help Marsha to find connection to her own loving authority that could help her heal her physical imbalances. Months later, she called to tell me about her tremendous improvement. When we find and engage our inner wisdom, we come full circle in finding help and being available to pass along the gift.

Sketching Our Wisdom Bowls

IT'S TIME TO SKETCH YOUR OWN Wisdom Bowl. The Wisdom Bowl is located near the crown of the head and relates to the Seventh Chakra or energy center. It governs your nervous system and seeks to link the impulses of your beliefs with those of The Creator. You may want to review the detailed steps of the Mending Your Bowls Practice in the Appendix before starting. Begin by imagining a bowl that represents your ability to believe in The Creator. To start the process, ask yourself such questions as: "Do I have faith in God, or in a Higher Power? How much does my faith in a Creator increase my courage in addressing daily difficulties by being true to my beliefs and values? Does my belief in a Greater Love bring me peace of mind when I'm afraid for the safety of someone whom I love? How connected do I feel to other people? Do I merely give them lip service, or do I feel a bond with them that influences how I act with them?"

Next, draw or sketch your Wisdom Bowl image. You don't have to be an artist to do this. Don't worry about what it looks like. You're interested in it only as a metaphor that represents your life experience. Make a note of every detail because your inner Wise Counselor is guiding you to places you've never been before. This is a voyage of discovery, and you are a courageous explorer charting a new course.

You can make your sketches on the blank pages provided at the end of each chapter or in a separate sketchpad or journal. This will become your personal record of your growth, emotional healing, and spiritual discovery on your voyage.

As the image of your bowl comes to life, draw it on paper. Keeping it only in your mind will short-change the full impact of the experience. Even if you feel resistant to drawing your bowl, keep going. You may think that you'll always remember the bowl image you envisioned, but trust me, it will slip away. You will want a record of your progress. Through the process of creating and mending your Wisdom Bowl, you'll discover a way to reduce pain and stress in your life, and you will uncover something brilliant about yourself that will restart a part of your life that had been languishing or lost.

Your Wisdom Bowl reflects your belief in a Greater Good. Your bowl, through its imperfections, will take you to what or who has shattered your connection to the Universal Creative Force. Don't stop at deciding who was at fault. Find the part of your authentic true self that is waiting to be reclaimed. This discovery is what will make you whole. Refuse to listen to the part of your Personality Self that says, "Why bother with this bowl business when I've been in therapy for years!" This isn't therapy; it's a healing practice that results in spiritual empowerment.

You might think that you should put off drawing the bowl until you have more time. There is no advantage to putting off what can help you right now. You're worth the effort. Take five minutes or two hours now, and know that you can return later for even more insights than those you get the first time.

When you use this bowl practice, tell yourself that you're doing it "as if" what you see is truly reflective of your feelings about kinship with the Creative Universe. In that way you bypass such thoughts as, "How do I know for sure what's true and what's not?" You'll realize soon enough the power of this visualization. Remember, there is no correct way for you to do this practice. *Your way is the right way.*

Every time you recall your Wisdom Bowl, remembering the blessing in your challenge and mending your bowl accordingly, you are enhancing the flow of energy into your Wisdom Bowl and bringing healing to your nervous system. For a while, you may want to use this process weekly, as a personal healing tool.

All too often we spend our days worrying and creating in our minds images that are negative and destructive. When we change the way we think about ourselves, we enhance our healing and our future well-being. When we learn to focus on healthy images, we slowly shift the old messages lodged in our bodies' tissues and energy field that have caused us trouble.

I saw a sign in a nursing home that said, "It takes 30 days to recover from a negative thought." Whether or not it takes exactly 30 days, our thinking creates the instructions that direct our energy flows.

Prayers in Our Wisdom Bowls

THE BEST WAY TO ENCOURAGE your nervous system to heal is through prayer. Prayer is the healing practice I urge people to use because it helps make real our inner knowledge that we are all one. Our energy bodies and our physical bodies operate by the principle that what we put out is what we get back because we're all part of one living system. When we are discouraged, angry, or put off by someone, we often react as if the person were separate from us. But at an energy level, we are only hurting ourselves by responding in ways that are detrimental to the other person. In each of our interactions, we either raise the level of positive energy within and around us or we lower it.

We know that praying is a good thing. We pray when we need help and when we're grateful, when we're happy and delighted, or when we're miserable and afraid. Praying is our most natural way of experiencing God.

There is no one way to create healing prayers. There is only *your* way to pray. Your prayer and my prayer will be different, but each will be heard, completely appreciated, and understood by the Source of Love. As we pray, we leave behind our jealousies and pettiness and realize our true brilliance.

I think God wants what we each want. God is the source of comfort and compassion for our struggles, not the one saying, "I told you so," but rather the one that says, "Let me help you." You can benefit from having a healing prayer in your life, whether or not it's connected to any specific religious or spiritual philosophy. God is love. Feeling that love will create a better life for you and those close to you.

■ *Healing Prayer Practice*

Create your own morning and evening prayers. They can be the same prayer or two different ones. Your prayer can be any length, but shorter is better. The only prerequisite is that it needs to come from your heart and be easy to memorize. To help you feel less self-conscious, you may want to put on some inspiring music or light a candle and some incense before creating your prayer. Do whatever helps you to feel quiet inside. Place your hand over your heart and ask your Wise Counselor self to be present and available to you as you say your healing prayer.

♦ Say your morning prayer as your first conscious thought of the day. Repeat your evening prayer as your last conscious thought before going to sleep.

♦ Say your prayer to bless your food.

♦ Say your prayer to bless your family when you feel especially loved or troubled because you don't feel loved.

♦ Say your prayer when you are grateful for all the people who make your life easier, or harder, because they are completely ungrateful and self-absorbed.

♦ Sing or chant your prayer to create a different energy effect. Choose a rhythm or chorus of a song that you especially like, and use it as the basis of your prayer.

♦ Strike a bell, chimes, or drum to the rhythm of your prayer.

This is my prayer:

Oh my Dear Lord
Bring me into your heart

*

Oh my Dear Love
Bring me into your life

*

Oh my Dear Lord
Bring me into your world.

Use your prayer throughout the day to enhance the connection to your inner Wise Counselor in order to access greater wisdom in your thoughts, decisions, and actions. You'll be surprised at the power and healing that comes to you from this deeply moving experience.

IN SUMMARY
The Wise Counselor's Gifts

HERE IS A SUMMARY of the types of guidance and mentoring available to you from your inner Wise Counselor. Call on him/her to be present in your life, inspiring your actions and attitudes. You will be amazed at how your life progresses, prospers, and fills with unanticipated blessings.

My inner Wise Counselor guides my life with wisdom.

◆ My Wise Counselor teaches me to see and use my wisdom and discernment in making the best possible choices for my life, as part of the larger family of all life.

◆ My Wise Counselor is the loving parent and mentor I've always wanted and needed.

◆ My Wise Counselor is my spirit telling me that The Creator is as close as my breath, and that I can stay out of the shadow of daily fears because God sees my value and embraces my life with Grace.

◆ My Wise Counselor helps me see the wisdom inherent in life's challenges, suggesting possibilities that I would ordinarily miss.

◆ My Wise Counselor is patient to a fault, never scolding but demanding my best efforts, for God knows my potential.

- ◆ My Wise Counselor helps me feel safe in an obviously unsafe world, daily deepening my belief and faith in my ability to love others even when they seem deeply flawed and unworthy of my love.

- ◆ My Wise Counselor helps me rise to new levels of courage and wisdom, restoring my faith in the power of love to heal.

- ◆ My Wise Counselor is the quiet inner voice, the whisper that, when I choose to listen, overrides the normal confusion and struggle in my mind.

As you review the drawing of your Wisdom Bowl, consider these statements about benefits you can derive from the exercise:

My Wisdom Bowl governs my quality of Divine Wisdom.

My Wisdom Bowl helps me feel kinship with The Creator.

My Wisdom Bowl governs the health of my nervous system (including the brain, spinal cord, ganglia, nerve fibers, and sensory and motor terminals.)

My Wisdom Bowl represents the actual energy center of my Seventh Chakra, which is located near the crown of my head in the envelope of energy that is my energy field.

Prayer is the most useful healing practice for influencing my wisdom and creating a stronger connection to my inner Wise Counselor.

How much you love someone has
nothing to do with how much they love you.

———————————

Cameron Gesto

VISION

Silent Palms

Light softens as the heavens come closer,
bending near to kiss the Earth.
Through her gentle blanket of solitude, night comes and goes,
and the days last until you can
no longer bear to look into the glare of your dismay.
Sometimes it's hard to see straight ahead.
Even more difficult is it to see into the shadows
and nuances of past loves and future dreams.
Yet here in the snowy wonder of visions lost and found
lies your new day.
God in the vastness of the heavens visits your soul each night,
bestowing the greatness of life eternal into folds of your beating heart.
Your vision sighs into intention
as silent palms come together in blissful night-time prayer.
Life is here and then gone in fleeting moments,
but your vision will live
as long as light bends to touch the Earth in each new dawn
as the silent slumber of children
sweeps vivid dreams across the hearts of all creatures large and small.

— Meredith Young-Sowers

VISION

To see others as they seem to be is human—
to see others as they truly are is divine.

THERE WAS NEVER ANY WAY this dream was going to happen. For as long as I could remember, I wanted to become a medical doctor. At first, it may have been a romantic notion, but it quickly became a genuine desire to explore how the miraculous body did its work to keep us alive. I worked in and around medicine just enough to keep my joy alive but never enough to find any real satisfaction. The first surgical procedure I witnessed, however, forever shifted the way I thought about healing.

The procedure was being performed on a young woman who had given birth to many children. Her name was Rose. I remember her soft brown eyes and the expression of quiet resolution on her face as the medical team put her under the anesthetic. The surgeon was a man of few words, intimidating to most because he would bellow his orders at interns and residents. But in the operating room he fully embraced his enormous responsibility to save lives.

As the operation got underway, with all the procedures necessary for opening Rose's heart and circulating her blood through a heart-lung machine, I stood in silent vigil, feeling as if God Her(Him)self had entered the sacred temple of the operating room. I reflected on the courage and faith that allowed Rose to agree to have her heart opened. And I imagined how her heart felt undergoing this invasion. But I was especially struck by the routine, matter-of-fact way that the operating room staff proceeded in preparing Rose to have her heart stopped and opened.

It never occurred to me that the woman would die. That wasn't supposed to happen in the miraculous world of modern medicine, where healing, I thought, resulted automatically from surgical interventions. Slowly, the surgeon's face took on a surreal look—whiter than the dying woman's face that lay in front of him. The horror, profound sadness, and utter helplessness of the situation settled into every line of his face like a tragic mask. For hours the entire team labored to save Rose, but the sutures wouldn't hold in her heart muscle, which was later described as having the consistency of tissue paper. She just never came back.

I never did become a medical doctor. Instead, I became a spiritual teacher and intuitive healer. I didn't choose my life path; it chose me. As we allow our authentic selves to guide us, trusting our inner vision, our way emerges in bits and pieces. We find the path we're meant to walk in the same way that we walk over rocks to cross a stream, one step at a time.

We yearn to have the entire picture of our prized career spelled out in front of us in block letters, but I don't believe that is how it works. We have to put effort, often for many years, into finding the parts of our sacred nature that will form the foundation of our life work. We want the edifice before we build the foundation. Concrete and rebar—steel rods that reinforce concrete—are very boring, but without a foundation and structure, no life work can stand. Before our sacred foundation of concrete and rebar is set in place, we look, but we fail to see the possibilities. Then, one day, we look again and see a new trail to follow.

Our spiritual journey gives us the tools to see differently. We are no longer fooled by what looks like a pot of gold at the end of the rainbow. The real pot of gold isn't out there; it lives within us as our sacred natures.

The real work we're to do in life is so close to our hearts and our passions that, for many years, we give it no attention. We are prone to look only at the obvious. We look at our skills and talents, our interests, our likes and dislikes, and we discount our passion, which is what drives us from inside. For most of our lives, we work hard to succeed at a career. Slowly, our life purposes take shape in spite of the roadblocks we put in our own way. We keep trying to do more of the very things that have left us feeling sick and unfulfilled. We know that we feel dissatisfied, but we think the reason is that we're just not successful enough. It doesn't occur to us that we're looking in the wrong place. If you want a drink of water, it does no good to pick up a stone.

We're very smart people. Once we realize that certain kinds of living and relating fill us up, we're able to see the big picture of our future. But rarely does the big picture become a reality. I think God and our angels want us to stay focused and content with today. In my own experience, every time I've gotten lost daydreaming about a wonderful future that awaited me, it evaporated. Our authentic selves love process rather than goals. It is our personality selves that are wedded to goals and accomplishments.

Figuring out our life paths and their visions is messy. We experience lots of starts and stops—green lights, red lights, and many, many years of yellow lights. Yet our purpose for living is an essential aspect, a major piece, of our sacred nature. We are propelled to know our visions—not our jobs, our visions. We ask, "Why did I come to this Earth? What am I doing here? How can I contribute?" Over the years, I've heard hundreds and hundreds of students, clients, and friends ask me these same questions.

A vision is a living fabric of our creation. It is ours alone; no other person can step into our shoes and live our visions. We see this play out when a company prospers under the original management that holds the company's vision, then collapses when the company is bought by some other, larger organization. Our visions flow from us like streams of energy. Our visions are the identifying marks of our existence. When a spiritual teacher says, "My life is my message," she means that her vision and its expression identifies and personifies the sacred nature of her life. Our every breath nurtures our sacred vision no matter whether we're aware of it or not. Our inner Vision Keeper tends the sacred fires of our Vision.

Vision Keeper Friends

Vision Keepers encourage us to discover our own inner Vision as an aspect of our authentic selves. A Vision Keeper is someone who has experienced the sacred in his or her own life and opens a doorway leading us toward the spiritual. Vision Keepers can be priests, rabbis, ministers, or teachers. They can also be people who express their loving intent without a title or mantle of authority. It might be the elderly woman next door who lovingly takes care of her invalid husband, or the teenager who rides his bike to his grandparents' house after school to help out. Another is the latchkey child who spends many empty hours playing happily with and feeding a stray cat that appears mysteriously at his house each day. It is also the company executive who brings more compassionate criteria to his company in order to produce products with less impact on the environment. These are all examples of Vision Keepers, who demonstrate spiritual authenticity in correcting morally untenable situations. Their visions flow from loving hearts, their deep sacred natures, to solve a problem and live the solution. Our own internal Vision Keepers want us to live the qualities that we're espousing for others, or those we claim we live by. Our Vision Keepers set a high standard.

Vision Keepers as friends and colleagues know they need the sacred in their lives, even though they may or may not identify with a particular theology or belief system. They know a deeper truth. They know who they are through actions that flow directly from their vision of how life ought to be. Vision Keepers do not wait for others to implement change; they begin with what is possible in the moment. They don't listen to what cannot happen; they see what can, and they are content to work small.

Vision Keepers respond with heart and certainty, as the following true story demonstrates. A young man was walking along a country road. As he rounded a bend, he saw some children playing near a small pond. As he got closer, he saw that the children were throwing sticks and stones at a calf stuck in the mud. The young man walked over to the edge of the water, waded into the muck, and pulled the calf out. The children said, "Why did you do that?" The young man replied, "Because it hurt my heart to see the calf struggling." Vision Keepers respond from their compassion and take immediate action to set things right.

Another significant thing about Vision Keepers is that they finish up old business in order to clear the way for their new vision. They may be experiencing significant family struggles that have haunted them for years, but they realize that in order to have a future, they must first deal with the relationships that drain their energy. Without energy, no one has the resources to awaken a vision.

Vision Keepers are different from Wise Counselors in this way: A Wise Counselor helps us to see the big picture and how we all have a place within it. A Vision Keeper inspires us to take action consistent with our sacred nature and to trust the process rather than worrying about the outcome. Vision Keepers help us believe in ourselves so that who we are is implicit in our vision.

Listening to Our Inner Vision Keepers

Our inner Vision Keepers want us to sense God in intimate terms. We've considered God in terms of the vastness of the Universe. Now, as we seek a vision for our lives, we're ready to experience The Creator in a more direct and personal way. The very essence of the Universe is personal. Every creature takes life very personally. Every child has a direct and personal relationship with his or her parents. Every grandparent treasures his or her life through the smiles of grandchildren. God isn't an absentee landlord. The Creator has given us the greatest gift of all: our own individual Divine Light. Through this personal light we can recognize our personal God.

Divine Light births our vision as we make our way in the world. Only when we become practiced pilgrims on the journey do we discover how to keep our energy levels high enough to continue to feed our visions. Sometimes we feel so drained by our daily efforts to keep life and limb together that we need some recovery time. Such practices as prayer, meditation, walking, reading, contemplating, or just being quiet help us replenish the light, turning us inward to receive the nourishment we need to stoke our vision fires.

When we imagine God in our lives as up close and personal, we find a different feeling in our hearts. If God were sitting on the couch next to you, what would you say? What would God say to acknowledge your life, give you comfort, and take away your fear? We may squirm a bit, thinking about God being so close, yet God is as close as all the life forms around us every day. We forget to see the man or woman behind the counter at the post office as God or the UPS driver as God.

God also appears in our lives in more evolved forms, as mentors and powerful "way-show-ers" presented through the world's great religious leaders. Jesus the Christ, Buddha, Mohammed, Krishna, and Sathya Sai Baba are examples of personal forms of God. We, too, are on our way to becoming "way-show-ers"—more realized beings. We have the inner equipment in the form of our inner light, our authentic selves. As we pick up the pace on our commitment to expanding our Divine Light, we are rewarded with a clearer, more dynamic sense of our own vision.

Imagine God in the form of your favorite "way show-er," sitting next to you on the couch or at the dinner table. Realize that the Almighty has your number! Not the number of things you've done wrong! Not the view of you as a failure or of you as less than meeting the mark! "All That Is" finds you a person who cares, someone trying to become a loving player in difficult times. To this end, you have been gifted with a Vision Keeper who is actively engaged with you in the pursuit of your vision, teaching you to realize your vision through the art of Sacred Seeing.

Perception as Sacred Seeing

Sacred Seeing is seeing deeply with awareness. Perception, like the awareness of "Kinship," helps us engage the qualities of our inner divinity, tracking the meaning of our lives by asking "vision questions."

Our intuition alerts us to changes in our emotional environment. Perception alerts us to shifts in our spiritual environment. Sacred Seeing takes us two steps deeper than our normal intuition, to the level of our authentic selves. It asks us to "hear" and respond honestly to the real questions for which we need answers.

As we identify our personal vision questions, we see how we are guided to the places that have meaning for our lives. Our vision is the process of refining and redefining, over a lifetime, that which provides the greatest meaning for our lives.

■ *Inner Questioning*

Using Sacred Seeing, Hearing, or Listening, we learn to pay attention to our inner questions. We're always tracking our truth, which is the way we seek to enliven and enhance our lives. Many times we ask "vision questions" without realizing that they come from our Vision Keeper, who is pushing us to pay attention to where we're going in life. Our answers to these vision questions help us understand what we love and where we find meaning.

The vision questions we need to answer are not necessarily the ones with which we begin our internal dialogue. Let's listen in to an imaginary conversation with Julian, who works in the kitchen of a large hotel, in order to understand the process that takes us from entry-level conversations to vision questions.

Julian asks himself, "I wonder if I'm going to earn overtime tonight? What if Joe leaves early? Will I need to clean up his section, too? Does anyone appreciate me for the work I'm doing here? Why am I in this job, anyway?"

At first, Julian thinks about the more mundane aspects of his work. His intuition allows him to consider the nature of his work and what he can anticipate. Then his perception takes over, and he finds himself asking a profound question: "Why am I in this job, anyway?" This is a genuine vision question for Julian. Were he using his Sacred Seeing, he'd be looking for such provocative questions, and he'd take them very seriously. Our Vision Keeper asks us to live with continuous awareness of our vision.

Let's assume Julian is paying attention and is struck by the significance of his question. He would consider whether his job was meaningful to him. He wouldn't consider any other sidetracks, like, "Yes, but it pays the bills." Or "I have no college education, so this is as good a job as I can get," or "The economy is depressed, so I'd better play it safe and just suck it up." When we clutter our minds with all the reasons we cannot possibly be successful in taking the next step, we foil Vision Keeper's insights. Either we give up, or else willpower takes over and we try to make our vision work by sheer muscle. We all know the results: disaster, and wasted time and effort. Our authentic selves fuel our vision effortlessly. We show up to do our best, with total confidence in the outcome because we've given the outcome to The Creator. I find it useful to ask myself, "Am I working for God, or am I working for myself?" Where I feel the reaction inside of me tells me the truth. If I feel it in my gut as opposed to my heart, I'm probably working for myself.

If Julian were staying true to his vision, he might conclude that, for him, the only value comes from working with the other staff members, helping them feel better about themselves. Realizing this, he might begin to understand that while his job provides a small slice of what is significant to him, he needs a larger slice of what he loves. Julian has choices; he can decide to get some training and begin working with troubled teens. He'd be moving closer to a full-time experience that would give his life greater meaning.

Vision isn't guiding us to just another job. It is guiding us into full-time participation in the experiences that offer us the greatest meaning. Vision Keeper is at work in everyone's life and cares only about spreading love, encouragement, and opportunity into every open hand and heart. Everyone has a fair shot at finding his or her vision and turning it into a living presence in their lives.

We might wonder about people who are very successful financially but seem interested only in making money no matter how they do it. Are such people being guided by their Vision Keepers? I've learned from experience that we're wise not to judge such people because we do not understand the bigger picture of their lives. One thing we can know is that, as we age, Vision Keeper has a distinct advantage, because our minds turn naturally to the legacy we will leave our children and the world. We all want to leave a positive mark. Money, power, and position may matter in the short term, but they don't count when we are ready to leave the Earth. The vision we lived is all that will comfort us. Money, power, and position are not necessarily evil things; the way we use them is what makes them valuable in the world. Money, power, and position, driven by vision from an authentic heart, can change the world.

Never underestimate the power of the Vision Keeper to make use of every one of our passions, turning our self-serving interests into community-serving ones. Vision Keeper is an equal-opportunity employer.

Creating a Vision

Vision travels beneath our career choices as the divine thread inspiring our efforts in the world. Our vision shapes us as much as we shape it. I may hold a thought, but once I've put it out into the world by teaching it or writing about it, it has a life of its own. Other people hear and respond to the thought, and now they are playing a part in my vision. They've added their energy to my vision, just as I add my energy to other people's visions. Think of the many people in your lifetime whose work you've admired or enjoyed. You are an active part of their vision. You spread their vision by telling others about it. In this way, we are all active parts of each other's visions. Together, our vision family is our spiritual community. We are connected through our passion to the same dream of spreading love and compassion in the world. Our spiritual community holds overlapping visions that are imbued with the sacred.

The energy of *Wisdom Bowls,* for example, is helping me expand my vision family because everyone reading this book is participating in my vision. I am also participating in yours. Together, we are a spiritual community. Discovering our vision family can make the essential difference in any needed healing.

Shawn's Story

Shawn was referred to me for a consultation because he had hypertension, was on hormone replacements, and had a benign pituitary tumor. Interestingly, he was a successful physician with a large and thriving practice. He worked constantly, spending little time at home with his family. At work, he found connection and support for his efforts that he didn't experience at home. While he struggled to trust and care for himself when he wasn't working, he felt fully alive when helping others. Shawn admitted that he was completely unable to accept kind comments. He told me how odd it had felt to have a woman patient he had helped kiss him on the cheek in gratitude and tell him he was wonderful. After the incident, he left the room feeling embarrassed and empty.

What was keeping Shawn from feeling his worth? He knew he needed to change his life but felt immobilized by the enormous shifts that needed to take place in his career and his failing marriage. He wanted the state of his world to be miraculously righted without having to face the pain of feeling wrong, or hearing the accusations he would confront, not only from family and friends but also from himself, if he chose a path not endorsed by others. He told me that he admired his father, yet he hadn't been able to please his dad, no matter how hard he tried.

Having a strong sense of self, a belief in the rightness of our efforts, and a path to a personal God are the only healing graces that work when we have so many changes to make. We find the courage to survive only when we face the people in our lives with as much honesty and consideration as we can muster. Many times life pushes us to a place where we throw caution to the winds and either fall in love with someone else or get up and move out without even saying goodbye. We aren't schooled in how to do or say difficult, unpopular things and survive the inevitable isolation or condemnation. Sometimes it's easier to die than face the consequences of our actions.

As we talked, I realized that Shawn, after years of therapy alone and with his wife, knew what the problems were but lacked the will and courage to move forward with his vision for his life. We can continue to dig at the imperfections that we and our partners display and to parry accusations back and forth, but if we're to find the confidence to trust our choices, we need to raise our questioning to the level of visioning.

Earlier in his life, Shawn had practiced Zen meditation. He confided in me that he had dreamed of becoming a Zen Master. I could see from his energy that in fact he had come into this life with deep compassion and a desire to serve humanity. He seemed to have all the rough ingredients of becoming a true Zen Master. Yet his life challenge, the piece he had to face and overcome in order to bring spirituality back into his life, was learning to deal with his tremendous fear of criticism. He criticized himself unmercifully.

He told me he'd grown up Catholic, gone to Catholic schools and a Catholic College. He didn't buy "this personal God stuff." I knew that Shawn and I needed to get at his feelings of being judged by God rather than feeling comforted by The Creator. In Shawn's mind, God, like his father, was an absolute judge. Shawn found it impossible to permit himself to work at what had meaning for him, or bridge his love from himself to his wife and children. He confided to me that his father had said, "I'll never tell you when you do something right, but I'll always correct you when you do something wrong."

I suggested to Shawn that we take part in the Mending Your Bowl visualization practice. I told him to close his eyes, soften his breathing, and put his hand over his heart. I asked him to imagine a bowl of any shape, color, or size, made of any substance he chose. I explained, "This bowl represents the power of your vision. It holds your ability to engage your vision to heal your relationship with your father and with God as judge. This bowl also holds your vision of your life's purpose. What does this bowl feel like to you?"

Shawn described his bowl as black, shiny, slippery and very small. He said it was made of alabaster, and there seemed to be no way to pick it up. As I played his comments through my thoughts, I knew this final comment was extremely significant. I also paid attention to the black color, which suggested deep change and transformation, a need to wake up spiritually. The slippery sides of his bowl suggested that he had trouble holding on to his vision of how he wanted his life to be and felt little confidence that he could find what held meaning for him. The fact that the bowl was small related to his feeling that his vision power was diminished. I found it especially helpful to realize that he was looking for a handle, some way to "pick up" his bowl, or to take hold of his vision.

I asked Shawn to identify any broken places, chips, or imperfections in his bowl. Shawn's response took me by surprise. He replied that a fog seemed to surround his bowl so that he couldn't see it clearly. I asked him to talk to me about the fog. He said, "I need help in seeing through it, and I don't know what to do or where to go." I asked him what else he could tell me about the fog. He continued, "I see the face of a dear friend, a woman who cares for me, and she's smiling. It makes me feel safe." Then, he said something quite uncharacteristic. He said softly, "Do you suppose that this woman is a symbol of some kind, telling me that it's safe to love myself?" I asked him to make it possible in his mind's eye to see the bowl again and to tell me how it had changed. Shawn said, with slow, deliberate words, "The bowl doesn't seem so dark. I see some flecks of gold on the far side. It looks almost like a smile."

Shawn had moved naturally from the trouble in his bowl to the source of his pain and then to the solution. We talked at length about the smile in the bowl being the power of Love guiding him personally. I suggested that he imagine a friend who had played or was playing the role of Vision Keeper in his life, a thought that might give him a better sense of his own powerful inner Vision Keeper. If Shawn stood a chance of connecting with his wife and children in a more meaningful way, he needed to engage his Vision Keeper to clear out the many years of pain from his family relationships. I continued, "Shawn, what does the brilliant gold of the 'smile' in your vision bowl tell you about the jewel in the suffering with your father?" His voice got very quiet, and he said haltingly, "That I can smile through uncertainty, and never lose my way again."

While Shawn had made a remarkable beginning in releasing years of self-condemnation, he realized continuous effort would be required to find the inner freedom he sought.

Shawn's Pituitary Tumor

I thought about the emotional and spiritual issues that lay behind Shawn's pituitary tumor. The pituitary gland is the master switch of the endocrine system. This amazing system is the "power behind the scenes" for our well-being because it tells our organs when and how much of our hormones and other essential secretions to release. The endocrine system involves the pituitary gland, the thymus, thyroid, pancreas, and adrenal glands as well as parts of the ovaries or testes. I knew that, for Shawn to decrease the size of his tumor, he needed to understand how it had come about from an emotional and spiritual perspective.

The Vision Bowl, or Sixth Chakra, is an actual part of our energy field resting between the eyebrows. The energy that flows through this bowl determines the level of balance and health in the organs of our endocrine system.

Shawn's lack of belief in his vision—his feeling stranded because of his father's criticism and his own inability to create meaningful relationships with others—was what was out of sync with his health. Symbolically, a tumor means that a person is trying to grow emotionally and spiritually but is unable to face particular issues. As a result, growth occurs in a destructive way inside the body. There are no accidents in the way diseases take shape. The pituitary gland was the point where Shawn's emotional suffering began as a child. The presence of the tumor meant he couldn't grow past this place of pain without a belief in himself and a vision for the future.

In addition to revisiting Shawn's Vision Bowl and deepening his feeling about the "smile," we worked with meditation. Meditation, quieting the critical mind, is the most useful practice for bringing healing to the endocrine system. Meditation is also the way we revisit our past relationships and embrace the quiet new authentic voice we're learning to hear as our Divine Inner Light.

Sketching Our Vision Bowls

THE VISION BOWL CONNECTS you directly with several key elements in your life: your family of origin, your ability to create a vision with your spiritual family, and your personal relationship with The Creator. The Vision Bowl is located near the center of your forehead and relates to the Sixth Chakra. It governs your endocrine system, stimulating good outcomes for your life by asking you to forgive old struggles and fears with your biological family.

Although many of the practices in this book bring you back to your family of origin or previous partner struggles, the Vision Bowl is the primary one for ridding yourself of old negative messages that obstruct your life. The Vision Bowl helps you find answers to such questions as, "Do I have a personal relationship with The Creator? To what degree have I healed my issues with my family and other important people in my life? How aware am I of the Vision questions I'm asking?"

In drawing your Vision Bowl, you enter a process of self-discovery about the way God can play a part in your life. We've explored faith in God as a concept, but now you might consider faith in God as a personal connection. We're not trying to give The Creator human behavior patterns, only a human form. In order to claim the Mother/Father God within ourselves, we need to realize that to help us along our path The Almighty takes many shapes. Finding a personal form for God helps us to build trust in our inner selves. It's the hand we reach out for at 2:00 A.M., to help us regain our footing.

Because our Vision Bowls govern the health of our endocrine systems, if you have a problem in this area—a thyroid imbalance, adrenal fatigue, pancreatic/blood sugar imbalances, or addictions of any kind—you'll want to make the Vision Bowl practice a priority. As you perform the various healing practices, especially meditation, which reinforces the link between you and the Universe, you'll develop a deeper appreciation of what lies behind your health problem. You'll also see marked improvement in it.

Healing and Empowerment Meditation

MEDITATION IS A TECHNIQUE for quieting the incessant thinking of our busy minds so that each day we feel calmer and more centered. Beginning to meditate means setting aside a time in the day, preferably in the morning, before the busy-ness of the day takes over. Sit in a quiet room on a comfortable chair or on the floor with your back straight. Close your eyes and breathe slowly, deeply, several times.

Sit with your feelings, breathing through them to find calm. You're learning to be with yourself without the continual stimulation of thinking. By sitting, you're inquiring into the nature of the authentic "you"—your God-self—that lives juxtaposed to your personality. Know that you are a genuine, authentic jewel of existence.

If you struggle with addictions or fears, meditation is a wonderful way to find the demons that feed these challenges. People have thoughts like, "Why can't I stop eating all the wrong things?" or "Why am I so unhappy in this marriage?" or "...with this child?" or "What will happen to me if I don't find a new job (get more money, get out of this deal, buy this new house, or move across the country)?" The panic we feel is because we don't yet see the answer or can't control the way events unfold. Through meditation we learn to be patient, not to assume that today's events are the final word on any subject. Meditation helps us live with the uncertainty of life and stave off the panic that we feel.

I remember hearing from a spiritual teacher that the reason we have a home is so that we have a place to meditate. Of course, meditation doesn't eliminate our difficulties. We continue to have pressing problems and situations that require our full attention. That doesn't change. What does change is the way we approach our lives and challenges.

Through meditation we develop greater equanimity, a more positive sense of coming out in a good place, no matter what happens in between the good feelings. We begin to experience the sense that the Creator is as close as our breath, and that we are prepared to face the suffering of being attached to things in life, the eventuality of our death, and the transition of those whom we love. Meditation can be difficult because to use it we need to set aside precious time in the day. But the twenty to thirty minutes reserved for meditation set us up for the day. We become clearer, less jagged in our efforts, more authentic, and less reactive. Most important, resting our minds generates peacefulness, and from peacefulness comes compassion, self-love, and love of others.

■ *Vision Family Meditation*

Use this meditation to create a true connection to several people you choose as your spiritual family. These are people whose life-work, vision, and passion inspire you. You can continue to add as many people as you wish.

♦ Sit with your back straight, close your eyes, and steady your breathing.

♦ Move your attention from your thinking to your inner self by placing one or both hands over your heart center *(the center of your chest)*.

♦ Become aware of the special, living or dead, well-known or unknown people whom you admire and with whom you wish to feel a deeper connection. These may be religious figures like Jesus Christ, or well-known humanitarians like Mother Theresa. He or she can also be your neighbor.

♦ Place yourself on a simple stage with these other people. You're all standing together at the same level. *(This indicates that all beings are made from the same universal creative essence—all are your family.)*

♦ Imagine a golden ribbon surrounding all of you.

♦ Feel your connection with these Vision Keepers, who can now be with you, guiding and encouraging you to find your own path.

♦ Slowly return to your sitting space and open your eyes. Write down your feelings of connection.

IN SUMMARY

The Vision Keeper's Gifts

CONSIDER THESE SPECIAL GIFTS available to us from our inner Vision Keepers. Which ones are you familiar with? Which ones draw you in? Ask your Vision Keeper to show you how to experience or benefit from these gifts.

My inner Vision Keeper remembers and holds my true life vision.

♦ My Vision Keeper is the God inside, who today helps me find contentment, knowing that nothing in my life is a mistake, and all has purpose and is useful in my journey.

♦ My Vision Keeper opens the door for my authentic self to learn from the collective goodness of all life, gently but firmly moving me to appreciate why I've come to "Earth-School."

♦ My Vision Keeper settles me into inner steadiness, even when I can make no sense of my own or other people's actions or hurtful ways.

♦ My Vision Keeper holds me close as I find the strength to forgive the unforgivable.

♦ My Vision Keeper leads me toward meaningful insights about my past, so that the road ahead is welcoming and less daunting.

♦ My Vision Keeper draws me into warm company of new dear friends and supporters.

♦ My Vision Keeper has no fear of what lies ahead so that I find comfort in trusting the experience of the moment.

♦ My Vision Keeper welcomes my guardian angel, guides, and messengers so that I may learn and grow in the rich spiritual heritage to which I was born.

As you review the drawing of your Vision Bowl, consider these statements about benefits you can derive from the exercise:

My Vision Bowl governs my quality of Divine Vision.

My Vision Bowl helps me find my true life vision.

My Vision Bowl governs the health of my endocrine system (pituitary, thyroid, parathyroid, adrenals, testes/ovaries).

My Vision Bowl represents the actual energy center of my Sixth Chakra, which is located between my eyebrows.

Meditation is my most useful healing practice in influencing my vision and creating more useful connection with my inner Vision Keeper.

Vision isn't guiding you to just another job
but rather to full-time participation in experiences that offer you meaning.

Cameron Sesto

JOY

Darkness Is an Illusion

Darkness settles into your life
as unexpected pauses that take you by surprise.
The sun sets and the moon arises and still the darkness persists,
settling into the bowels of Mother Earth.
You can't see outside, nor can you make out the shapes dancing in your soul.
But darkness is an illusion,
for there is only the brilliance of the eternal flame.
Let inner darkness never become your excuse for hurting others.
Let darkness never again block your clear view of your path.
May the light of all eternal knowing descend upon your life
like moonbeams dancing at midnight on an unsuspecting lake.
May the eternal flame of the Mother and Father of all disguised truths
respond to your call for mercy.
May darkness and lightness find their oneness in your soul
as life resounds in joy.
May you never again be seduced into believing
that you are alone.

— Meredith Young-Sowers

CHAPTER FOUR

JOY

Dare to believe that you
can grow flowers in Jerusalem.

 I FELT SICK IN EVERY CELL of my body when I thought about getting divorced. I'd been married for twenty-three years and had two lovely children. Jim and I had planned a great escape to rural New England. We wanted more time for ourselves and our children. Time was the precious commodity we lacked. Time to be peaceful. Time to enjoy planning a child's birthday party. Time to write a book. Time to walk on hidden paths in the woods.

Jim felt that the struggles in our marriage were the result of too much pressure. When you have children and an active life, you can easily find yourself without a moment to breathe. We engaged in too many activities and had taken on too many obligations. And Jim was commuting by train an hour and a half to work every day. We suffered from a lack of time when we weren't planning, fixing, moving, or thinking. We wanted to be part of the living world again—trees, plants, animals, streams, sunsets, and a small-village atmosphere. We wanted out.

We'd taken a year off to help build a post-and-beam home in the hills of New Hampshire. Our marriage was supposed to get better. It wasn't supposed to end there. Yet, if truth be told, I'd been deeply unhappy for many years before I would even allow myself to silently mouth the word divorce.

Like a spider in a web, I went round and round in the memories and experiences we'd shared. I often felt trapped and saw no way out. I considered how divorce would affect our two children, our families and friends, our shared business colleagues. It just seemed hopeless to imagine unweaving this intricate web of a shared life. Yet, every time I came back to the idea of divorce, I knew with a quiet inner certainty that I was heading for that terrible precipice.

Interesting how we have fleeting moments of quiet certainty and clarity about our futures! We can see where we're going, what's going to happen, and we watch in slow motion as if the events were suspended in a non-reality beyond feelings. Perhaps the watchers are our individual true selves, showing us where we are going. We want to leave a marriage without animosity. But it seems impossible to do so unscathed. My mind said, "stay," but my heart said, "I can't."

Divorce, the pulling apart—the "Putting Asunder," as the wedding vows suggest—is one of life's most difficult experiences. We want our partners to understand our dilemma—our good feelings toward them but also our need for a different future. Of course, they don't understand, and the pain and rage that fills them soon clouds our own good and loving feelings. We move toward wanting to make the other persons wrong. This would be so much easier; the responsibility would be theirs.

We "love each other in spots," is what my grandmother used to say when, as a kid, I'd have a falling out with a friend. She'd say, "You'll see her differently tomorrow." In marriage we both love and admire certain aspects of our partners, and dislike, even rage, against other parts. It's very confusing. There were parts of our life together that had been good, strong, creative, and loving, but other parts put us in a continuous power struggle, a miserable tangle from which we could never entirely extricate ourselves. Our partnership was either going to grow the new buds of more intimate sharing, or we were going to tread water hoping to avoid the inevitable. I asked myself, "Can I find peace in this partnership? Is joy still possible?" I knew what my answers were and what that meant for my life.

Reality hit slowly over the next few months as I tried to spread myself around to meet everyone's needs: the children's, my company's, and the maintenance of a large property. There was little time to consider my own needs. But when I did find a scrap of time to be quiet, I had a sense of doom. What had I done? What right did I have to break up this marriage? Had I made a terrible mistake? Who could help me now?

Learning to trust my choices and decisions, even those that had been made painstakingly over many years, was a lesson that would haunt me for a long time. I realized how very unsafe I felt in my own skin, let alone in my life. How would I manage with no one to look out for me? I wondered.

Standing on our own as adults can be more terrifying than the first time we stood on our own as toddlers. At least then we knew we were walking toward someone who loved us. Yet the difficult times after Jim left eventually laid the groundwork for recovery from a serious lack of self-worth and confidence. I would come to see that self-confidence lies juxtaposed to faith in God.

When we strip away life as we've known it, we must find what remains that we choose to take forward, and what we want to let go that will disappear forever. What we can't do is think that we'll duplicate the best parts of our past by simply replacing the main player. If we're wise, we take time to rediscover who we are before entering another partnership. We've spent so many years giving to our partners and families that we've erased or detoured our own emerging interests, unique talents, and spiritual directions.

What I did take forward in my life was my spiritual work. This work would grow to become the very core of my world, my still point. And through Grace, I finally came to appreciate that it had been my Divine Mother/Father God I'd been walking toward all my life.

Peacemaker Friends

Peace Maker is the voice of Joy from our authentic selves. As we appreciate the people in our lives who exert a calming influence over us, we become better prepared to identify our inner Peace Maker.

People are not by nature peaceful. Peace Makers are the exception, because they seem to have a quiet understanding and ability to guide us that is refreshing. Peace Makers don't overtly teach us; they show us. They are the ones who don't need to be the first to be heard, or the first to receive applause. Peace Makers are usually found in the back of the room. They are the ones to whom others congregate, are eager to share with, and want to listen to deeply.

Peace Makers seem to have their own direct link to The Almighty. Their words hang in our consciousness. What they say isn't divisive or provoking but soothing. In an argument, they seem much less concerned with who is right than how both people can cooperate toward a new end. Peace Makers are usually loners, although they inspire everyone who knows them. Peace Makers are the people who walk simply and quietly on the Earth. I think of the scriptural passage from the Beatitudes, Matthew 5:9, in the Christian Bible: "Happy and blessed are the Peace Makers. They shall be called Children of God." Thus we might conclude, "Peace Makers shall inherit the Earth."

Peace Makers are unflappable in conflicts over values and ideals. Their commitment to nonviolence restores our own inner rhythms when we're around them. When we're in the presence of Peace Makers, we feel a quiet steadiness, a joy.

Listening to Our Inner Peacemakers

Of all the ways that we get in touch with who we really are—our authentic natures—none is more obvious or significant than the way we express ourselves through the words we use and the intentions behind them. We're usually unaware of our true intentions, even though we have various agendas going on all the time. We hope and need others to give us love, money, attention, respect, or other forms of approval and appreciation. But the most powerful and useful intention we can have is peace. Our inner Peace Maker is the voice of Joy asking us to accept the gift of reconciliation with life.

Joy wears many faces and is expressed in a multitude of ways through people who are part of our spiritual community and who are our partners or immediate family. We want to feel greater closeness and happiness with those we love, to deepen our tender connections with our partners, and to experience intimate union.

Peace Maker is the voice of Joy that speaks to us through our families, partners, and circle of friends. We can enhance Joy in our lives in three ways:

First, we can ask our minds to be in harmony with our hearts. This is the practice of congruence.

Second, we can be more consistent in creating peace rather than its opposite. This is the practice of continuity.

Third, we can experience Joy as an ecstatic state of closeness to God.

■ *The Practice of Congruence*

The practice of congruence requires us to pay greater attention to our words and actions as expressions of our desire for peace. With repetition and patience, we can become Peace Makers every day in our own right. We can find many opportunities: the neighbor who dumps his garbage into your bin; the person in the car in front of you who cuts ahead of you; the parking attendant who overcharges you; the manager of the company who overlooks your contribution; the child who forgets your birthday. These are all opportunities to practice peace instead of war.

I read a comment that the Dalai Lama made when asked why he never felt that military force was called for against the Chinese after their invasion of Tibet. His response became a bookmark on the page labeled "Peace Maker" in my consciousness. He said, "To go to war with China would create irreconcilable alienation between my heart and my mind. War was not a possibility." The practice of congruence allows us to become more aware of our true intentions so that we, too, can promote peace by seeking harmony between our hearts and our minds.

To practice congruence, take a slow, easy breath, and find your inner intention for peace. Imagine that this intention becomes words of truth, harmony, love, right action, and nonviolence. With this vocabulary, imagine how you can now respond to your family and friends. When something or someone upsets you and you are tempted to retaliate in word or deed, take a slow, steady breath and move back into the space of your inner Peace Maker. From this place, imagine the words you would most want to use, if you dared. Now believe that you dare—that you are the Peace Maker. Have faith that you've been given an opportunity to break out of a cycle of pain, fear, secrecy, abuse, or neglect in your life, your family, and your world. You have the power to shift out of whatever in your life comes from anger or fear. You can help rather than hurt, encourage rather than discourage, promote love rather than fear.

A Bullet for My Coat

When we remember to think "peace" instead of "war, " we create far greater intimacy and happiness with others, because we've removed the divisiveness that says, "You're on one side, and I'm on the other." We have common ground for finding a solution.

Holding an inner intention of peace is a personal commitment. We may fool other people, but we can't fool ourselves. When we make an effort toward peace we can't always know the ramifying impact of our gesture. This story demonstrates the point.

Thich Nhat Hanh is a Vietnamese monk and a world-renowned

spiritual teacher. He was ordained a Buddhist monk in 1942 at the age of sixteen. Eight years later, he co-founded what was to become the foremost center of Buddhist studies in South Vietnam. In 1963, when he was studying and teaching comparative religion at Columbia and Princeton Universities, his monk-colleagues in Vietnam pleaded with him to come home and join them in working to stop the war. He immediately returned and helped to lead one of the greatest nonviolent resistance movements of the century, based entirely on the principle of nonviolence that Gandhi used to free India from British rule. He tells this story.

During the war, he was walking through a rice paddy when he met a soldier. He asked the soldier if he would trade his gun for his coat. The soldier refused, saying that he needed the gun to stay alive. Next he asked if the soldier would trade his ammunition for it. The soldier said that he could not. Finally, the monk asked the soldier to trade one bullet for his coat. The soldier agreed.

One bullet for the monk's coat may seem like a very poor trade, but the monk didn't see it that way; he saw one life saved. We may feel that our individual efforts can do little to heal the troubles in our families, our towns, our countries, or the world. We are tempted to feel that our tiny gestures aren't worth it. But our individual actions become giant guideposts, energetically, helping shift the collective viewpoint from war to peace. I can only imagine the impact that exchange with the monk must have had on the soldier. I'm sure it changed his life—as the story has changed mine.

We all encounter situations in our homes where violence and hatred create emotional and physical havoc—another kind of war. We spread these without meaning to by reacting in rote ways, passing on a desperate and unwanted legacy to our children. It would be better to teach our children to plant gardens instead of digging bunkers. We are all afraid our children won't have enough materially, but we'd be better off ensuring that they have enough spiritually.

■ *The Practice of Continuity*

Joy and happiness are cousins. Joy is the personal experience of living in harmony with our inner Peace Maker. Happiness is the experience of sharing Joy. When we use our intention for peace with others, we share happiness. Our hearts don't want to be at war with our partners and children, and we don't want pain and confrontation with friends or in our communities. No one's heart wants war anywhere in the world.

If our hearts want peace, then why do we create such unhappiness, pain, and sorrow for ourselves and those we love? If our hearts want peace, we can, through daily practices, train our minds to listen. We can find joy through connection to our efforts rather than to outcomes and results. Throughout the day, we can reinforce our intentions for peace by taking several slow and nourishing breaths. In this way, we recover from the stress around us and bring renewal to our bodies, especially our lungs, as well as to those around us.

The practice of continuity allows us to see each day's effort as contributing to the next day's peacefulness. Each day that we practice peace in our thoughts, attitudes, and actions, we become stronger in the Peace Maker aspect of our authentic selves. We find it easier to think of peace instead of anger, hostility, and war.

To practice continuity, imagine you are playing a game of dominoes. Each day that you breathe your intention for peace and are peaceful with those around you, you set up another domino. In a very short time, you will see how many dominoes you have lined up—seven, fourteen, twenty-eight, fifty-six. Each domino represents your daily effort to act out of an intention for peace.

Now imagine that many, many people around the world are also engaging in this same practice. What do you think would happen? One day, as we set our dominoes, we might sense a dramatic change. All the dominoes everywhere, all around the world, might slowly begin to collapse, falling down to create a new path for humans to walk on—a path of peace! As if the All-Knowing Source were saying, "And now you're ready for peace in your world. Enough of you realize the power of peace in your hearts, and you can do whatever is required to never again let joy die."

This is the way it would be. We can hope that our efforts will contribute to such a magnificent world event. If we believe it, we can begin to practice being Peace Makers in earnest. It is up to you, and me, and all of us who are part of this *Wisdom Bowls* "vision family." We can make this dream a reality, one domino at a time.

■ *Joy as Divine Bliss*

The search for ecstatic joy may seem a long way from washing the family's clothes, picking up the children from soccer practice, or slipping into a chic black outfit for a night on the town. The outer expression of our lives is not what has lasting significance. The inner expression is what needs our attention.

We find many references to ecstatic joy in the spiritual traditions of the world, including those in the writings of early Christian Mystics and the Rishis of ancient India. Poets and philosophers from all cultures and religions have marked the path of wise men and women, saints, and gurus as leading to ecstatic joy or bliss. Yet today we realize that we each have the potential for joy because joy is our own true nature. Joy is within reach for all of us, and wherever joy appears, bliss follows.

Joy heightens our awareness and receptivity to love of all kinds; it is being strong with our children, compassionate with our parents, and tender with our partners. Joy is a light in the normal denseness and dimness of our daily challenges, reminding us of our true selves and our potential. Consider joy your soul's perfume. It permeates our being and diffuses an aroma that invites others to share the journey. We have that precious treasure trove within us. Joy as bliss is within our reach.

The joy that is Divine Bliss can be seen in the Goddess rituals of our ancient sisters of Avalon. The holy isle of Avalon was where the living representative of the Goddess, the Lady of the Lake, lived and trained novice priestesses in the wisdom and magic of Goddess worship. Now lost in the mists of time, the great Druid priests and high priestesses of Avalon gave Arthur his sword, Excalibur, and installed him at Camelot, in exchange for a pledge to aid Avalon when needed.

The Wise Woman tradition of the Goddess was based on a dedication to the Oneness of God and Goddess, body and spirit, magic and worldly power. The human form was considered a natural and beautiful part of the power and grace of the priestess. The ritual marriage of a Druid priest and priestess of the Goddess celebrated the joining of night and day, male and female, the mystical and the mundane. Their ceremonial coupling during the annual Feast of Beltane was a magical act of passionate power in which the God and Goddess revealed themselves and joined in an embrace, signifying the integration of the human spirit and the renewal of life on earth.

Imagine the most wonderful experience of closeness to a lover you've ever felt. Imagine the most profound orgasm you've ever experienced, and imagine that at the moment of climax you burst into a million brilliant stars shooting out into space, joyfully scattering to the far reaches of existence. This state of being more, knowing more, being lost in joy is erotic as well as ecstatic. Experiencing Divine Bliss is joyfully ecstatic, and in many experiences of the saints and mystics, it was also erotic.

In time-honored traditions, we find Divine Bliss by eliminating the barriers to our inner clear light—our radiant presence—through prayer, contemplation, meditation, and living in awareness of the preciousness of all life. The Divine Lover encourages us to rise to the level of belief in our own inner divinity in order to "love on purpose." By practicing this belief, we replenish our own hearts and fill the hearts of others with joy.

Flowers in Jerusalem

We can "grow flowers in Jerusalem" by living our intention for peace and wanting it for all people everywhere. When women live in peace, they empower women everywhere to do the same. The same is true for men and children. At the level of spiritual energy, we are kin. Whatever one of us experiences anywhere on the Earth is experienced by all of us and every form of life.

As we tend our animals with compassion and our gardens with loving care, treating our natural resources as if they mattered to us, we create the energy of one world. As we water, nurture, or simply admire a single flower, it is as if we are growing that flower in Jerusalem.

Jerusalem is an ancient city where Christianity, Judaism, and Islamic cultures and beliefs clash today. As we imagine our intention for peace, we can envision growing flowers in parts of the world where flowers—the brilliant symbols of life and beauty—are being destroyed by conflict and hate. As we imagine a flower blooming in a place without hope, we deepen our commitment to peace. When I get discouraged about the state of the world, I try to remember that like the aspirin I take to relieve a headache, I must do more than think about taking it. I must take peace into my life and make it live in my heart. That is why, when I think about Jerusalem, I imagine flowers filling the streets and yards of everyone who lives there.

Bobbie's Healing Journey

Bobbie came up to talk with me after a lecture I'd given at a local bookstore. She told me that she was very much interested in the field of mind/body/spirit healing, but she was most concerned about her husband, who was seriously depressed. She confessed that she didn't think her husband would be interested in doing any counseling with me, since he didn't believe in anything spiritual. She lamented that she had too little time in her life to have me do an energy evaluation of her, even though she was having some trouble with a knee. Bobbie continued to tell me about her overly busy life and her perseverance in holding things together for everyone. It seemed like a well-rehearsed story. She had been trying to convince herself that she didn't need to pay any attention to the lack of joy in her life or her unhappiness at work. She repeated to me what she had no doubt said to many other willing helpers: "I'm too busy taking care of my husband and my three small children, plus working full time, to consider my own happiness."

When people go to great lengths to tell me they don't have time for themselves, it often means that they believe they don't deserve time for themselves. We assume that, unless we have a pressing and diagnosable physical problem, our feelings aren't significant. Bobbie, unfortunately, was to discover that the lack of joy in her life had serious health implications.

Two months after I met Bobbie, she called me in utter shock. She'd been diagnosed with stage IV lung cancer. She told me that she'd had a raspy cough for a while but assumed it was an allergy to the family's new puppy. She said that when she looked at the x-ray she wanted to throw up, it looked so bad. But she was a "fighter," she told me, and she was sure she could "beat this thing."

Her words rang bells of alarm in me, more for her feeling that she needed to "fight" the disease than for the actual diagnosis. It's been my experience that people can heal even from what seem to be the most incurable conditions. But Bobbie's sense that she needed to fight with the cancer suggested the way she dealt with all her inner demons. She would need to see that her body wasn't the enemy and that neither was the cancer. We all have cancer in our systems all the time. Cancer cells begin to grow out of control only when we fail to allow our lives to grow naturally. Growth happens in destructive ways when healthy ways to grow are for some reason precluded.

Bobbie was going to wrestle this cancer to the ground like an opponent. Cancer or any other illness is like the canary in a miner's hat. Miners used canaries to signal poor air quality. Just so, illness signals that our bodies are seriously out of balance. This is supposed to encourage us to listen to our bodies rather than feeling we need to pound them into submission.

As I did my intuitive assessment of Bobbie to find the emotional patterns and life experiences that were lodged in her tissues, I considered the nature of her greatest suffering. Our lungs hold the "message" of what we feel about ourselves that has been our greatest lament, our greatest suffering. For Bobbie, this message was, "I have no right to my own voice." She'd spent her life surrendering her right to make choices for herself and about her circumstances. Like a bystander, she'd lived her life assuming that the circumstances in which she found herself dictated an unalterable path. For years, she'd pushed aside feelings of unhappiness. She redirected her energy to helping others rather than to understanding and meeting her own needs. She didn't understand that she could attend to herself first and still have the means to help those who depended on her. Just as we're told by the flight attendant on a commercial airliner, you have to put on your own oxygen mask first before you can help others.

Bobbie had lived in denial of her own joy, and now she was being pulled deep inside to where it was dark, yet healing. She was being asked to address the source of her suffering so that she might again breathe joy into her body.

When Bobbie called me, we spent time talking about the illness as her opportunity to change her belief system. Even though she was terrified, she agreed that she could view the cancer as an imbalance in her ability to receive joy and inner peace. I knew that her healing might hang on the issue of giving herself permission to be nurtured. I asked if she was willing to give that permission to herself now. She said she hoped she was.

We began the Mending Your Bowl practice. I asked Bobbie to go inside herself and to imagine her Joy Bowl. I explained that her Joy Bowl was an actual energy center located in the area of her throat. I went on to tell her that this Joy Bowl governed the health of her entire respiratory system, especially her lungs. I talked briefly about her authentic self and her untapped resources of the Peace Maker.

Bobbie described her Joy Bowl in this way. She said, "The bowl looks like a night sky. It feels open, with stars twinkling in the corners. It feels wide open, like the Universe—expansive." I asked, "Does it feel as if your Joy Bowl is able to hold your energy of joy?" She said, "No, it's too wide open; it's almost flat. There is very little curve to the bowl." She continued, "The bowl doesn't seem to want to hold anything. It keeps turning upside down." I asked her to move inside the experience that she most vividly remembers that might suggest that she's unworthy of being happy. She was quiet for a long time. Finally she said, "I've never been happy. My mother was mentally ill. I had to take care of her. It was terrible. She was in and out of hospitals. I became the mother to the younger kids. I never had time to be with my friends. I was forced to be the mother in the family. My father missed my mother so much he used to come into my bed late at night and lie down beside me. He put his hands where he shouldn't have. It was my fault, though, because I wasn't being a good enough mother. I should have tried harder. I had no right to resent helping the others."

I asked her to tell me what authentic aspect of her true self was emerging from the loss of her mother, her father, and her friends. She said, "I guess that I did my best. No one should be faulted when she does her best." I agreed with Bobbie, and asked, "Now, do you feel you have a right to have a life, too?" She replied, "I gave up everything, and it still didn't make things right." I asked her what conclusion she could draw from the past that applied to her life now. Bobbie said, "I guess I'm doing exactly the same thing in my life now, hoping that if I do enough, someone will listen to me." "Bobbie, the jewel in your pain is that you have an authentic inner voice that can guide you to Joy, if you will listen to it," I told her.

I asked Bobbie to return to the bowl image and make it whole. I suggested that she could turn the bowl over so that it still looked like the night sky, but that it could hold her joy, as well. As she began to imagine this shift in her bowl, she started sobbing. I knew these were healthy tears from bringing home a newly-discovered part of her true self. She never felt she had a right to her own voice. To heal, Bobbie would need to use her voice to articulate her feelings, needs, fears, and dreams to those closest to her. Whether or not *they* listened, *she* needed to listen to the tone and timbre of her voice, to speak up and say what was in her heart. It takes courage to become our own Peace Makers, wanting peace instead of the old, familiar state of inner war with others, or feeling as if we can't do enough to find inner satisfaction.

Bobbie described her newly-repaired bowl: "The night sky is so beautiful, I want to keep my bowl the same way, but I'm turning the bowl over and making it deeper so that it holds my joy, not just my role of protecting others." I suggested that with the bowl able to hold her joy, she might imagine that the darkness was the unexplored, undiscovered parts of her authentic voice. The twinkling stars were her spirit lights guiding her on a new path of discovery.

As we finished our session, I could tell Bobbie felt stronger. She planned to undergo a rigorous regimen of chemotherapy and radiation. We made a second appointment. I said, "Bobbie, remember who you are!"

She never kept her second appointment. I called several times to see how she was doing. She was extremely weak from the chemo but still slowly tracking in her new direction. I was hopeful that she would continue moving ahead on her healing journey.

Sketching Our Joy Bowls

YOUR JOY BOWLS show how you feel about using your authentic voice—the Peace Maker's voice—with the people closest to you. The Joy Bowl is located in the area of your throat and relates to the Fifth Chakra. It governs your respiratory system, making it possible for you to continually exchange sorrow for joy with the people you love the most. The amount of energy in this bowl, represented by the shape, color, and texture of the bowl, tells you how much joy energy is flowing to your respiratory system. As you change the way you approach your life, your energy shifts to support your healing. When you find your inner joy, you also help others who touch your life and are searching for fulfillment. You come full circle in finding help and passing along the gift. As you begin imagining your Joy Bowl, here are some questions to consider: "How often do I search for peaceful solutions to arguments with my partner, family, or close friends? How quick am I to assign blame when things don't go my way? Do I listen inside in order to be authentic in my answers? How peaceful am I? Does the idea of being peaceful suggest to me weakness or strength? How do I respond to others who refuse to fight?"

The Sanctuary of Inner Peace

MANY TIMES WE FORGET about breathing. That is because our breathing is handled automatically by our autonomic nervous system. Breathing takes care of itself, drawing in oxygen and eliminating carbon dioxide. We can take back control of our breathing for short periods when we choose, but when we lose interest or forget, our bodies take over.

In spiritual practices, we are told to pay attention to our breathing, so that we can find deep peace and relaxation by tuning out the world and tuning in to the rhythm of our breath. We are guided to breathe fully with each breath, to be in harmony with the movement of prana (life-force energy) into and out of our bodies. We become our breath, losing awareness of everything but our breathing.

Breathing creates a rhythm that is soothing. Paying attention to our breath offers us a way to reunite with our Divine Selves or, as the Buddhists call it, the place of "clear abiding," or ground luminosity.

You can live without food and water for extended periods of time. But if you have any doubt about how long you can live without oxygen, try holding your breath. Our lives hang by the slimmest of margins: one breath.

Here are some thoughts you might want to take in with each breath. Repeat a thought and breathe with it, into it, taking it deep inside. No need to struggle to find an answer. These thoughts have no answers, but they do prompt greater awareness of what we're doing in our lives—and why.

■ *Thoughts to Breathe With*

♦ I hold today by the fragile effort of one breath.

♦ Tomorrow will bring me more of what I focus on today.

♦ May my intentions for peace be more obvious in my words.

♦ Joy is worth my investment.

♦ Contentment comes from resolving issues with myself.

♦ Life is precious even when it seems all wrong.

♦ I will never come this way again with the people who are in my life now.

♦ I will watch what I say to find clues to what I believe.

♦ I will allow synchronicities to attract my attention.

Use breath awareness as a means of entering and/or leaving meditation, or as a way of interrupting the busyness of your day to help you remember to be the Peace Maker. You'll be better able to quiet your mind, to find and maintain greater focus on your work and your joy.

IN SUMMARY
The Peace Maker's Gifts

REFLECT ON THESE unique qualities of your inner Peace Maker. Observe the way your words and intentions enhance the positive feelings of those around you.

My inner Peace Maker creates joy and the intention for peace with my partner and my closest circle of friends.

♦ My Peace Maker knows the difference between genuine inner peace and capitulation.

♦ My Peace Maker has many ways of being heard without saying a word.

♦ My Peace Maker speaks loudly on the inside, continually showing me that if I am to create peace in my life, my intention must be for peace.

♦ My Peace Maker is never afraid to quiet my chatter and to insist that I experience the power of silence.

♦ My Peace Maker wants me to understand my family of origin rather than to blame it.

♦ My Peace Maker allows me to sit comfortably without the need to be seen, or to stand before thousands commanding attention.

♦ My Peace Maker shows me authentic ways to be powerful, one step at a time.

♦ My Peace Maker shows me that my mistakes are stepping-stones to self-realization, always helping me to know that those I love the most must stumble similarly.

As you review the drawing of your Joy Bowl, consider these statements about benefits you can derive from the exercise:

My Joy Bowl governs my quality of Divine Joy.

My Joy Bowl allows me to breathe into my intention for peace—to create joy instead of war with those I love most.

My Joy Bowl governs the health of my respiratory system (including nose, pharynx, larynx, trachea, bronchi, and lungs).

My Joy Bowl represents the actual energy center of my Fifth Chakra, which is located in the area of my throat.

Breath Awareness is the most useful healing practice for enhancing my Joy because it creates a more direct connection with my inner Peace Maker.

We feel a quiet inner joy when we're
in the presence of a Peace Maker.

Cameron Sesto

LOVE

Love Is Not What You Expect

Love is not what you expect....
Never where you look with piercing eyes
or sit with expectations hung like Auntie's mildewed tapestries.
Love is behind the door and under the carpet
when guests come to call with pasted smiles and comments too lacking in love.
No, love has good taste and fine manners.
Love is quiet until spoken to.
Love knows its place.
What thinks the high and mighty One of Light when Love is so abused?
How, then, is Grace delivered to those with swollen eyes
and outstretched arms?
And then, lo! you know,
one quiet day when your grief dares life to open its curtains for one more day
and even flowers bow their heads in pain.
Then and only then the Grace of the One Most High,
anointed with the breath of love,
touches your cheek, and you are healed.
Life is restored, and your dead heart begins again to beat.
You awaken like Sleeping Beauty with the kiss of her prince.
You are renewed, and without further ado,
life begins again.
Love is not what you expect!

— Meredith Young-Sowers

CHAPTER FIVE

LOVE

We want to find the "I am" that creates life
rather than only the "I" that has been created.

THE RAIN PELTED AGAINST the windows as I leaned back on the pillows in bed. I didn't feel like getting up. My excuse was that I had a cold, but the real reason was that something was terribly wrong. "You have no reason to be unhappy," I said to myself sternly. "True," I responded. I was blessed with a loving new husband, healthy children, and a company that had been brought back from the dead. So what was this sadness? I pushed a little further. This disquietude had a voice; I wondered if I dared listen. The internal dialogue continued with the thought that I'd been trying to avoid hearing: "You had to have things your way, and now you've messed up your life."

I considered what the voice was referring to. I had been impulsive in falling in love too quickly after my divorce from Jim. I wanted my life to go back to feeling normal, to put the scary, lonely times behind me. I wanted to pick up the pieces of my life as if nothing had happened. It dawned on me that the whole scenario had been about what I'd needed. I paused for a moment to think about the man I loved. "He loves me with his whole heart, and he's a good man," I thought. He came into my life when my company was in a shambles after the divorce, and he rescued me—and Stillpoint—from the brink of disaster. I felt I owed him everything.

I took a breath. "Yes, I owed him everything," I thought. As I continued my internal dialogue, I realized I had assumed that, by marrying

Errol, I would no longer need to face my deepest fears and sorrows. Loving him was my escape from having to look at the parts of me that I didn't like or understand. With lead in my heart, I realized that what I had succeeded in doing was to give away my self-determination. I had traded security for learning how to take care of myself. I hadn't been true to myself—I'd been true only to my need to be loved at any cost. I knew that I'd missed the opportunity to put my attention on my own desires and growing edges. I'd been so afraid and unprepared to take care of myself emotionally and physically that I had totally flunked the Universe's test.

"I've bought into a classic fairy tale," I said out loud, "the one where they stay together and never have any messy times, and everything is always easy and perfect. Errol was my knight in shining armor, and I was the damsel in distress." But my personal distress wasn't fixed as easily as that of an ailing company. I felt I'd betrayed myself. I'd taken the path of least resistance and never put my courage on the line to become strong on my own. Now I was stuck in the same old constrictive dynamic where my every thought and action felt controlled. I needed to grow up and be a woman and not a child. I hadn't realized how desperate I felt about our relationship until I put it together this morning. My pattern was to always back down, swallowing my feelings. I had no idea how to change this pattern.

"What should I do?" I asked out loud. I realized that Errol, my second husband, and I would need to rework our relationship so that he wasn't always the rescuer and I wasn't the one who needed rescuing. We needed to trust that our love for each other would bear the weight of our being honest about our feelings. We needed to stop enabling each other emotionally and start seeing each other with all our imperfections and sharp edges. We needed to stop trying to live in lock-step in both our marital partnership and our business. We needed the emotional distance to develop a new way of being together. Now I understood what my being rescued meant. The question was, what could I do about it? I felt honor-bound to remain the "damsel" Errol had married.

I needed a new level of love not just for my husband but also for myself. I doubted seriously that he would understand my dilemma. I was afraid he would see it as betrayal.

I wanted to scream, "Loving you isn't all there is to me! I need to find my own strengths and abilities. I need to take back the running of my own company. I need to have a say in my life and to not feel beholden to you forever because you saved me once."

It was fine to think these things, but there was no way I was up to doing anything about it. I wondered what God thought of me and of this situation. "He's probably totally disgusted with me," I thought. Deep down, I realized that this was the true source of my pain.

As women, we need to learn to care for ourselves and to take our needs seriously so that we can shift the focus of our relationships. We don't have to push away those we love, but we do need to assume control of our own destiny. Loved ones, especially well-meaning husbands, want to control our lives in order to keep us from harm. But we must all venture into the world and stumble around finding our own songs, our own words, and our own creative expressions. I'd been sheltered my entire life. I'd never had an opportunity to discover the borders of my personality. Being out of touch with one's own inner rhythms is not only an unsteady place but also a downright dangerous one. It leads to hopelessness and, potentially, even disease.

The more I thought about my dilemma, the more I realized I needed to ask God for help. I was facing a hurdle too high to jump alone and too fearsome to even consider without help.

We can feel that we want greater freedom and self-expression, and yet we're afraid to act for fear of losing the one person we love. It is so easy to give ourselves away without realizing that we're doing it again for the second time, or even the third. We want so much to feel solid inside that we're willing to give up everything for an illusion. I had told myself I'd never again give up my life's path for a man; but in my heart, I realized that I'd done just that. My concern was more about feeling safe than about taking hold of my own life.

"This is an impossible situation," I thought. With a deep sigh I turned off my thinking and stared out the window. Babe, our audacious tawny-colored cat, leaped up on the bed, knocking down a small book from the nearby stack. It fell into my lap. As I picked up the book I saw that it was a collection of stories about an East Indian spiritual teacher named Sathya Sai Baba. I didn't remember being given the book. I tried to remember where I'd heard that name before. Then I recalled that my friend and former Stillpoint business partner had sent me some Vibhutti—sacred ash that this teacher manifests for healing and spiritual help. She had received it in an unexpected way and wanted to share it with me.

I opened the book and began to read the stories of people's miraculous and life-shifting experiences in the presence of this Master. I felt strangely familiar with this teacher, even though I'd never laid eyes on him, and generally I was suspicious of gurus. I read voraciously. As I came to the last story, I felt a strange sensation in the pit of my stomach, as if I'd stumbled onto something so profound I couldn't quite get wrapped around it emotionally.

I wanted to experience the love and comfort the people in these stories had found. Dropping the book to my knees, I found myself filled with a deep sadness that overflowed as tears and then cascaded into deep gut-wrenching sobs. I heard myself praying out loud, "Please Lord, just move me in whatever way I need to be moved; let me do whatever I'm to do—only, please," I sobbed, "help me feel your Love and support."

The phone rang. I tried to ignore it. Then I thought, "Maybe it's one of the children." Reluctantly, I got out of bed and moved to the telephone on my desk. My 83-year-old mother, who lived a half-hour away from me in a neighboring town, was on the other end of the line. After reassuring me that everything was fine, she said. "I was just sitting here when I got this overwhelming urge to call you and tell you, 'God knows, God Knows!' Does that mean anything to you?" she asked. At first, I couldn't put the pieces together. God knows what? I thought. And why was my mother telling me this? Although we often talked about our spiritual journeys, she had never told me anything like this before. What did it mean? She was saying that God had told her to call me and tell me that he knows my grief, that he heard me.

I was dumbstruck. Things like that don't happen to ordinary people like me, I thought. My mother waited for my response. I didn't have one. My mind stubbornly refused to believe that prayers were really answered like this, in real, everyday terms that we can understand and appreciate. It was a miracle! Did I believe it? Could this be real? Did God put that thought in my mother's mind? Why else would she have called me with that exact, perfect response?

Hanging up the phone, I sat very still. I felt free-floating, as if my body had disappeared and I was tilting around the room, trying to find which way was up. I was speechless, afraid to find words that might upset the euphoric feeling that was building up inside me. Leaning back in my desk chair, I let my eyes wander up the large, white expanse of wall that lead to the cathedral ceiling of our bedroom. There, plainly visible on the wall, was a full-scale outline of a human figure, in gold. In the area of the heart was a brilliant pink light. I shut my eyes and opened them again. I saw the picture was still there. It was a person with only the heart space filled with a brilliant fuchsia-pink light. I stared at the life-size shape in absolute disbelief. The image didn't fade away but stayed long enough for me to accept that it wasn't shifting sunlight or a trick of the eye. Where did this image come from? Who made it appear? My mind couldn't compute an answer that made any sense. But inside, in the place that had held the grief of my self-betrayal, I felt something split open. Love took hold of my heart in some powerful way.

I knew in my heart that all things were possible for God. My question was, what had I done or said that could possibly be important enough to elicit a response of this magnitude? I wanted to stay frozen in that moment, to let myself feel that God really loved me enough to show me that he knew my pain. He was there through all my difficulties. I could trust that he was close. Here was God's answer, saying, "Love alone heals. Let me love you and Errol enough to help you get things right."

Deep and abiding comfort began to move around inside me like cloudbanks shifting so that the sun could shine through. Could God so love each of us that our heartfelt despair causes Him to want to heal our pain and help us? What kind of love was this that didn't blame or accuse but said, "I'm here; let me show you how Love heals"?

Errol and I have been doing just that—working with The Creator's love to strengthen and shift our relationship. I am no longer a damsel in distress, and he is no longer my knight in shining armor. We've slowly forged the partnership we always wanted. Day by day we find renewed value in being together even as we continue to work on the rough edges of our relationship. Knowing that God's love is so real and present in our lives gives us the courage to confront the fears and insecurities that show up daily. When I'm angry and feel invisible I think to myself, "I have the ability to love my husband enough to be honest, not hurtful, to be clear, but without blame."

This new loving support keeps us out of the old arguments about who is right and who is wrong. We now realize we are both right and both wrong in various ways. In other words, we're both learning. It's not about who is right; it's about getting it right for both of us. Staying open to listen to each other from our hearts rather than our personalities allows us to use compassion and empathy rather than self-righteous indignation. We realize that to continue to thrive in partnership, each of us has a responsibility to his or her own life and needs.

Daily, we practice meditation and quiet reflection, putting effort into staying on track. We are serious about becoming the people we are each meant to be. Our journey over these past twelve years, even the difficult aspects, has deepened us and made us more worthy partners. Now I can truly say: Errol is not only my lover but also my spiritual companion. Self-love has taught me to love my partner freely without losing myself. It has brought me to a more compassionate place where I can consider my feelings, my partner's feelings, and the feelings of all living creatures on God's Earth.

Compassionate Healer Friends

Our own personal Compassionate Healers are the voices of our authentic selves that encourage us to experience love and compassion for others and especially for ourselves. This powerful energy radiates from the area of our hearts, our Love Bowls. The more we become aware of Compassionate Healers in the world around us, the greater the likelihood that we will learn to respond to the voice of our own Compassionate Healers.

People who are Compassionate Healers teach us to love, with passion, other people—all people—including ourselves. Compassionate Healers don't take sides; they see beneath the patterns of our prejudices and speak to the oneness that unites us under the healing banner of humanity. Compassionate Healers have come to us in the form of major religious figures who taught love and compassion: the Buddha, Krishna, Jesus Christ, Mohammed, Moses, Sathya Sai Baba.

Compassionate Healers can be ordinary people who have an extraordinary capacity to love life and people. They see every task as a means of enhancing goodness in the world. Nothing is too menial or unimportant, because it's all useful for serving a higher good.

Compassionate Healers are spiritually alive, creative, and intensely passionate people, with a kindness that shines through to us just when we most need encouragement. They have a way of gently drawing us back to ourselves when we aren't sure who we are or what we want to become. Compassionate Healers help us see that our choices and our mistakes are learning opportunities rather than judgments against our characters or our innate goodness. They realize that life is a spiritual journey, and they encourage us to look more deeply into our loving hearts. They accept unequivocally that we are the embodiment of love even if we are painfully slow at recognizing that.

The following story illustrates the nature of a Compassionate Healer's heart. A long time ago, there lived a wise old woman named Hannah who wore a beautiful, expensive gold ring. One day she was traveling to a nearby town and stopped to rest for a while under a large olive tree. Seeing the older woman sitting under the tree, a young woman passing by also stopped to rest. The young woman couldn't help noticing Hannah's beautiful gold ring, which was worth a great deal of money. As they sat and talked, the young woman realized that here was the answer to all her problems: If she just had the gold ring, she would be happy, and everything would be perfect. When she told the older woman her sad life story, the woman quickly took off her ring and placed it in the young woman's open palm. "Take it," she said with a smile. Shocked and shaken, but deeply grateful, the young woman got to her feet and hurried off to tell her family and friends. Arriving home, she told her entire family about her amazing good fortune, and all congratulated her. Later, as she lay in bed, she had a revelation. The gold ring was not the treasure. The real treasure was the loving heart that so easily gave a gift of great monetary value to someone in need.

A Compassionate Healer would say, "I'm not special—I'm awakening to my powers." He or she is awakening to the importance of love and compassion in a world largely devoid of those essential human qualities. He or she is helping, encouraging, and acting as a guiding light and driving force for opening people's hearts to find greater love and compassion.

Compassionate Healers see their lives as opportunities to do something that feels good in their own hearts. They know the eternal secret that when we fill our hearts with love, we attract others who are also capable of loving. They help us change the dynamics of our lives from fear to love.

Compassionate Healers realize what has lasting value and what does not, and they invest their efforts in what has genuine value. People with love to share are around every corner, prompting us to consider how we, too, are awakening to the passion of love within.

■ Listening to Our Inner Compassionate Healers

The passion to love unconditionally is the most significant gift offered to us by our authentic selves. Love can be like the fierce March winds, full of passion and desire for intimacy. It can be the poignant goodbye kiss you place on a dying mother's cheek or the laughter you share with your small kindergartner as you push him higher and higher on the swing. Love is the glee we feel as we give thanks that we have a healthy family to return to each evening after work. It is our feeling of gratitude for seeing beauty around us, and it is our delight in finding ways to touch the still point in our own hearts and in the hearts of others. Touching without needing anything in return is compassion.

Compassion is a deep and abiding trust in the value of life, above and beyond obvious suffering and injustice. Compassion is the sensitivity and kindness that we extend to ourselves as well as to friends, family, and even people on the other side of the world.

Compassion allows us to find our centers and stay there rather than spinning off into our personal, emotional dramas. It holds us steady, allowing us to experience life in all its many forms, for only in this steadiness can we overcome resistance and move beyond fear, anger, anxiety, and suffering. As we soften our hearts with empathy, we enter our sacred still point, the embodiment of The Creator's Love manifested in our hearts and lives.

Compassion is the essential component of all loving—although, typically, we give ourselves little of this caring. We are consumed with try-

ing to stay safe and in control so that we can avoid the inevitable difficulties of life. We seduce ourselves into thinking that if we don't
acknowledge our discomforts, they will disappear. Like the child who
closes her eyes and imagines she's invisible to others, we pretend that we
can go about our business even when there is unresolved suffering in our
hearts and those of people around us.

Compassion alerts us to our shared human condition. We can undertake many different kinds of compassion practices, but by simply being
aware of the need for compassion, our thoughts and feelings become
more compassionate by being more inclusive and less judgmental. Our
words become less harsh, and our minds seek greater connection. We
become more aware of our needs and the feelings that circulate through
our physical bodies when we run on empty. In a deficit condition—lacking connection to our compassionate caring—we get sick. Circulatory,
lymphatic, and immune system problems are the direct results.

The first major sign of a "compassion deficit" shows up in a lack of
self-worth. It is natural to value ourselves: just watch the delight little
children take in what they draw, build, or discover. We, too, have that
capacity to delight in our discoveries and creative efforts.

The second major sign of a "compassion deficit" is devoting attention
to material desires that drain our passion and place us in compromising
situations. The more we lack self-approval for our decisions, the more
difficult it becomes to make good choices. We jump more quickly and
with less forethought into sexual liaisons, unwise career shifts, and other
risky scenarios, hoping to get it right.

Our desire to feel the thrill of new love drives us into a cycle of spi-
raling levels of personal dramas. We have more traumatic blowups with
partners, parents, and children, and we spend more money than we can
afford. We engage in daredevil recreational sports. We work too hard
and too long, and we overeat, over-drink, and over-drug.

Filling our Love Bowls starts with changing our lives in small ways.
We can ask ourselves, "How can I treat myself with greater compas-

sion?" Eventually, compassion leads to cherishing our originality, creativity, endurance, courage, willingness, and honesty.

We fill our Love Bowls every time we listen to ourselves with openness and acceptance. It doesn't matter whether we're right or wrong, or if we did something that was applauded or ignored. Self-acceptance helps us move in the direction of our inner knowing. Just listen!

Rather than telling ourselves how we should feel, we can ask ourselves, "How do I feel?" Rather than telling ourselves what we should do, we can ask ourselves, "What do I yearn for?" Offering ourselves recognition, acknowledgment, approval, appreciation, and the ability to use restraint are all ways of being more compassionate with ourselves.

The greatest kindness to those we love is taking care of ourselves, because so many people depend on us. How does it feel to say these things to yourself? "You're an amazing woman [man]. I was so impressed with your resourcefulness in that meeting." Or, "Well done. How extraordinary that you have completed that difficult assignment so well." Or, "Thank God you knew what was wrong with that car, since no one else did."

The approval we really want the most, more than from our mothers or fathers, more than from our bosses, friends, or partners, is from ourselves. Give it with openhearted delight. Get past the hurdle that says, "I'm being selfish if I do what I need because it takes time and attention away from others." Of all the ways that we derail ourselves, that is the most common. When we go to the dentist to have our teeth cleaned, are we being selfish? If we have radiation to shrink a tumor, are we being self-centered? If we take a new job and work harder and longer to provide additional dollars for a daughter's education, are we being self-focused? No, the contrary is true. Meditation, prayer, self-reflection, journaling, walking, and service to those in need are essential for making the quiet shifts that prepare us for love in our lives. We're not talking here about being self-indulgent. We're talking about giving ourselves what is essential to stay healthy in body, mind, and spirit.

Taking time to stay steady means tuning into our inner guidance and the peacefulness that allows us to be kind to ourselves and others. While love and compassion are qualities we often share willingly with others, we must remind ourselves that we, too, need this care.

Consider the ways we've learned to love that taught us to ignore our feelings and needs. Consider the deals we made to guarantee that we'd be loved, the co-dependencies we accepted in order to feel protected. Compassionate loving can help us see through our fear and find the strength to be more fully present in our lives.

Ways We Learn to Love

Who taught us to love? From whom did we learn how to love ourselves, our family and friends, our partners and children? How did we develop the understanding of how to grow emotionally and spiritually to sustain loving relationships? The way we've learned to love, of course, is an amalgamation of perceptions, words, demonstrations, and feelings. We know what happens when parents violate the sanctity of our bodies and our emotional well-being, destroying the safety we need as children. But even if our parents weren't the best parents in the world, we need our own learning experiences in order to love compassionately. Eventually, we realize that only by loving ourselves can we stem the tide of empty feelings, loneliness, and traumatic memories of love gone wrong that haunt us. The journey is in learning to love who we are, our faults and our strengths—the entire picture of our bodies, minds, emotions, and spirit.

As we begin to find the best ways to love and care for ourselves, we begin to recognize the unspoken agreements we've made in order to be loved and accepted as part of a family, a friendship clique, or a partnership. We can let ourselves finally reveal the truth that we've hidden for so long: the nature of the quid pro quo bargain we made for being loved.

■ *Private Agendas*

In each love experience, we quickly learn what is being asked of us in exchange for love. "I'll do this for you, or be with you, or give this to you, if you understand my troubles, respond to me in the ways I need, and don't ask me to change." These subtle agreements become the basis of our behavior patterns in friendships and partnerships. We think that these secret pacts are the way the game of love is played. We assume that love isn't about being honest and telling what we feel or what we believe; we assume it is more about saying and doing what lets us keep the peace. We think that only by keeping the peace can we get our needs met.

I remember that feeling of needing to keep the peace. I'd been trained in childhood to be a lovely and loving chameleon—to be invisible while being ever vigilant to the needs of others. My task was to be certain that all relationships ran smoothly. Of course, this way of getting love isn't very successful. We must be visible in our relationships and encouraged to take part in life rather than hanging back from full participation. We can be kind and thoughtful, but being given no choice, being unable or unwilling to step into life, leaves us disappointed and afraid to trust our own feelings. Because we've focused exclusively on taking care of others' needs, we have no time, energy, or motivation for taking care of our own needs.

We tell ourselves, "If you are always happy, always giving, and completely available to others all the time, others will always love you. But any transgression, any failure to measure up, and you will be all alone, because it will be perfectly clear that you're unworthy of being loved."

These inner deals do immeasurable damage and are difficult to undo. Like the proverbial can of worms, what began as a way to find love and appease our parents becomes the core pattern of our lives and what we believe is the best way to love ourselves and others. Our challenge is to realize that we need to give and receive love without making secret deals. We are who we are: brilliant embodiments of the Sacred. We're worth loving, each and every one of us. We have The Creator's own exuberant joy sprinkled into our hearts. The beautiful qualities of the sacred are folded into us. We need only listen to find out that we are completely loved and deserving of love.

■ *Patterns of Power*

We struggle in adult life to undo the imbalanced patterns we saw in our childhood homes that became an integral part of our relationships as adults. Not only do we make deals to be loved, we also emulate the way the most powerful people in our lives got what they wanted. No matter how hurtful those patterns were to us and how often we rebelled against them, we use some or all of the very same patterns as adults. If your mother always told you and showed you that you were unlovable and ill-equipped to be successful, a below-average plain Jane or John, you accepted it. You may have fought valiantly against this unfair evaluation, knowing in some corner of your heart that it was false. But you slowly accepted the false assessment and believed it. Eventually, as an adult, you realize that you are different from this early sense of yourself, but by then it's too late. The patterns have become part of your survival fiber, and they are invisible to you.

If this is our background, we continue to meet with disasters in all our relationships, building up impressive records of betrayal but never understanding why. Even when we do understand why, our "them" versus "us" beliefs are already deeply ingrained. Changing our way of being is tantamount to having all our teeth pulled in one sitting without an anesthetic. It is terribly difficult and painful, because anything that came to us in the package called "love" feels sacrosanct. We try to make it fit our hearts no matter that we destroy ourselves and others in the process. This is the tremendous power of wanting love in our lives. If we take this power, this tremendous passion for love, and redirect it as benevolence and compassion for ourselves, we find the passion of love flowing fully into us, uniting us with others in empowering ways.

■ *Throwing Yourself on the Rocks*

Of all the patterns that I've confronted in my counseling, the most persistent and insidious is what I call "Throwing Yourself on the Rocks." This is a pattern of repeating, over and over again, the same arguments that we know will end in the same place of disempowerment, tears, anger, and resentment. But worst of all, it short-circuits our ability to reduce our burden of anger and resentment by developing our love and compassion. Instead of throwing ourselves on the rock pile, we can resist the engagement, staying steady in our compassion for ourselves and for others.

When I felt the worst about myself in my relationship with Errol, I prayed about it. I'd take my dilemma into my morning meditation and try to find a new way of approaching the same old feelings of distress. One day, having talked God's ear off about my confusion, I closed my eyes. And God answered. He said, "As long as you are willing to throw yourself against the same pile of rocks, you'll feel only battered and broken. Sit, be steady, and love him."

The mental picture was so vivid: a body thrown mercilessly upon a giant stack of sharp-edged rocks. I was shocked at the feeling of remorse I felt for being so unaware of the impact my continual struggle was having on my entire being. This is what I'd been doing to myself as I cajoled, argued, and tried to "guilt" Errol into being what I wanted and needed. I reasoned that his attitudes and behavior were in my way, and that if he would just change, I'd be happy. The idea that I was to feel love and compassion for him when I was so distressed seemed at the time quite beyond me.

We change behavior not when we're pushed but only when we choose to. We change because we see our partners, business associates, or friends happier and getting more enjoyment from their lives. We decide we want some of those feelings. "What do I need to do to feel the same way?" we wonder. Wanting to love those persons instead of condemning them becomes a powerful practice for relinquishing the old pattern of hurling oneself against the rock pile.

■ Our Need for Love

The need for love is so essential to us because on some level we realize it is the only true antidote to our personal troubles and our world's overwhelming travails. How can we begin to undo the patterns that keep us from fully embracing our lives? We can make a new arrangement with ourselves that all previous deals and secret pacts are no longer applicable. We can dismantle the patterns that have kept love and true tenderness away, and we can stop throwing ourselves against the rocks, giving our energy to useless arguments. We can also begin to ask whose voice we've been listening to all this time.

The voice sounds so reasonable, so self-righteous, about how life is unfair and others are misguided. While this may be true, what we really need is a voice that says, "Take a look at your own motives instead of focusing on what others are doing. What did you do? What was in your heart? How loving were you?" Be suspicious of the voice that always makes you right while others are at fault. This familiar voice isn't your friend; it is the voice of an old tape you play called Directions for Loving.

The voice we've been listening to is our insecurities. We can learn to listen to The One who has the real answers for us and is as close as our hearts.

The Voice of The One

To find the spiritual directions we're seeking—the ways to love and have love returned—requires us to visit the voice of our spirits to show us how to live without an agenda. At first we're frightened and disbelieving. We think it's impossible for us to love without a deal that binds us at the level of our weaknesses rather than our strengths. But the voice of the sacred doesn't dangle relationships in front of us, whispering, "If we just do or become something, then... ." Instead, this inner voice tells us we are more than enough—we are Divine. We can, of course, have relationships that are nourishing and fulfilling as soon as we learn to be ourselves without apology. This voice speaks with the assurances we need. This is the voice of our authentic selves, with a capital S.

By comparison, the voice of our personalities is the one that, until now, we've always believed. This very familiar voice separates us from others by telling us that we're not enough: we must do better, try harder. This is the voice that is relentless in pushing us to better secure the material needs of our life, even at the risk of our health and sanity. We push and struggle for our rightful share, and we are convinced that our responsibility is just to our little corner of the world and our individual families. This is the voice of our (small s) selves—our personalities.

This duel of voices, and the way I found The One true and essential voice inside me, unfolded one sunny, summer morning. I was on vacation in Maine with Errol. My morning routine was to sit quietly for a time watching the water, read a few pages of an inspiring book, and then walk for a while. I often found insights while meandering alone, along quiet back-country roads.

This one day, I had an amazing realization. I'd been working on trying to love and care for myself, not out of fear or resentment of others but out of compassion and acceptance for myself. But I wasn't sure how I could find this inner voice of my authentic self. I reflected on a statement I'd read earlier that morning from spiritual master Sathya Sai Baba. The study piece suggested I try to understand my true nature, my authentic self, in much the same way I think about my children, my home, my work, my friends, and my physical body. When I thought, "This is my body," I was to consider who it was that was announcing it possesses a body. It isn't my body itself, but a part that guides and directs my body;

it's not my mind, because it, too, is part of my physical composition. It is my spirit. And my spirit is none other than The Creator.

I read a concluding thought that made a lasting impression as I tried to grapple with realizing that the "me" that was making decisions about what I'd think and do was none other than my authentic self. I realized that the path to greater understanding, love, and compassion was to find the "I am" that creates life rather than the "I," my physical body and mind. I was looking for the part of me that is the originator of ideas, the genuine Creator within me. My inner voice was the place where The One abided. This voice was my authentic self, and one aspect is my Compassionate Healer.

Renewing Passion

As we take ourselves by the hand, giving ourselves permission to be who we are—our own original mold—we step more fully into the center of our lives. Our steps may be halting at first, but slowly and steadily we rewrite our old patterns, and we cease making the damaging secret deals that allow us to be loved. We learn to distinguish the inner voice of The One from our mental voices. This journey to selfhood is life-long and a process lasting for as long as we draw breath. There isn't a single destination. We keep finding more and more to love and appreciate about ourselves, and more and more that we're willing to shed. We shed layers of excess emotional and psychological baggage that we've been carrying around for years. As we come to know ourselves better, we find new flows of passion.

Our passion, both sexual and spiritual, moves in predictable cycles. Our closeness to ourselves, as well as to a partner, begins with what we might call "Banking the Embers." These are the quiet times of self-absorption, times when we're journaling, meditating, spending more time in solitary activities. This is a time to be especially sensitive to inner conversations that are extremely insightful and open us to our true spirits.

After "Banking the Embers" comes a time of "Blowing on the Embers" of love and desire for closeness. We reawaken to the relationships around us as if coming out of a deep sleep. We feel new love, joy, and delight, drawn back toward life with our partners. We become more aware of them and slowly want to be closer, both physically and emotionally.

"Blowing on the Embers" leads to the full flush of "Rekindling," when we are in the full flush of passion for ourselves, our partners, and others who mean a great deal to us. This is a heady time, when we're sure that our intense passion for life and love will last forever. We revel in this invigorating and fully-awake state of loving, finding satisfaction every place we look. When this high point inevitably lessens, and we move back toward "Banking the Embers," we worry, "What has happened to the passion? Why do I want to be alone or with friends and not as close to my lover?" It is easy to think that something has died in our relationships, but actually, we're just moving through an emotional and spiritual cycle of renewal.

When we seek friends and activity apart from our partnership relationships or marriages, we need to see that we're in our "cold-to-cool, warm-to-hot cycle" that repeats itself over and over, perhaps monthly or perhaps every few months. Whether or not women are of childbearing age seems to make no difference to this ebb and flow of our passion. Men, by contrast, manage to deal with their flows of passion in a different way. They daily take in what has meaning and then consider its implications. Men often experience their renewal within several days, while it takes women a month or longer. Women need time to bring inside the opportunities for love in order to decide how they feel about the people and experiences that have expressed this love. Women and men renew their passions in different ways. I like the thought, "Women need to feel love to make love. Men need to make love to feel loved."

Understanding our needs and the flows of our energy can help us convey our inner feelings to one another so that neither person feels rejected or left out. The old thought that our partners can meet our every need is poor advice. We are individual souls coming together for nourishment, learning, and warmth. We need each other, and we need the many others that make up our community of friends, colleagues, biological families, and spiritual families.

Lighting the Way for Others

As we expand our desire to experience love in honest and lasting ways, we can spread love to strangers. Every morning I use a simple little practice that shows me how welcoming love is even when we're rushing to get to work or take the kids to school. I go out for my morning walk along the country roads near my home. I wave to everyone in every car that passes. I wave to strangers. As they drive past, I bless their day and wish them well. When I first began doing this, many people didn't wave back, but now they all wave back. The love we're spreading around helps each of us. I can almost see them smile as they, too, feel the impact of our shared wish for a good day. We're more apt to be awake to the expressions on other people's faces when we're feeling valued ourselves. The more accepting we are of ourselves, the more accepting we can be of others, and the more effective we are in facilitating change.

Love comes to us in many ways—even through television or in movies. You may find that when you're watching a movie, a character so touches you that you feel yourself caring deeply about that character's plight. You may be in the grocery store and see someone who is in distress. You see the look in the person's eyes, the set of his jaw, and you know that place of desolation. In the moment, you may feel centered enough to make eye contact, to offer a smile, or just be aware of the person's suffering and hold it in your consciousness for a few moments. All love makes the world a better place and makes us happier and more aware of the blessing of our passion for living and loving.

Sathya Sai Baba talks about the various ways we love. He says:

Love is like a lamp kept in a room. The lamp illumines only the room. This kind of love is self-focused and limited. It does not extend to others.

*

Love may be compared to the light from the moon. Moonlight is visible both outside and inside. However, it is not very effulgent. The light is dim. This kind of love extends to a wider group but is not very intense.

*

Love can be compared to sunlight. It illumines both inside and outside with brilliance, but it is not continuous in the sense that the sun is not visible at night. Actually, the sun is always there. Likewise, selfless love may appear to be absent sometimes but it will reappear again.

*

Love, finally, is Divine Love. This love is always present, inside and outside, in all places, at all times, and under all circumstances. It is imperishable. It is eternal. It is immanent in everyone. When this love is manifested, the individual achieves peace that passeth understanding.

Sai Baba asks us to learn to love God in any form that is near to our hearts. He explains his mission as encouraging and guiding people to see God within themselves. Most people try to make the world a better place. Some people, however, are actually "wired with Divine Love" to take an active part in addressing the needs of the poor and needy. People who respond to these needs are some of the Compassionate Healers of our time, the spiritual warriors of love and compassion, the Bodhisattvas. We are each growing into our awareness of Divine Love. As we practice being authentic, we grow in the ways that preserve love and life on our beloved planet Earth.

Ramsey's Story

Ramsey had been referred to me for spiritual direction and an energy evaluation to help heal the pain in her ears. She had experienced an unfortunate accident the previous month when she'd gone to have her ears tested. The technician had inadvertently injured her eardrums. Now she was experiencing significant pain and continual ringing in her ears. She wanted to understand what these ear injuries meant spiritually and what she might do to restore her hearing. While she was furious over the injury, she was also curious to know if the incident had any additional meaning for her.

In the intuitive evaluation that I completed before our phone appointment, I saw that Ramsey had a great deal of genuine love that she was pouring out to help others. She was clearly a mentor and fine teacher. From the lack of self-love apparent in her Love Bowl, however, she needed to learn to deal with herself more compassionately. I began to look for clues in her energy field that would show me exactly which patterns needed to be addressed in order to release them. I found that her relationship to her mother was toxic. A wall separated them emotionally. We would start with this relationship to learn more about what Ramsey "didn't want to hear," and why.

Partnership was another subject we'd want to discuss. There was no energy to speak of in this aspect of her Love Bowl. This lack indicated there was no passion moving her and her spouse toward greater intimacy.

The energy of the Love Bowl governs not only the heart but also the entire circulatory system, the lymphatic system, and the immune system. In order to help restore health to Ramsey's damaged eardrums, we would need to enhance blood flow to her face and ears. The blood is sacred to our bodies and carries our ability to truly give love to ourselves and receive it from The Creator. We'd want to discover what the messages were that were "too painful to hear." In considering her ears, I felt intuitively that she had a good chance of lessening the pain and ringing. We would do some hands-on healing to jump-start the flow of healing love.

Ramsey began our appointment time by talking about how blocked she felt at work and in her marriage. When I asked her what the block was, she felt it was other people's behavior and attitudes. I asked her how it made her feel to have others overlook her abilities. She reported that it made her feel terribly invisible. I asked her if she'd ever felt invisible before. She thought for a minute and said, "All the time." The continual ringing in her ears had forced her to pay attention not only to her physical healing but also to the emotional patterns that she'd been living with, the feelings behind not wanting to hear criticism.

As Ramsey and I talked, she brought up the subject of her husband. She told me that she commuted between two places, an apartment close to the medical center where she was a nurse practitioner and a home with her husband three hours away. She tried to go home on the weekends. Nonchalantly, she said that it didn't make any difference whether she was home or not, since her husband hardly looked up even to acknowledge that she was there. I asked her how she handled this. She said, "I cry a lot."

I asked Ramsey to envision her Love Bowl, along with all the ways she loved herself, her husband, and other people for whom she felt compassionate. I instructed her to let the image appear gently in her mind's eye and then to describe it to me. She reported to me that her Love Bowl "was made of rose-colored crystal. It was the size of my mother's berry bowl." I asked her if her Love Bowl could hold her own love for herself. She paused and said, "The jagged edges of the bowl seem to make it an uninviting place to come. I'm not sure I've ever invited love into my Love Bowl for myself."

"What do these jagged edges remind you of?" I questioned.

"My mother was always very particular about the way I set the table for meals and cleaned the house. I never seemed to do things the way she wanted, no matter how hard I tried." She went on, "After a while I just tuned her out and didn't listen." So this was how Ramsey handled criticism, by tuning it out. Ramsey's pattern was to react to criticism and lack of attention by recoiling from her mother and her husband and then turning a deaf ear and closed heart to their voices. I realized how much we would need to stimulate and activate the power of love to rebalance her entire circulatory system.

Next, I asked her to imagine her Love Bowl in relationship to loving her husband. "It loses its pink color and just becomes plain old glass," she stated. I asked her to consider why the bowl lost its color. She thought for a moment and said, "Because our relationship has lost all of its color, too. We haven't slept together in months, and I've given up trying to change him."

I said, "The most important way to change him is to stop trying and focus on restoring passion to your own life. Passion is more than sex," I continued, "it is about loving compassion for you from your sacred self."

We went on to explore her Love Bowl in relationship to strangers. She said, "The bowl is brilliant; it's like the sun just came out. I've never seen anything so brilliant. It's hard to even look at." I asked her to tell me about the brilliant light and what she felt it meant. She said, "It's easy for me to love people, and this looks like liquid love shining all over the world."

I asked her to go back to the bowl as it appeared in receiving love from her own sacred self to her life. I said, "How might you change the bowl so that it is more accepting of love and care for yourself?" She told me that she would "file down the jagged edges" so that the bowl was now inviting to her energy. She continued, telling me she polished the edges until the uneven edges of the crystal bowl resembled a flower more than they did sharp teeth. She announced quite proudly that the sun was now shining on her Love Bowl, and all the individual crystal prisms of the bowl were radiating a magnificent brilliance. I asked her what she felt this meant about loving herself. She was quiet for a time. Then she said in a very serious voice, "I have never seen an image so striking. I realize that the reflection of light is coming from me. The sunlight is my brilliant inner light. When I'm not receiving my light, I can't send it out to help others. Meredith," she said softly, "I'll never forget this moment. It has changed my life."

Ramsey was deeply moved by the understanding she gained from the visualization of her Love Bowl. I encouraged her to take her own precious life in her hands and begin to value who she was and what she had to offer without its being a reaction to the needs of her mother, husband, or employer. We talked about paying attention to the times when she tuned people out. I asked her to pay attention to when her mind wandered from the flow of conversation. I suggested that she ask herself, "Why am I so upset, and what do I feel inside as a result of this person's comments?" I continued, "Place your hand over the center of your heart and just breathe into the feelings without battling them. They will slowly recede."

In all likelihood, years of closing down to unwanted conversations placed her hearing mechanism at risk. I assured her that while accidents such as the one she'd had might seem unrelated to her emotional issues, they were directly connected. The parts of our body that are injured in an accident are the parts that are the most vulnerable from years of stress and lack of energy.

Ramsey would need to build a bridge between trust in her own authentic voice and the outside world of people who were not in sympathy with her. She could no longer hide from criticism. She needed to work on relinquishing the patterns that made her interpret incessant criticism and indifference as love. Ramsey came back several more times. Eventually, she was able to begin to communicate her feelings to her husband. He assured her he wanted to improve their relationship. She continued to focus on giving herself the nourishment that she realized was essential to feeling love in all the ways she wanted.

Sketching Our Love Bowls

As you draw your Love Bowl, realize that this image represents how you love yourself, your partner, and other people beyond your immediate family. The Love Bowl is located in the area of the heart and relates to the Fourth Chakra. It governs your circulatory, lymphatic, and immune systems, making it possible for you to circulate your natural energy of love and compassion to better care for yourself, your partner, and others in the world. If you are single, your "partnership" piece may be reflective of a previous relationship. It may also be related to preparation for a future relationship. Everyone has a place for partnership in his or her life. Use this practice to discover more of your feelings and growing edges in partnership.

By focusing on your Love Bowl, you bring loving energy to your immune system, your lymphatic system, and your circulatory system. Any physical problems you have will be addressed as you focus on the energy of love flowing freely into your heart center, your Love Bowl. Questions you may want to ask yourself to begin the process of imaging your bowl might be: "How willing am I to care for and love myself? How much effort do I put into meeting my own needs? Do I feel selfish when I care for myself? If so, where does that false premise come from? What tenderness do I experience (did I experience, or might I want to experience) with my partner? How does our relationship stir up my feelings of inferiority, superiority, animosity, anger, resentment, compassion or understanding? In what ways do I find myself caring about strangers? Am I awake to the power I hold to Love others who suffer or feel lost or lonely? Am I a spiritual warrior?"

Loving Touch™

LOVING TOUCH IS SOMETHING we all do all the time. We just don't call it that. When we hug a friend, pick up a crying tot, or touch the hand of an aging parent, we are practicing Loving Touch. When you stroke your new puppy's head or brush your kitty, you're practicing healing. Whenever we touch other living things with the intention to help them, to send them love, or just to share a special moment, we are creating a healing environment, and healing energy passes from our hearts to theirs. The intention for love and healing is what brings special power to our hands for healing practices.

In seeking to love ourselves, we're reminded to watch the words we automatically use in disapproving and criticizing our motives and efforts. Being compassionate with yourself means using your own sacred passion for love to help you through difficult times. When no one seems aware of you, become aware of your own needs. Practice Loving Touch to awaken the voice and energy of the Compassionate Healer. As you begin practicing placing your hands over the center of your chest, you practice Loving Touch for yourself, facilitating the flow of healing energy into your total presence.

■ Loving Touch for Yourself

You can practice Loving Touch throughout the day with yourself and with friends and loved ones. To bring greater love, compassion, and self-confidence into your life, follow these simple directions.

♦ Place one or both hands over the center of your chest.

♦ Say a prayer or state an intention that the power and passion of love and compassion flow into your heart and your life.

♦ Mention any particular needs. You might speak to needing comfort from an unhappy ending of a friendship, or endurance to finish your chemotherapy treatment. You might pray for a deeper connection to Spirit. You could pray for greater faith in moving through difficult financial times. Love is the great healer, and your Compassionate Healer reflects all the power and majesty of God as the Master Physician and Healer of all ills and troubles.

Remember this: When you pray or create your intention, do so believing that you are being heard specifically and directly. Before the words are out of your lips, they are in God's heart.

Here are a few loving intentions and affirmations that you can use as variations in your Loving Touch practice. As you rest your hands over your heart, repeat a single phrase or several phrases in order to strengthen your understanding and the Grace in your life.

I am worth loving.

The Source is guiding me.

All I need to be happy and to feel safe is to remember that
God is inside me.

I benefit from being quiet and still.

Quiet times allow me to rest in God's love.

My steadfastness comes from confidence in The Creator.

I am steady in loving my Self as a Compassionate Healer.

The Creator knows my every movement, thought, and feeling.

Allah answers my prayers in the best way.

I am a brilliant work in progress.

The Great Spirit is within and around me every moment.

My Spirit reflects and enhances the spirit of all people.

■ *Loving Touch for a Friend*

To work with a friend, ask the person to place his or her hands over the Love Bowl, the center of his or her chest. You can then say a simple prayer out loud; ask your friend to say a prayer silently. You can also place your hands over the other person's hands folded across his or her chest. Now share a prayer aloud. You can begin, and the other person can add a piece to it, or finish the statement. This meaningful exchange will bring enhanced capacity for love in all its many forms, and for greater health. The exchange will help you and your friend.

IN SUMMARY

The Compassionate Healer's Gifts

HERE ARE SOME OF THE ways our inner Compassionate Healers imbue our lives with love, passion, and compassion. Choose one or several to consider each day. See where it leads you on your journey of self-discovery.

My inner Compassionate Healer inspires me with deep love and compassion
for myself, my partner, and for strangers. As I embody this presence,
I become a spiritual warrior.

- My Compassionate Healer has a deep caring for others.

- My Compassionate Healer allows me to address with sensitivity and kindness the needs and concerns of others.

- My Compassionate Healer realizes my need for acknowledgement and offers me approval that silently fills my empty inner places.

- My Compassionate Healer believes in my value, giving me the means to sustain my passion for life by helping me set appropriate boundaries for myself and others.

- My Compassionate Healer offers me the continuing confidence to share my Sacred Heart Song—my special way of bringing love into the world.

♦ My Compassionate Healer links my love to meaningful attitudes and activities that support my body and its health.

♦ My Compassionate Healer recognizes that I am body, emotions, and intellect in one miraculous and never-to-be-duplicated spiritual package.

As you review the drawing of your Love Bowl, consider these statements about benefits you can derive from the exercise:

My Love Bowl governs my quality of Divine Love and Compassion.

My Love Bowl allows me to bring my loving attention to myself, to my partner, and to strangers.

My Love Bowl governs the health of my circulatory system, lymphatic system, and immune system (including the heart, blood vessels, blood, spleen, lymphatic vessels, specialized immune cells and substances).

My Love Bowl represents the actual energy center of my Fourth Chakra, which is located in the middle of my chest.

Loving Touch is the practice most directly connected with Love and Compassion and links me with the energy of the Compassionate Healer.

Whenever you place your hands on another lovingly,

healing happens.

Cameron Sesto

POWER

Contribute to Life

When you close your heart,
pain happens, and power leaves.
When you close your heart,
suffering begins, and trust vanishes.
When you close your heart, your effort to contribute to life slows.
When you close your heart, the work you contribute stops contributing.
What you've thought belonged to you, doesn't.
What you wanted to contain, control, and be the sole proprietor of
slips between your fingers like favored trinkets from a dying woman's grasp.
Nothing belongs to you. All is rented!
Rented house, rented job.
Rented family, rented children.
Rented body, rented thoughts.
Let go of feeling you own life.
It owns you.
It owns you as the water fills the creases of the sun-parched earth
and the sky flows into the brilliance of Universal light.
It owns you as the candle flame consumes the wick.
Contribute to life, realizing all the time that you're renting space.
You belong to God.
And God lives only in the effort to love and not in the outcome.

— Meredith Young-Sowers

POWER

Power is found through your awareness, acknowledgement,
and translation of your creativity into the world arena.

MY FIVE-YEAR-OLD DAUGHTER, Melanie, had a fever
of 105 and a deep, nasty cough. I called the pediatrician, and
his receptionist managed to fit us in for an appointment later
that morning. Since we wouldn't be leaving for another hour, I tried to
think what I could do to calm down and quiet my fears. With Melanie on
the bed near me, I decided to meditate for a few moments.

Sitting on the seedy brown shag rug, I looked around the bedroom
of our rented summer cottage. The walls were gray, and plastic flowers
were on a table in the corner. Not my taste, I thought, absently. We were
moving to New Hampshire, and we had to sell our home in order to
build a new one. The plan was to stay in the cottage for a few months
while we made the transition to our new home.

My stomach churned as I thought about taking Melanie to the doctor's
office again. Once before, we had to rush her to the hospital with a high
fever. I remembered only too vividly the dash to the hospital, the screaming child, terrified as they packed her in ice to bring down her fever, and
then the nightmare of her veins collapsing. I recalled the terror of feeling
helpless as the medical team rushed to keep her alive. With great relief and
God's grace, we'd survived that ordeal, with all of us intact.

I'd waited a long time to have a little girl of my own. Melanie was the
daughter I'd longed to hold for so many years. After my son Mark was

born and following two miscarriages, I was ready to consider adoption. I wasn't concerned at all that this child wasn't coming from my body; I felt she was coming from my heart. I knew I wanted a child from an Asian country, a little girl who wasn't going to have much of a future if someone didn't adopt her. We would adopt each other, I thought wistfully. I'd help her settle into her life in America, and she'd help me feel complete as a mother. I realized that children are only on loan to us, and while I loved being a mother, I also needed to find my life work. I had no idea where my contribution lay.

My lovely little Soon Young Lee, five months old, arrived on Thanksgiving Day at O'Hare Airport in Chicago. She had thick black hair that stood straight up, and beautiful dark, round eyes. She looked like a doll. She'd come all the way from Seoul, Korea. We'd named her Melanie Soon Young, since my own married name was Young.

Melanie coughed, and I returned quickly from my reverie to the role of vigilant mother. I closed my eyes, steeling my nerves for whatever was to come. I prayed. Did God really hear my words? For a moment, I wondered if God would or could act to relieve the misery of one small child, with so many children in the world in worse situations. It seemed unlikely. Nevertheless, I asked God to help her.

As I closed my eyes, I heard a soft and gentle voice speak to me. I heard this voice so clearly that I opened my eyes to see who was standing in the room. No one was there. I closed my eyes again and the voice said, "You can heal your daughter." My eyes snapped open again. I looked over at Melanie, who was dozing fitfully. I looked out the window, but all was just as it had been before. I closed my eyes. The voice continued, "Love will heal your daughter; just try." I was speechless. Preposterous, I said out loud! The voice continued with infinite compassion. In that moment I was starting to believe that the experience was real. Was this God? I asked myself. Who else could it be? Was it safe to listen to this voice? The voice said, "Pick up your daughter, hold her in your arms, and see her filled with love." I couldn't imagine that I wasn't making this up. Still, I felt a glimmer of hope that this was a miracle. "This isn't any miracle," chimed my personality, "it's your wishful thinking." But something inside of me said, Maybe I should try it. But try what? I didn't know anything about healing.

The voice repeated the same instructions. "Pick up your daughter and hold her. See her filled with love." I gently picked Melanie up and sat down on the shag rug with her in my arms. She hung in my arms listlessly. I thought, I have no idea of the right way to do this. "How do you see someone filled with love?" I asked out loud. I could feel myself fighting a panic that I might miss an extraordinary opportunity to help Melanie because I didn't know how to see her "filled with love."

I decided to try the best I could. I began by imagining love as a bright light, as if it were God's love filling her body. I started at her head and let my eyes slowly move down her body, imagining this special healing light making her better.

The phone in the kitchen rang so loudly I nearly jumped out of my skin. Placing her quiet little body carefully on the carpet, I went out to answer the call, thinking it might be the doctor. Coming back into the bedroom several moments later, I stopped abruptly in the doorway to see if my eyes were deceiving me. There was Melanie bouncing on the bed. She was smiling and laughing. "Come play with me, Mommy," rang out her little voice. She wasn't coughing, and when I put my hand on her forehead, it was cool. Where did the fever go? "This can't be happening," I said to no one in particular. How was this possible? Did I imagine the fever? But then my eye caught my hastily scribbled message to the pediatrician. I hadn't imagined that she was in trouble! But how could this have happened? It wasn't possible. But in fact, healing is possible through the power of God's Love.

When we act from love, we never know what the consequences will be. Love is the pathfinder for our life purposes. Through love, we move into our authentic nature and attract the passion that is our work—the work that serves a greater good. My love for Melanie provided an opportunity to see love in action as a healing agent. I'd participated in a most amazing healing experience demonstrating the power of love to heal. I was hooked, enthralled, intrigued, and afraid to ask more about it.

For so many years, I'd longed to find the direction for my life, instead of working at one job after another, with none of them filling the empty place inside me. I wanted a meaningful career, but I saw only confusion. I thought about returning to school to get my degree in nursing, or about becoming a full-time potter. I considered the wide range of my skills and interests but didn't see any option that I was passionate about. Now, by listening to the Voice of Love, I found something that touched my heart. My career in healing had found me.

Acting in accord with love, we come to our sacred life purposes. When the time is right, a nudge from God and our angels opens the door. This means we're ready to engage life more fully, with less fear and less need to know how things will turn out. After Melanie's healing, I realized I needed to understand more about what had happened. Months later in New Hampshire, as I continued to hear this gentle Voice of Love, I learned more about spiritual power, the power of God's Love, and how this power had flowed into Melanie. I hadn't realized that Love was anything more than an intense emotion, or that love could also be a healing tool. Or that we could focus love from our inner selves into our bodies and those of others to help them heal. This gentle voice said to me in a statement I'll always remember, "Whenever you lay your hands lovingly on someone, healing happens."

We think that we must find our proper careers through a process of deduction, from opportunities we generate through our mental efforts. But many times The Creator offers us a chance to use our talents in a new way, one that teaches us about our lives at the same time it encourages us to help others. The loving voice I heard taught me about the human energy field and the ways we sabotage our own efforts for a good life. I learned the impact that fear has on our bodies and the ways in which love from our inner selves—our souls—opens us to the healing grace of love that is our birthright. We are love incarnate. We have the power of love in our hearts. Our challenge is to get our intellect out of the way because it keeps telling us what is and isn't possible. And it's often wrong! Instead, we can let Love take hold of us, moving us into our authentic lives and our true work in the world.

I kept my appointment with the physician the morning of Melanie's fever, but I was embarrassed when he pronounced Melanie a healthy child. I know he thought I'd wasted his time by imagining that something was wrong with her, but I needed his confirmation of her good health to put the puzzle pieces together, to understand that through love, healing happens, and all we need to do is show up. Clearly, my fumbling efforts were the means God used to offer Love through me to her. We can't know how God's love works. It's too vast to comprehend. But we don't need to know how this powerful current of love works. We need only know that it does, and that we can access it.

The loving voice became my guiding light as I entered the many rough years of my divorce from Jim and the search for the inner power to pursue my life work. I wrote about my experience with the Voice of Love (Mentor) and learning about the power of love to heal in *Agartha: A Journey to the Stars*. When the power of love speaks to us, it awakens our authentic selves so we can come into our unique contribution for this lifetime. Our Empowered Creator gives us the guidance and power to trust what we love and see that, in fact, it can and will turn into our special work in the world.

Empowered Creator Friends

Empowered Creators show us ways to find and manifest our life work, our purposes for coming into this life. Empowered Creators are people who embody power and know how to encourage others to feel empowered. They show us through their example that the work we do, the effort we make each day is meant to contribute to all life rather than to serve only as a personal statement.

An Empowered Creator may be a teacher, professor, first boss, or friend standing next to us. They have presence, are not unduly humble, nor are they braggarts. They know who they are without over-inflating their accomplishments, and they're on solid footing even when they've been fired or have left a job and are unsure of the next step. They trust that spirit will unfold their next opportunity as soon as they absorb the learning connected with their last job experience.

Empowered Creators can have a great deal of money or not know where the next meal is coming from. They are not overly concerned with the outcomes of their efforts. What counts for them is being true to their own convictions. They are the epitome of an authentic person, whether they are milking cows or sitting on the New York Stock Exchange, invested in being the best they can be rather than overly competitive with others. They aren't obsessive about controlling events, and they trust what life offers as their way of finding connection with spirit.

They are enormously compassionate and effective in motivating others. They accomplish their work with Grace, seemingly effortlessly, because they know how to tap the power of love.

Listening to Our Inner Empowered Creators

The voice of our Empowered Creator encourages us to trust that we are born with power. True Power, like Wisdom, Vision, Joy, and Love, is latent until we seek it as a means of nourishing our inner lives. As we deepen our inquiry into the nature of power, we realize how best to engage it to enhance our lives and to preserve all life in the global family.

When we go to work, tend the children, manage the family, friends, and social engagements, we're actually assessing our power in relationship to others. When we meet other people, we know without saying a word who has more power by the way we react: do we defer to them, or do they defer to us? This constant dance of power is what fills our day.

We each need to know our place in the "pecking order," as do animals and other species.

Understanding what power means to our very survival helps us appreciate our drive to be the best, to overcome the competition, to prosper and to thrive. Males and females of other species handle power differently. The male confronts, intimidates, and dominates his rivals in order to protect his family and create a safe haven. Male power comes from an assertion of dominance. By contrast, a female may hide, but she will fight to protect her young even with her life. She prepares the food but eats last, makes peace and negotiates with others in the pack. Her power comes from cooperation, maintaining peace and continuity from day to day. As human beings, we carry both the power of dominance and the need for inclusion. Our challenge is to meld the two in order to create the power of "presence."

The Power of Presence

Having "presence" means we've combined self-assertion with the desire for inclusiveness. We've integrated power into our psyches both as the ability to be seen and the urge to step forward and assume a position in the world. We've also embraced concern and empathy for others with whom we work or share our lives. People with presence automatically live at the top of everyone's pecking order, because they embody the ability both to lead and to follow; to be in charge and to work within the framework of what has been agreed upon. We each have the capacity to be leader and follower, teacher and student, in various ways.

The energy of presence is found most directly in the work we do, the effort we put forth each day. Whether volunteering at a local homeless shelter, raising our children or grandchildren, taking care of parents, or helping friends, we can define ourselves and assess our contribution. When we don't have an occupation we consider important, or when we see no worth in what we're doing, we slide into disempowerment.

Whether we work at home or outside the home, manage a multi-million-dollar company, or raise a family , we all have the opportunity to be Empowered Creators. Whether we stamp a name on a plate for an automobile chassis or run a nursing home, our efforts make the world work better and more harmoniously.

■ *Cherishing Our Values*

Authority based on the power of presence promotes inclusiveness and demonstrates empathy for colleagues and friends. Those in positions of authority involve others, embodying values and ideals that bond people together. Leaders we trust espouse values in which we believe. To develop presence we must know what we believe, the essential values that we impart through the various roles we play: mom or dad, grandpa or nanny, corporate CEO or switchboard operator. Our values need to be the first thing we pack in our briefcases in the morning as we head out the door to work. Our beliefs and values need to be imparted to our children so that they, too, have a basis for developing presence.

We bring the issues of the world to the microcosm of our offices and homes. What we value influences the quality of our lives and our work environment. It is easy to strain against the rules that others set. "If only things were different," we moan. But as Empowered Creators, we can use our power to decide what we'll agree to and what we won't. Ultimately, it is each of us who has the power to make positive change.

It's easy to be generous-hearted and profess life-enhancing beliefs when our wallets are full and our families healthy. But when events shift and expressing our beliefs jeopardizes keeping our jobs, getting promoted, or our very lives, then we get to put our beliefs on the line. These are difficult choices for everyone, and standing up for what we believe doesn't always win us plaudits. But our actions make a difference in our own hearts and, ultimately, for the global family in ways we may never realize. When we say "no" to a deal that is not quite legal or "yes" to an opportunity that shares our company's resources with those in need, we are making choices that stem from the strength of our values. Average everyday people often step up to a challenge that would daunt the rest of us. Ordinary people sometimes do extraordinary things that demonstrate their presence. Pastor Dietrich Bonhoeffer is an example.

Bonhoeffer lived in Germany in the 1930s and taught at the University of Berlin. He began to draw serious criticism from Nazi authorities for speaking out against the persecution of Jews. Just before World War II broke out, Bonhoeffer visited the United States, where he was offered a prestigious position at Union Theological Seminary. If he had accepted, he would have had a safe haven throughout the war, but instead he took the last boat back to Germany, where he was arrested and put to death just three weeks before Hitler committed suicide. He was 39 years old.

Bonhoeffer's career was based on principles of friendship, inclusion, belief, and faith in the goodness of human beings. A peaceful man, his deep belief in the innate goodness of humans included even his persecutors.

Pastor Bonhoeffer had a choice, and while I'm quite certain he didn't want to die, he chose the path that held the greatest meaning for him: returning to Germany and speaking out against Nazi oppression, even though that path meant risking and, ultimately, forfeiting his life. His beliefs and values were stronger than his fear. We must grow our children with such presence. We must insist on world leaders with true presence, and we must live with presence ourselves.

■ Honoring Our Creativity

We are totally unique and original beings. Just as no two people are alike, no two gifts or sets of opportunities are the same. Each individual expresses power differently. To feel fully empowered, we need to accept ourselves as the creative beings that we are. Usually, we tell ourselves just the opposite—"I'm as creative as a stump"—because we confuse creativity with artistry. We may not be able to draw a straight line, but creativity isn't just drawing, painting, dancing, or being a musician. Creativity is the way we express our originality, imagination, inspiration, ingenuity, inventiveness, resourcefulness, and vision.

Creativity is "the cut of our jibs," the way we are put together, what we love and how we use, demonstrate, and express it. It's impossible not to be creative, but it's easy to deny our special form of originality.

Our opportunities are pertinent to our unique gifts and skills. Although five thousand men and women may be master plumbers, when they show up at our homes to repair a pipe or fix a toilet, the way they do it, the tools they use, the dialogue they carry on while working, the attitudes with which they work, the follow-up they seek, and the insight they glean while working are all entirely unique. No other person can fully comprehend our attitudes, desires, beliefs, or sacred alliances with God. We alone speak for the space we take up on the Earth and the contribution we've come to make, and we have original and unique means of expressing our gifts.

The way we become aware of our creativity is to notice what we love to do, how we enjoy participating, and what turns us on. What would we choose to do, even if we didn't get paid for it, for the sheer delight of the experience? I've often joked about the fact that, if I were locked in an eight-by-ten-foot cell, the first thing I'd do is inquire into the troubles of the other people locked up with me. I can't help doing what gives me pleasure and a sense of helping someone. This is the way I express myself.

Think of what you love as more than an activity. What you love may involve your imagination, your way of viewing a situation or event, your inspiration in approaching a problem or shifting other people's thinking. Your creativity may take the form of ingenuity in finding solutions, putting out the fires of others' discontent, or approaching a problem by thinking "outside the box." We assume that we aren't original or creative because we discount what we love, what comes so easily and naturally to us.

Why do we have trouble acknowledging our gifts? We hear the voices from our past informing us that we have no originality, no gifts that are worth anything, that we're lacking in talent, boring, and unimportant.

We hear our own inner critics assuring us that we have nothing creative to offer. But the invitation to explore our authentic selves takes us into new ways to view our lives and our gifts. We have a choice as to which voice we'll listen to: our false selves or our true selves. We find our power not only through awareness of our unique offerings but also through our acknowledgment of our contributions. We are one-of-a-kind human beings, so we must have one-of-a-kind contributions to make.

The place where we most often run into trouble is in offering what we love to the world. We often have difficulty finding acceptance, approval, appreciation, and compensation for supporting our talent. As a result, we assume that we're inadequate, unprepared, and inferior. But the truth is that, because we are original pieces of work, we need not take what others offer as criticism; we can accept it as our learning. The problem is not with our gifts but with translating who we are and what we're offering so that people can understand our vision and creative work.

I recently experienced a perfect example of this "need to interpret effectively." I was finishing the writing of *Wisdom Bowls* and had sent the manuscript to a friend's agent, whom we were considering to handle foreign language rights. This literary agent was a lovely and intelligent woman, who was certainly interested in working with me. We sat down to talk. She told me all the things she loved about the book. Then she began to give me a long list of ideas on how to make the book better and ways to direct the reader through the book more effectively. In times past, I would have seen her comments as criticism and confirmation of my inadequacy. I would have instantly jumped into the familiar hole of "I'm not enough, and neither is what I write." But as she talked, I said to God, "Okay, show me what this is really about." And just then she said, "When I send book-length manuscripts to publishers and they are rejected, it's upsetting. So now I send work out asking, 'What can I learn from this experience?'" I got it! I was to hear her criticisms as suggestions, ways to improve my communication of the ideas in the book. What she was really saying was, "I want to understand what you're saying, but I need more information." It had never occurred to me before that when someone criticized something I'd written, it simply meant that I needed to recast the writing so that others could better understand and appreciate what I was trying to say.

As we approach managers, investors, clients, teachers, or physicians, consider that our job is to continue to interpret our work, our discoveries, or our understanding so that they can find the creative gift in our work. Not only do we need to earn a living by having our work valued, but even more important, we need to feel satisfied with our daily efforts and be able to go to bed at night knowing that our unique creativity has been expressed with love. This is the way to produce elegant work that is valued and recognized. Just remember: what you love will need to be translated and communicated effectively to those with whom you want to share.

Our creativity is the direct link with our empowerment. When we are unable to frame our natural gifts in ways that we can appreciate, we send ourselves into repeated cycles of self-damaging denial of our value and contribution. Accepting our gifts, acknowledging them, and continuing to teach others how to appreciate our efforts is the path to true and lasting presence.

Stacey's Discovery

Stacey was referred to me by a friend. She had chronic fatigue syndrome and a variety of other difficulties. After reading her intake form, I performed an intuitive assessment to discover the root cause of Stacey's chronic fatigue.

Chronic fatigue syndrome is a condition of generalized malaise, erratic heartbeat, and trouble with digestion, joint pain, and nervous reactivity. The condition can be mildly or totally debilitating for many years. I've worked with many clients with chronic fatigue and I've concluded that, from an energy point of view, it represents a "time-out" in the way a person earns his or her living. The person is unable or unwilling to shift his or her work toward what brings greater meaning.

Often we can't imagine ourselves not being the doctor, lawyer, or Indian chief that we've been trained for and/or that our parents/family want for us. We want to please them, and we crave their approval, so we become certain of "the right" thing to do. What our spirit wants for us, however, isn't always what our personality self is convinced will keep us out of trouble. But then, living isn't about hiding in the bushes to avoid life. Living is about stepping up to the plate and taking a swing at the ball. Our yearnings may not look like what we think of as our careers, so our personality may tell us to forget it. We want a comfortable lifestyle and to make good money, but our hearts say, "Making money isn't the first criterion. Let the money flow from what gives you meaning and lets you feel you are contributing something of value." Our personalities or false selves may tell us that we need to do what is in the mainstream and not get too far off the beaten path, or people will disapprove of us. Our hearts ask us to consider the delight in our adventure and our dread in pursuing work without joy. Our hearts tell us that we're strong enough to handle whatever negative fallout comes from choosing our own paths, but our false selves say, "Are you kidding? You'll collapse! Be on guard that you don't miss out on your fair share of material possessions." Our hearts say, "There is plenty of everything to go around, and we haven't a minute to waste." A battle such as that going on inside us can close us down totally.

Deciding how to spend our time and talent takes maturity and finesse. Finding our direction isn't a straight line; it requires sorting through many choices and learning to trust decisions that feel right in our hearts. What we're looking for isn't a cookie cutter career. It isn't a label. It's our tender love and caring for life on a journey of great benefit and enjoyment. Why would any people be satisfied with spending two-thirds of their waking hours doing what leaves them feeling empty? When it's too frightening to ask the deep questions about what we're doing, our bodies close down to give us time to find out who we truly are. From this flows our recognition of what to do with our creativity.

From my evaluation of Stacey, I realized that the fear that was immobilizing her was concern about being inadequate in the work she would love to pursue. I understood from my workup that she had a rough childhood and was afraid for her safety on many levels. She also had tremendous rage at feeling blocked from love that didn't come with a price tag: a spiritual connection. I leaned back in my chair and considered Stacey's situation. Here was a woman who had amazing spiritual potential, gifts of considerable magnitude that would surely lead her to help others directly, if she could face down her fears of not measuring up. She seemed to be on the lookout for ways to prove that she was inadequate; the truth was that Stacy was exceptional.

Stacey called on the telephone for her initial session. She had a melodic voice, soft and sensitive. I explained about energy and how we wanted to find what was keeping her from regaining her health. She told me that she had been sick for so long that she was desperate. She needed help to do everything from getting out of bed to getting to a chair and eating and dressing. She lived with another woman whom she didn't feel especially close to. This friend had attached herself to Stacey, insisting on being her caretaker. Stacey felt she had no other choice except to stay with this friend until she was healthier. This, then, was to become Stacey's theme song, "I have no choice but to…."

Stacey told me that she had worked for a small organization that made maps for the government. She liked her job well enough, but she always felt tense doing the work. She enjoyed her colleagues, was considered a bright, rising star, but was afraid others would discover her fear. The stress of her double life gradually eroded her energy until she could no longer drag herself to work. She finally quit her job. She was glad she had saved some money, so she could manage to stay home and take care of herself for a while.

As we explored Stacey's childhood, the reason she was so afraid became clear. She had been traumatized by an emotionally abusive father and an emotionally and spiritually absent mother. While the trauma

from the father had deeply scarred her, it was the lack of love and atten-
tiveness from her mother that had left the deeper wound. Her mother
had been unavailable because she, Stacey, was inferior, she told me, so
how could she trust that she had any worth?

On the surface, Stacey seemed to be fully in charge. She made good
comments in response to my suggestions and sounded ready to take
charge of her healing. She insisted that she wanted to heal from the CFS.
She had chosen issues that would take a great deal of effort and years of
God's direct love to help her find the inner Divine Mother that would
never desert her.

I suggested to Stacey that we perform a Mending Your Bowl practice
that would show her where to begin to reclaim her trust in herself and to
unshackle her spirit from her fears. Telling her to breathe slowly and
from her heart, I suggested she imagine a bowl of any color, shape, or size
that could show her power. This bowl, I continued, was located in her
solar plexus, and it did actually represent the aspect of her energy related
to her power. "Take a moment and tell me about your Power Bowl," I
said, "the bowl that holds your inner power, your trust in yourself, and
your confidence in sharing your gifts and talents with others."

I heard her take a deep breath before she responded. She said, "My
Power Bowl is navy blue, and it's starched. The sides are rigid, as if they
are holding the bowl prisoner." I asked her how she felt when she considered that this bowl represented her personal power, her presence. She
said, "The bowl makes me feel that my power is so unbending that it's
without any freedom to become its own shape. My power is in some-
body else's mold." Reminding her to continue to breathe, I suggested
that she allow this "starched" feeling about her Power Bowl to suggest
where this way of feeling had come from. She hesitated and said, "I
don't know if I dare go there."

I said softly, "Where do you need to go?"

She said, "I'm looking at my mother, and she looks dead."

"How old are you?" I asked.

"I'm little. My hands just reach to the sheets," Stacey answered. I asked her to describe what was happening, feeling that this may not be something she has shared before. "My father is standing against the wall, and he is yelling at me to leave the room. But I just have to stay. I'm afraid he'll hit me, but I need to see my mother. I haven't seen her for so long. She looks so strange. As I stare at her face she opens her eyes. But there is no smile of recognition, no loving words. Her eyes don't see me; they are empty."

Stacey stopped because her voice was so filled with pain that she needed a few moments before she could regain her voice. The suffering that Stacey felt was palpable. All these years, this feeling of horror and loss had weighted down her heart and her power. Returning to the story, she said, "I'd never felt so totally empty and bereft in my life." She added in a whisper, "In that moment the bottom fell out of my life."

Stacey continued, "That picture of my mother haunts me to this day. She just didn't care about me at all. Later, my father told me she had died. I never went to any funeral and I was told never again to mention her name in the house. I knew my father thought that, somehow, I had killed her. If I could have changed places with her, I surely would have."

Stacey continued to tell me about her adolescence and the rigidity with which she was raised and severely punished for no apparent reason. She said, "I remember that every morning, I'd watch for the door of my bedroom to open and my father to come in to tell me what I was to do that day. He always wore navy blue."

I directed Stacey toward a spirit-to-spirit dialogue with her mother. At first she was afraid, because she was convinced that her mother would rebuke her for doing something terrible that had lead to her death. But gradually, with gentle reassurance, she agreed. She asked her mother why she had died, and what she, Stacey, had done. Her mother said, "I had pleaded with your father to send you to my sister's so you'd be spared seeing me die. You did nothing…how could you have ever thought that I didn't love you? I was so worried about leaving you, but it wasn't my choice. I never remember seeing you that final time you describe; I was already far away. Can you still love me?"

Stacey and I both cried, so moving was the story and her mother's plea to her daughter to love her! Slowly, as she recovered her composure, I asked her what part of her authentic nature, her power, she might reclaim from this experience. Stacey said, "My right to be me and," she hesitated, "to believe that I'm worth loving." I asked her to revisit her original bowl image and to make it whole. She said, "The color is softer, more of a sky blue, and the rim of the bowl is fluttering, as if it's moved by a gentle wind." I asked her, "How do you feel now about your Power Bowl?" She was quiet for a few moments and said, "Meredith, I feel like I've started to take back my life."

Stacey became a regular client, and I'm happy to report that this was, indeed, the beginning of her recovery. She is now almost entirely well. She's moved to her own home and is actively exploring the field of holistic healing. Stacey is a major success story; she has worked diligently to reclaim her power. Through God's love and some important spiritual experiences, Stacey is embarking on the work she was always meant to do.

Sketching Our Power Bowls

Y OUR POWER BOWL ALIGNS YOU with your personal power and presence. The Power Bowl is located in the solar plexus and relates to the Third Chakra. It governs your digestive and muscular systems, allowing you to nourish your creativity and move fully into your life purpose. You use your inner power as you trust the contributions you make through your work in the world. It shows you how much trust you have in your creativity and confidence in manifesting your work in the world. Your Power Bowl governs your digestive and muscular systems. Your entire alimentary canal, from the mouth to the anus, is influenced directly by the energy in your Power Bowl. No matter what the problem you may have with digestion, no matter what part of your body hurts, this bowl is the one that holds the keys for your healing. The digestive system involves the processing of food and, in relation to energy, it handles the processing of your feelings about your work. It deals with how you genuinely feel about your creativity and what or whom may be blocking it; the degree of control and competition that you live with daily; the degree of sweetness or satisfaction that you derive from your efforts; and the amount of stress that is created by people at your workplace—all are giant markers for the health of your digestive system.

All the muscles everywhere in your body are also governed directly by the Power Bowl. Your muscles contract and relax in order to help you to move and to transport food through your system. Symbolically, too, you have to contract and relax your power, knowing when to step forward and take action and when to relax and regroup.

As you begin to imagine your Power Bowl, you may want to ask yourself these questions: What have I done that made me feel in my power, and conversely, what work or efforts left me feeling flat? What people do I credit with building my belief in my gifts, and who eroded it? What part has God played in strengthening my self-confidence? Am I doing work that I love? What part of my daily activities or career adds the greatest value to my job? How might I take part in more of these activities? What would happen if I did engage in more of these activities? Who would be upset? How would I handle that?

Draw your bowl, and then after spirit-to-spirit communication in which you find the answers you need from another person's authentic self, mend your bowl. Be certain to reclaim a part of your power and presence, which you can now allow to fuel your creative contributions— the work that you do—the effort that you make—to bring your unique talents to the world.

Moving with Intention

ANY INTENTIONAL MOVEMENT will build your inner confidence and encourage you to trust your creative efforts just as you trust your body. Walking is an especially valuable means of encouraging self-trust and enhancing your personal power. You can practice walking with intention any time and anywhere, in the country or in the city, in the morning, the afternoon, or the evening.

Use walking not only as good exercise but also as a time of quiet enjoyment and self-acceptance. As you begin walking, notice how many thoughts you have about what you ought to be doing with this time, and what you're prepared to do when you return from your walk. Let your thoughts slowly unwind like the clock that you refuse to wind too tightly. Take several deep breaths and blow the air out through your mouth. Steady your breathing.

Ask your feet how they are doing: Do they feel sluggish? Are your feet telling you they are sore, achy? Listen without comment. Are your feet telling you that you must move more quickly, not a moment to waste? Send loving attention to your feet; they carry you into your future.

Listen to your heart and ask how it is doing. Is it hurting? If so, why? What does your heart need today? What can you offer it? Just Listen. Put your hand over your heart and send loving attention to it, grateful that it is continuing to beat without interruption through the day, giving you life.

Enjoy your surroundings without judging them. Find something to smile about, and feel the regimentation ease up a little. Identify a place in your body that is feeling renewed; pay attention to that spot, and watch it grow, spreading fresh confidence throughout your body.

As you round the bend for home, breathe in confidence to trust your heart and your natural gifts. Ask your Empowered Creator to guide your efforts and all your activities today.

IN SUMMARY

The Empowered Creator's Gifts

Here are some of the roles our inner Empowered Creator plays in our lives. How many of them resonate with your spirit? How many new roles can you incorporate into your way of being in the world?

My inner Empowered Creator activates my inner power and presence.

- My Empowered Creator deepens my understanding that the work I do today is meaningful and useful.

- My Empowered Creator expresses my creativity with complete originality, trusting that I'm capable of grander and grander insights each day.

- My Empowered Creator takes delight in the excellence of others, knowing their success is also my success.

- My Empowered Creator allows me to relish my accomplishments, showing me always that they come from within my heart, where the Source is unlimited.

- My Empowered Creator sees my value even when others seem to overlook my contributions.

- My Empowered Creator expresses my effort as a true and meaningful purpose in the world so that I feel the delight of contributing to the welfare of all life.

- ◆ My Empowered Creator allows me to enter or leave a room or a career with true Presence and spiritual elegance.

- ◆ My Empowered Creator gives me permission to feel my shining in the world.

As you review the drawing of your Power Bowl, consider these statements about benefits you can derive from the practice:

My Power Bowl governs my quality of Inner Power and Presence.

My Power Bowl allows me to bring my creativity into my work/effort.

My Power Bowl governs the health of my digestive system and my muscular system (including the mouth, esophagus, stomach, small and large intestines, rectum, anus, liver, gallbladder, pancreas, and the muscles, tendons, and ligaments).

My Power Bowl represents the actual energy center of my Third Chakra, which is located in my solar plexus.

Movement with Intention is the practice most directly connected with the Inner Power and Presence that links me to the energy of the Empowered Creator.

Life isn't about hiding in the bushes.

Life is about stepping up to the plate and taking a swing at the ball.

———————————

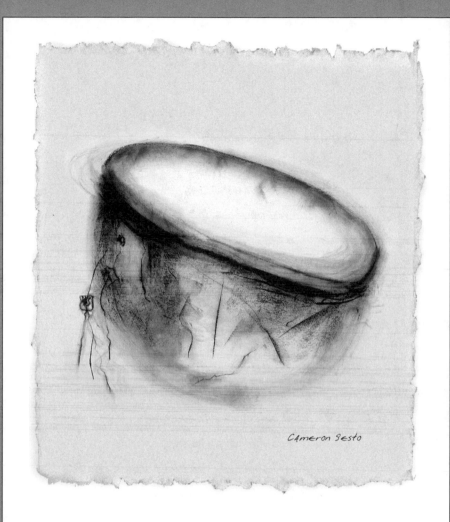

CAmeron Sesto

INTIMACY

God Is Great

"God is Great," you pray.
But who listens as tears fall?—reminders of
days long gone and dreams blown away,
like end-of-season dandelions gone to seed.
Beloved family put to rest on sheets faded from the summer winds;
new life born, nestled in the same old sheets that endure beyond hope.
"Now I lay me down to sleep..." who listens?
In the doorway between Heaven and Earth, Grace arises,
winging her way from beyond the beyond,
light years away.
She moves with benevolent hand and heart
to stroke a burning brow and hold a hopeless soul.
She sweeps through barefaced windows with missing panes
and attends to business.
What change has happened...and who would know?
Kneeling on tired knees, beside the bed with covers all askew,
all is well, you sigh.
God is Great.

— Meredith Young-Sowers

CHAPTER SEVEN

INTIMACY

*The purpose of change is to initiate us into intimate resonance
and dialogue with our soul.*

"CHANGE IS DIFFICULT," I said half-heartedly, wondering how to keep my voice steady when my heart was breaking. Joan and I walked slowly across the gray macadam parking lot of the Dartmouth-Hitchcock Medical Center in Lebanon, New Hampshire. The skies were overcast, with huge cumulous clouds pushing each other angrily across the sky. The weather looked the way I felt. We'd been to see Joan's oncologist. The liver cancer had returned and was inoperable.

For seven years Joan and I had an extraordinary history together. I'd been woven into the fabric of her healing, and now I was to be with her for her final curtain call.

I first met Joan the evening I was invited to talk to a group in Walpole, New Hampshire, that was studying my book, *Agartha: A Journey to the Stars.* Over coffee, Joan asked me to "check her out" because she had indigestion. Later that evening, at home, I scanned her body intuitively and saw two very small spots on her liver that I felt certain were malignant. Subsequently, Joan and I met with a physician friend who ordered a liver workup to study what was going on.

Weeks later, the surgeon reported that the tests had identified the two spots on Joan's liver and that they were malignant, just as I thought. Liver cancer is treacherous because, by the time a person experiences symptoms, often the condition is too far advanced for there to be many viable treatment options. But in this case, Joan's indigestion, which had nothing to do with her cancer, had given us precious lead time. Joan was operated on, and the diseased section of her liver was successfully removed.

The gift of time allowed her to see her daughter, Phyllis, married and to be part of her granddaughter's young life. Now, seven years later, she was in trouble again. Joan, who was like a second mother to me, was a talented writer and a student of the world, especially of French culture. She dreamed of a life of travel, art, and spiritual discovery. Instead, now, after her divorce, she lived alone in a small apartment, struggling to make ends meet. I sensed an inner sadness in her; she was full of life on one level, yet empty on a deeper level.

Joan had grown up in considerable wealth but with little personal attention. Her nanny, Mimi, was her true mother, the one person who was her confidante and heart's companion. Apparently, Joan's mother became jealous of Mimi's relationship with her daughter, and on one unforgettable night she sent Mimi packing without even giving her a chance to say goodbye to the child who had been her ward since birth. Joan awoke to a world that would never feel safe again. Her emotional and spiritual growth had been frozen at that early age, and like a carelessly pruned tree, she would never fully recover.

At the time of her terminal cancer diagnosis, Joan was in her early sixties, yet the pain of losing Mimi was as fresh and raw as it was the morning she awakened to her life-shattering loss. Joan's fear of dying was tied to a memory of terrible things happening when you go to sleep and are unable to do anything about them. Where had God been when her Mimi had been ordered away? Why had He allowed that to happen? How could she trust Him now? The injustice seemed too monstrous to get past. Yet, as the fall turned to winter and the dark, cold days ebbed to the beckoning of spring, it was evident that Joan had come to her final days.

One late evening, when I was about to leave Joan's apartment, I procrastinated, sensing that it might be the last time I would see her in this life. Her daughter, Phyllis, and I sat on either side of her on the bed. Joan wanted pretzels to dip into peanut butter and a cup of cocoa, even though she couldn't eat much. She was in a particularly good mood, and the three of us reminisced about the many experiences we'd shared. She told us we were her two daughters and how much she loved us both.

At around five o'clock the next morning, Phyllis called to tell me her mother had died. I took a shower, dressed, and headed for Joan's home in Keene, a town about twenty miles from my home. As I drove through the early morning dawn, I thought about Joan and wondered where her soul was at that moment. I reflected on the many conversations we had shared through the years about spirituality, death, reincarnation, and God as the Great Mystery.

I remembered a special evening six months before Joan's death when we sat on her back porch talking about her life. She knew she was dying. She told me how her heart still ached over the loss of Mimi, the nanny who took care of her for the first three years of her life. She still wondered what had happened to Mimi. I asked Joan if she really wanted to try to find Mimi or her spirit. Her answer was an unequivocal "Yes." We both sat in silence for a few moments, pondering the seriousness of what I was asking. I couldn't imagine that I was considering such a thing, but my overwhelming love for Joan prompted me to go to any lengths to help her become less fearful of death. I didn't really know if it were possible to reach the spirit of another soul who had passed on, but for Joan's sake, I was willing to try.

Joan and I were overwhelmed with the possibility that she might hear from Mimi. When I asked the Voice of Love if such a connection were possible, I was directed to be quiet and wait. A few minutes later I heard that "Mimi is available." I couldn't imagine how this would happen, but I simply listened and closed my mind to any internal thinking or feeling. I stayed deeply focused on the words I heard, repeated them out loud, and waited for Joan's response.

So beautiful and touching was their reunion that, as I relayed the dialogue between Mimi and Joan, tears streamed down my face. Mimi reminisced about the good times they shared and the special gifts she had given Joan as a child. She recollected events and clothing that Joan had worn and that Joan remembered, too. Mimi asked if Joan recalled the photograph they had taken of Joan when she was about two years old, dressed in a long white outfit and sitting on a stone wall with Mimi standing behind her.

The dialogue ended, and Joan and I settled into a long silence. We were overcome with what had just taken place. Joan got up and went into the other room. Several moments later she returned, holding the picture that Mimi had described. It was a small black-and-white photo, crinkled and faded. There was Joan, about two years old, and her wonderful Mimi, big and black, standing beside her with a large, protective hand on the child's shoulder. You could feel the love between them. I left for home awed by the gift of love I had witnessed.

On the day of Joan's passing, I was driving for the second time to her home, returning to witness her friends saying their final goodbyes to her, wondering just what it means for our souls to "go on." Does that mean the soul is real, not just a symbol, but an actual presence? I silently asked the Voice of Love whether Joan's soul was alive somewhere. I was told that Joan's soul was very much alive and aware of what was transpiring. I asked for proof. I heard, "Ask Phyllis how her foot feels this morning." Not understanding how one's foot had anything to do with the soul, I decided to follow up when the opportunity presented itself. It wasn't until the end of a long day of visits from friends that I finally got the chance to ask Phyllis about it. Her face turned ashen, and she asked me how I knew about her foot. When I explained, she told me what had happened. The night before Joan died, Phyllis had gone in to check on her mother at 2:00 or 3:00 A.M. and noticed that she was still breathing. As Phyllis turned to leave, she inadvertently jammed her foot into the leg of the hospital bed. She let out a yelp because it hurt, and she was afraid the noise had awakened Joan, but when Joan didn't move, Phyllis crept back into her own bed.

We stared at each other, trying to decide what this experience meant. The only way I could have learned about Phyllis's foot was from Joan herself. Since Joan never again regained consciousness, the only way I could have received this information was directly from Joan's spirit. If Joan's spirit could communicate with me, Phyllis and I wanted to try communicating with her again. I decided that I would ask the Voice of Love for additional details the next morning. I didn't expect that we would be successful because such a possibility seemed so surreal. However, that communication from Joan became the first of many.

I left Phyllis and went home, knowing that representatives of the funeral home were coming that evening to collect Joan's body and to prepare it for cremation several days later. In my meditation at home, I asked for more insights from Joan. Again I closed my eyes and asked the Voice of Love to connect me to Joan's spirit. And again I could hear Joan talking to me. She relayed the details of her death in fascinating detail. I wrote down what she said so that I could check with Phyllis the following day to see if any details could be corroborated.

Joan's voice told me that dying wasn't what she had expected. To her utter delight, her beloved Mimi, surrounded by a brilliant rose light, appeared to her. Joan said that as she left her body she floated toward Mimi and then right through her image, as if Mimi were a doorway or mirror to another dimension. Once she was on the other side, she saw several images and realized she could choose with whom or with what she wished to be reunited.

As Joan described her experiences to me, I could see a "movie" of what she was describing, and I was afraid to breathe for fear the images would disappear. I saw a log house surrounded by tall pine trees and a woman who, I later learned, was Joan's biological mother, and an older man with a mustache. I wondered if he might have been her grandfather. I asked Joan who this man was. She said, "It's Frank."

After each of these miraculous encounters with Joan's spirit, I'd try to piece together what she'd told me in order to learn more about the way we leave our physical bodies. From Joan's death experience, I realized that some people don't go through what is often described as a golden tunnel leading to the realm of spirit. Instead, they see a person whom they loved dearly and that person's image becomes the doorway to the spirit world. Rather than being afraid, the person who is passing to the other side is joyful. Once there, the person's spirit is attracted to the images of those they loved in life. Joan had often joked about wanting to get her hands on her mother to tell her just how she ruined her life. When Joan actually had the chance to do so, she declined the opportunity and headed toward the man with the mustache.

I called Phyllis the following morning with my astonishing information. I asked her if she knew of anyone named Frank and if she had ever seen the log house. She told me the log house was Joan's favorite childhood summer home in the Pocono Mountains, where she and Mimi had spent time. Frank was an uncle who had died before Joan was born. Every time Joan saw a picture of Uncle Frank, she would hesitate and say, "I know him—something about him is so familiar." I concluded that he must have been close to her in a previous lifetime.

At home again, I sat in meditation listening to Joan's spirit voice. She had already told me about her actual dying experience and what she'd seen on the "other side." I couldn't imagine what she might tell me next, but I was unprepared for what I heard. Joan's spirit described how the men from the funeral home came to take her body away for cremation. She related the exact experience, complete with the place where her daughter and sister were standing and what they were doing. Joan's spirit said that the two men, one heavy-set and burly and the other very tall and thin, had picked up her body and placed it on a stretcher. When they came to the top of the steep steps leading from her apartment to the first floor, they set the stretcher down to discuss how to maneuver the body down the steps. Joan relayed this to me without emotion. She seemed serene, interested in what was taking place but not tied to it.

Again, Phyllis was able to confirm every detail, exactly as it had transpired. Joan had told me that they had taken her body in a hearse, and she described the blue sheet they used to cover her. It was the only time after her death that she reported she was afraid. She tried to re-enter her body but was unable to do so. Once she arrived at the crematorium, the "mirror" through which she had observed the events she described to me clouded over, and she could no longer "see" anything in the physical world.

I marveled at the loving way that her spirit had been released. It would have been frightening to see her body lowered into the burning fire, so she was protected from witnessing it. The moment her body was no longer present, her physical life was complete and could no longer be seen by her spirit.

Joan continued to talk with Phyllis and me once a month for almost a year, and each time our communication was very different. The experience was disconcerting because Joan had trouble remembering who we were and needed to warm up to the conversation. One time the Voice of Love was unable to locate her spirit to converse with us, and I never found out why. Joan's passing was especially difficult for Phyllis, who was in her early thirties and still longed for her mother's guidance. Joan sometimes talked directly to Phyllis, and other times she would talk about what she was learning in the spirit world and how she felt. I could sense the growing distance between Joan's spirit and our physical reality. It was always a stark reminder that we were witnessing a process that was beyond what one was allowed to see ordinarily.

In one dialogue, Joan told us about three black horsemen she'd seen in a dream when she was alive. I recalled that, when she first told me she'd had the dream, she had been terrified. Now she reported that the three horsemen were actually special teachers who had come to help her understand her fears. From this comment, I surmised that what we are most afraid of manifests as a person, a situation, or—as in Joan's case— three dark horsemen. Once we face the fear, we are ready to let it teach us rather than haunt us. Apparently, the process of overcoming fear continues in earnest in the afterworld.

Each exchange with Joan was unique and precious, and we tape-recorded every word. Finally, almost a year after her physical death, the time came when Joan announced that she would no longer be able to speak with us. She told us that she was "entering a time of preparation for a new life." In our final session together, Joan responded to Phyllis with great warmth, as if, just for a moment, she recalled her deep love for her child. "Do you know why I nicknamed you Phoebe?" she asked. "I named you after Phoebe Artemis, which is another name for the Greek goddess of the moon. Remember how we used to watch the moon together? Every time you look up at the moon, remember that you and I will always be connected." And that was the last word we ever heard from Joan.

Phyllis and I sat in silence dissolved in tears. "She's really gone, she's really gone...she's really gone," we repeated numbly. We had lost her twice, and it was gut-wrenching.

I learned a great deal from Joan, both in and beyond physical life. She made an enormous effort to educate us so that we might do the same for others. It was her final gift to me, given so that I could allay the fears of other people facing their own transition. Death is often portrayed as the "grim reaper," but this was not Joan's experience. Death was a doorway to a place where she was free to choose her own balance between love and fear, forgiveness and hate, acceptance and revenge. The only grim reaper is the fear that keeps us out of balance, eroding our appreciation of the lives we've been given.

I felt privileged to have shared Joan's and Phyllis's journey beyond the physical world. But I do understand why there is a veil that separates life and death. We do not grasp the rules of spirit until our death forces us to live by them fully. Once we are in spirit, we cannot undo the choices we've made in our lives; instead, we must live with the results. Only when we are given the opportunity for the Power of Love to heal our lives can we recognize fully how important that is. I was an interloper allowed to peer beyond the veil for a brief time to view the generosity of spirit that is the norm there. As a result, I've become more settled within myself, so that when my transition time comes, I will have no need of fear.

We move toward love—always toward love. So many people ask me why their dear departed loved ones aren't able to communicate with them. This is what Joan told me about communication from the spirit realm: "It is extremely difficult to communicate, because I have to take my words apart and make them very small and different so that you can understand them." She said this type of communication was similar to "trying to push an entire armload of energy through a single straw."

We think of our physical lives as if they were the greatest treasure we could own, terrified that losing our physical identification means the end of everything—a dreadful fate. Yet, according to everything I've learned, that is far from the truth. The process that joins us with other loving souls in the realm of spirit offers us the opportunity to experience Love as the true power of all creation. Change is the natural order, and death is a part of that. When we become intimate with change—including death, the inevitable companion to life in the natural world—we encompass our true natures.

Life Steward Friends

Life Stewards are those friends, mentors, and associates who teach us how to survive change. The Life Stewards in our lives enable us to appreciate and call on our inner Life Stewards, who are part of our authentic selves.

Life Stewards are intimately connected to the physical world. They share our struggles, seeing them with clarity, passion, and assurance that all is well. Life Stewards love the Earth and her life forms. They are the sacred ecologists of our world, reminding us that a sustainable environment is essential to life, allowing us to derive from its splendor the natural abundance that benefits all people. Aware of the past but not circumscribed by history, they know that invention and innovation are the agents of change intended to stir the times and stimulate renewal of the culture. They are idealistic in envisioning new ways of working with Nature and realistic in understanding that change requires making life different—not just better or worse, but different—by creating a new balance. Life Stewards aren't rooted to a home or a country, because the entire Earth is their home. They understand balance and help us to find our shifting center, the fulcrum point that steadies us between past and future that we call "the present."

A Life Steward is someone like the young woman who told her local Humane Society that there was a large colony—a hundred or more—of wild or feral cats in uptown Manhattan in New York City. The cats had every kind of known malady and disease, but no one could catch them, so they remained untreated, hiding from people during the day. The Humane Society was too overburdened to respond.

This Life Steward, whose name was Shauna, was deeply distressed by so many sick cats fending for themselves under deplorable conditions. She decided that, despite her busy work and school schedule, she would do something about it. Shauna worked all day as a secretary and was earning her degree at a local college at night. When she came home from school she'd catch a few hours of sleep, then head out to some of the scariest parts of the inner city to try to capture some of the cats. She brought them home to her tiny apartment to tame them, treat them, feed and groom them enough so that others would be able to handle them and they could be put up for adoption. She jokes about the fact that she wasn't evicted because of housing a continuous stream of a dozen or more cats in her tiny apartment. Shauna didn't see that what she did was special. "Anyone would have done it," she told me. But the fact is, no one else had!

■ *Listening to Our Inner Life Stewards*

Our inner Life Stewards teach us that change is inevitable, and as we change we become more intimate with our own natures. Inner Life Stewards help us sense the rhythms and ripples that are the feedback from our efforts in the world. We are urged to participate in life for the sheer pleasure of experiencing the Unrevealed and to uncover the possibilities that lie before us.

■ In Search of Our Inner Beloved

It is easy to see love and intimacy as the gift that comes from bonding with another person. It is more difficult to recognize it as a desire for closeness with our inner Source of Love. Either in this life or a future one, our universal search for meaning and stability ultimately brings us to intimate and tender connection with our own internal beloved.

Through the centuries, visionaries have written about their search for God as a pursuit of the Beloved. The thirteenth-century poet, philosopher, and scholar, Jalaluddin Rumi, is one of these remarkable mystics. His writings take us to our own unexplored inner spaces where we, like Rumi, can invent a language with which to reach our own inner "Beloved." In *The Illuminated Rumi* by Coleman Barks and Michael Green, Rumi tells us, "To change, a person must face the dragon of his/her appetites with another dragon, the life-energy of the soul."

Trying to love ourselves and those close to us with forbearance and forgiveness daily, challenges the dragons of our appetites. We can imagine the standoff between our two dragons, the one breathing the fire of getting our own way at any cost or feeling victimized by life, the other breathing the clarity, sweetness, and power of our union with our inner Beloved. Every one of our experiences strengthens only one of our dragons. Every acknowledgment, judgment, belief, spoken word, and action we take strengthens either the dragon of self-interest or the dragon of soul-interest.

Just as we search for ways to demonstrate our devotion to a loving partner, so too we can look for the special endearments to use with our inner lovers. Our souls' interests are in giving us an expanded perspective on life so that we understand how to best use our time on Earth. Our souls want the best for us and from us. The Life Steward says, "Learn from Nature and its intimate relationship with change. Observe how life grows, shifts, and weaves together the systems that support all life." We are interwoven and intimately connected with The Beloved. That connection is what allows us to handle change.

■ *Managing Change*

Change can either hurtle us into a loop of continuous reactivity to distress, keeping us off-balance and unable to remain on our chosen path, or it can offer us ways to enter into the rhythms of life, creating harmony and balance rather than cacophony and struggle.

Change is like a revolving door. When we step into it, we need to keep a steady pace in order to move comfortably toward our destinations. If we stop, or if we walk too quickly, we move out of the rhythm and begin bumping into people or feel pushed by them. Staying in harmony with our inner rhythms also helps us to activate our intuition for our personal health.

In working with women healing from breast cancer, I ask them to tell me how they sensed the rhythm of their lives before the diagnosis, while in treatment, and now, several years later. Usually they start out feeling pushed, unseen, afraid, and uncertain. Gradually they become more aware of their disempowered feelings. Instead of accepting them as judgment of personal failure or deficiency, they choose to forge new agreements with life. Putting our heads in the sand is never the answer. Answering the call of a discordant inner rhythm requires us to attend to our needs, staying steady as we breathe through the distressing feelings and seek out genuine options.

The purpose of change is to initiate us into intimate resonance and dialogue with our souls. We may know a great deal about our emotional likes and dislikes, our preferences and wants, but we know little about the language of our souls and how to grow closer to our Inner Beloved.

When we are sick and when we regain our health, life looks different to us. We are changed whenever we gain or lose in the stock market, plant a garden, buy a horse, visit our grandchildren, start a business, merge a business, lose a business, bury a friend. The best way to honor change is by anticipating that we will experience an internal shift with every pleasure and pain. Sometimes we assume that change will be unsettling rather than fulfilling, disastrous instead of euphoric. Staying steady, anchored in courage and compassion, we can wait out the storm calmly, allowing events to unfold fully so that we can see the bigger picture. I try to remind myself of this both when I'm feeling invincible and when I'm feeling vulnerable and unable to cope. I remind myself, "This too will pass." We are in the process of "becoming," and the final word has yet to be written.

Our spirits love reaching out toward the unknown, giving us new ways to experience our authentic selves. Our personalities, by contrast, prefer familiar conclusions, ultimatums, and definitive answers. To stay steady even as we move into unknown territory, think of the ski instructor who says to her students, "Plant your pole and then move into the turn." In life, when we plant our poles, symbolically, we are reminding ourselves who we are—aspects of the Creator's Light—and then, when we move into change, we can continue to head in our chosen directions. It's important to plant our poles where we know we can count on consistent and supportive ground—in our souls. When we plant our poles in the unstable soil of events, material success, or stormy relationships, we're signing on for a rough ride. Life around us is always in motion, with much ado about nothing. We no longer need to be embroiled in these tempests in teapots. By contrast, our inner selves generate movement that is completely dedicated to our well-being and to our most purposeful directions.

To manage change well we must be intimate with our personal preferences, both our emotional, physical, and spiritual ones. Emotionally, we can make creative and self-nurturing choices, infusing our lives with enjoyment and delight. Physically, we can surround ourselves with beauty, friendships, play, and work that strengthen and expand our lives. Spiritually, we can seek to fathom the nature of Spirit and practice devotions that hold us steady in The Creator's love. Too often we fail to remember that by satisfying our own preferences we stay steady, balanced, and resilient. Instead, when we invest all of our energy into the three roles that society says are paramount: those of parent, spouse or partner, and bread-winner, we may have little left for ourselves, especially when we run into inevitable life challenges. When these roles are threatened, as when we face the prospect of a divorce or a job loss, we feel done in—without the endurance and the steadiness to accommodate to change and refresh our spirit.

The Seasons of Our Nature

When Nature changes her seasons, the shift seems effortless, predictable, and inevitable. The new season approaches and the old one retreats. Just as Nature doesn't stay forever in a single season, like it or not, neither do we.

Just as there are four seasons in Nature, our inner natures also experience four seasons. Spring is the season of new beginnings. In Summer, we grow the fruits of our new beginnings, and in the Fall, we harvest the rewards of our efforts, including opportunities to be acknowledged and appreciated for our accomplishments. In Winter we rest, rediscovering our true selves. Without Winter we cannot move into Spring.

We recognize the season we're in both by the way we feel and by the movement of energy in and around our efforts. We know when we are putting forth our greatest efforts, but we don't always realize when we are internalizing our greatest learnings. It's not the level of effort that tells us what season we're in, it's the return on those efforts.

In the Spring of our inner natures, our efforts begin to bring us returns, and we feel compelled to begin new projects, even some that have rested on our shelves for many years.

Our growing bank accounts and acclaim from peers tell us we are now in the Summer of our inner natures. Other people recognize us when we are in Summer and want to celebrate with us. We feel stronger each day, a direct reflection of the intense heat of the Summer sun.

In the Fall of our inner natures, we feel invincible. Everything we touch turns to gold. We are celebrated for our achievements, and we seem to be headed for a permanent place in the winners' circle. Then we feel the first signs of Winter, and everything begins to shift.

In the Winter of our inner natures, we slow down and feel the loss of outer accomplishments, public acclaim, and/or material possessions. We are doing nothing differently, yet there are fewer returns on our efforts. We feel as if we're coming undone; an old fear we thought we'd put to rest resurfaces. The more attached we are to worldly success, or to old patterns and people with whom we've identified, the harder we struggle, and the more we struggle the more life unravels before our eyes. We push and pray, ask and beg, but to no avail. Our undoing has a life of its own, and we seem its victims.

If we could stop the action at this point of desperation and say to ourselves, "I realize I'm being asked to grow in new ways," we might consider that this is a time for someone else to shine and be successful. We would say: I wish all who are in the Spring, Summer, and Fall of their lives the joy of their success, knowing that I, too, will enter the Spring of success again. But in the meantime, I can rest, renew, and reap spiritual rewards.

We're like a spent flower in Winter, tired and needing rest and recovery, not from the outer world but from our inner selves. Instead, many of us enter Winter desperate to hold on to the energy of Fall, which slips through our fingers no matter how tightly we clench our fists.

Winter is God's time, the time of spiritual renewal. It doesn't mean that we have to lose everything, or even that we have to lose anything. What falls away in the Winter of our inner natures are the outworn trappings with which we identify ourselves.

Whether we're stressed beyond reason or deeply unhappy doesn't seem to matter. We persist in staying where we think the power, money, or prestige lives. Even though we may be suffocating, Winter releases us from our burdens. We continue to want the things that are identified with outward signs of success: financial status, career, marriage, appearance, clever wit, or brilliant physical prowess. Once relieved of what is burdensome, we climb quickly back into the fray again until Winter once more shows us what really matters now.

As we grow spiritually, our Winters deal more with the interior of our lives. We are prodded again to give up the fears, anger, desires, and jealousies that have grown up along with material success. At first we lose what we think we want; then we lose what we are ready to give up. I like to think of my Wintertime as coming into dry dock to get rid of the barnacles.

◼ *Illness is a Winter Opportunity*

Mental and physical illnesses are experiences of the Winter of our inner natures. We can't run away from them, so we have no choice but to stay and learn. People talk about the gift of an illness. The gift is that we've been given an opportunity to heal a dysfunctional behavior or a useless emotional pattern, perhaps from this life and perhaps from past lives. We are offered an opportunity to move to an advanced level of awareness, releasing unwanted patterns of anger, resentment, envy, jealousy, regret, judgment, and loss. Sometimes we're able to release the patterns and the illness instead of our lives. In the broadest view of life, healing isn't just about changing the body, it's about adjusting our perception and about learning to love. Healing happens when we believe in the power of Love that is in us.

◼ *Winter Offers Renewal and Clarity in Partnership*

Marriages and partnerships also move through the cycle of Spring, Summer, Fall and Winter. We tend to get divorced in the Winter of our inner lives, and we tend to come together in the Spring, Summer, or Fall. In long-standing relationships, Winter holds the potential for rediscovery or bailout. We enter and leave Winter with different minds and hearts. We may come into Winter determined to leave a relationship but emerge knowing we'll stay. Just as Winter snows moisten the earth so that Spring flowers can grow, Winter's tears may awaken a new and glorious Spring for our hearts.

Trish's Healing Journey

Trish desperately wanted to attend the Stillpoint School Program in Intuitive Perception and Energy Diagnosis. I wondered why she felt so driven to come this particular year. She lived in Paris, France, but felt the travel wasn't an obstacle. Because I never "scan" someone without the person's permission, I just accepted that she was deeply motivated to study the work and knew that as I got to know her, and we moved through the year's program together, I would understand in what way I was to work with her.

Trish was one of the first people I met at the School's initial orientation session. A slender blonde with short curly hair, she was full of energy and seemed ready to take on the world. I loved her enthusiasm. At the conclusion of our first six-day learning intensive, Trish asked if she could call me for a special health consultation. We set it up for the following week, since she was staying in the States for a few days to visit friends. She told me she would be getting the results of some medical tests and wanted to review them with me.

When I did my initial evaluation of Trish before our phone consultation, I realized that breast cancer was the issue we would address, and that, in all likelihood, it had returned. Breast cancer, in my experience, focuses around the need for greater self-nurturing. Healing is most effective when it focuses on helping a woman identify the loss that has drained her vital self-love, giving her the support she needs to acknowledge the pain and grieve for the loss, and finally, to accept the Grace to know that she is authentic and has the necessary healing resources within her.

From my reading of Trish, it seemed that she had lost confidence in her career or had perhaps actually lost her job. As if that wasn't enough, she seemed to have little intimacy with her husband and much confusion around her children. I could feel that she was searching for God, with the unanswered questions that come through having a life-threatening disease. This is why she is coming to School, I thought. She's ready to find answers to the essential questions.

When Trish called, it was clear from the muffled tone of her voice that the news was bad. She told me that she'd had a mastectomy for breast cancer several years earlier and believed she had dealt with what needed to be taken care of. The cancer was now in her second breast and she wanted to know what to do. When clients ask for my opinion about an operation, I know that what they really need is a chance to explore how they feel about their situation, and from that discussion they will find the right choices for their healing. My work isn't to direct them to or away from surgery but to help them find the procedures they trust will work for them. Belief in our healing choices goes a long way toward enhancing the effectiveness of the choices we make.

Trish told me she believed she needed the surgery. She said, "I want to get this over with and get on with my life." I thought to myself that breast cancer is a powerful and difficult teacher, because it is relentless in causing a woman to dig deep for the quality of self-nurturing that can truly heal and satisfy. I was concerned that she was treating the diagnosis as if she were sweeping unwanted crumbs off the table after an unruly guest. I thought briefly about all the women I'd worked with and how many of them were doing well even after repeated challenges. Breast cancer is a demanding teacher and is a serious call for spiritual direction.

Trish and I talked about the spiritual resources that would add energy to her body and help unblock emotional patterns of distress that stood in the way of her healing. I told her that there are three aspects of her authentic self that would be important in healing her breast cancer, because each responded to a different aspect of her body needing attention. I told her about her inner Life Steward and the need to strengthen her reproductive system, including her breasts; about her Compassionate Healer and the importance of enhancing her immune system and her circulatory system; and about her Vision Keeper and the necessity for bringing stability to her endocrine system, the hormones and secretions that maintain her feminine power.

We moved from this discussion to her reactions to the business loss she'd sustained, which I believed might have triggered her cancer. The year prior to her initial diagnosis, the mail-order business selling children's educational materials that she had run went bankrupt. While a malignancy can go undetected for many years, a serious and unresolved loss often gives the cancer permission to settle in. Trish told me that her beloved son was in school overseas and that her daughter was a very challenging teenager. She also told me that her husband and she were going in different directions. I took that to mean that she was considering separation. Clearly, there was a lot of work to do to determine what she wanted for her own life.

I suggested we begin with the Mending Your Bowl experience, because I knew this would put her into her heart instead of her head, where I sensed she lived 98 percent of the time. I told her to close her eyes and breathe slowly. I suggested that she visualize her Intimacy Bowl. I asked her to imagine that this bowl could show how comfortable she was with intimacy with her inner self and in managing change. I said, "Trish, this is the Bowl that allows you to learn to see that your feelings and attitudes about the past are the basis for your future. Tell me what your bowl feels like." She immediately said, "My Intimacy Bowl is made of sandalwood. It's dusky brown and smells sweet. It's soft and pliable." I asked what she noticed about how her bowl could hold her energy of Intimacy. She said, "The bowl is so malleable that it seems unable to hold its shape. It moves with my every thought."

"Where did your inability to hold your own shape come from?" I asked. She paused a long time, searching for the right answer. I added,

"Trish, you have to move into your feelings to answer this question. Your mind doesn't have the answer."

She responded, "I feel such a failure. I tried everything to save my business. I'm really very creative, you know! I listened to everyone's opinions but my own. The business just seemed doomed after the first year. Everything went wrong."

"Whom do you blame for your failed business?" I inquired.

"Myself," was her immediate answer. "I should have known how to do it right."

I smiled to myself, thinking how often I've said the very same thing. "Trish," I continued, "imagine that you are sitting facing yourself as if you're looking in the mirror. I want you to address your mirror self as you looked and felt at the time of the bankruptcy." I was taken aback by the force of the verbal attack that Trish leveled against the mirror image of herself. Her words were deeply cutting and challenging. "Now," I continued, "put your hand over your heart in a loving manner and imagine that you're moving down to your heart to listen to what your mirror image has to tell you."

Trish didn't say a word at first. I could tell she was struggling to get her reactive self into a calmer and more loving heart space. I waited. Eventually, she found the passage to spirit and said, "I feel like a little girl again talking to my father. I loved him so desperately, but I never felt he cared about me. He was so critical. I never knew what to do to please him."

I continued in a slow, steady voice asking, "What is your father saying to you from his heart?"

Her voice began to shake, as the power of the experience with her deceased father took on a life of its own. She said between sobs, "He says he only wanted the best for me—wanted me to be prepared for hard times." Trish continued with "I told him that instead of preparing me, he left me feeling I would have nothing but hard times my entire life."

I thought: here, then, is the real loss, not her business but the love and support of her father. I asked her what she needed to hear from her father. She said, "I need him to tell me he's sorry for never allowing me to thrive." She talked further and finally felt satisfied with her father's positive response that he truly cared for her.

"What part of your authentic self do you now claim, Trish?" I asked softly.

"I claim my right to be successful in life, in all ways," she said with strong feeling. I asked her how she could now mend her original bowl image. She replied that she would pour a sturdy lining into the bowl to keep it in optimum shape. I thought how important an image this would be in our work together, since the lining was clearly her own self-generated power to love herself.

Trish and I had many sessions over the course of the school year. She graduated and was filled with delight over her accomplishment. The rest of the students admired her ability to take hold of life. We kept our fingers crossed as she returned home to France, away from the safe environment of the program.

But slowly she lost herself again in the struggles of the family. The cancer returned. She had been granted the time to return to her family and begin to sort things out. She was stronger, more honest, and more committed to life. But joy eluded her. She struggled to accept the realization that she was worth loving and that she could have a future.

The difficult thing about regaining physical health is that by the time we have the power to remake our reactions to old pain, the disease may have gained so much momentum that it is unstoppable. The solution seems to be to take seriously any threat to our well-being at the inception, realizing that we are being called not only to address our body's needs but also to explore our emotional reactions to life and love, and to rediscover the healing connection to our own souls.

I knew that Trish was originally an American and that she yearned to return to the States. She had a sister in the Northeast, but they weren't close. I asked her if she would like to come and stay with my husband and me for a while. Part of me realized she was probably trying to choose where to finish her physical life; the other part of me had grown to love this gutsy woman, and I was hoping for a miracle.

She accepted our invitation and shortly was set up comfortably in our guest room. Trish stayed with us for three weeks. The cancer was not to be denied—but neither was her new spiritual power. We spent many hours together praying, meditating, and talking about The Creator. She grew calm, thoughtful, peaceful, and aligned with spirit. The miracle was watching her find her true power. One morning she reported to me that she'd had a significant dream. In the dream, she dove into a beautiful, clear pool of water, and when she came to the surface, giant luscious-smelling white-and-pink lotus flowers surrounded her. We both knew what the dream signified. From that moment on, I knew she was in safe hands. God had officially taken over. We all decided that it was time to contact her sister, who was aware of her condition and that she was staying with us. Trish wanted to be with her sister and make things right. She was taken to a hospital close to her sister's home, and the rest of the family flew in from France and Japan. Everyone was assembled around her bed when she said goodbye to this world. She had made it safely and powerfully through the doorway to spirit.

Healing is taking away the pain—sometimes physically, usually emotionally, and often spiritually. Our physical bodies are the last part of our presence to come into healing because the inner levels have to find balance first. Many times our bodies can rebalance themselves even with life-threatening diseases. Physical, emotional, and spiritual healing does happen, all the time and all around us. But healing in the true sense of the word means coming to peace in our hearts and realizing that the Beloved's signature is written across our lives so that we no longer need to fear change, whether we stay in our present lives or leave them.

We have set up a Stillpoint School Scholarship Fund* in honor of Trish's grace and bravery. Her gift to us is to live with joy and enthusiasm even when we have problems and little control of our futures. One new student each year is the proud recipient of this scholarship, making it possible for him or her to attend the program to learn to practice a healing modality that helps people live fully.

Sketching Our Intimacy Bowls

AS YOU DRAW YOUR INTIMACY BOWL, realize that it holds the energy of your deepest feelings about yourself, the way you accept both the challenging parts of your personality and the parts that are filled with grace. The Intimacy Bowl is located in the pelvis and relates to the Second Chakra. It governs your excretory and reproductive systems, allowing you to eliminate what no longer serves you so you can nurture your new beginnings and deliver yourself into a meaningful future. As you imagine this bowl, you'll find how hopeful you are for a future that is more than just a continuation of past struggles. Your Intimacy Bowl holds the energy of change and reveals how steady you stay with the support and comfort of the natural world.

In preparation for sketching your Intimacy Bowl, you might want to ask yourself questions like: Do I feel my stomach tighten when I think about changing where I live or whom I love? Am I comfortable allowing my life to unfold differently? What do I really want for my future? How powerful is my connection to the natural world? Am I comforted by seeing that nothing in Nature dies but instead is transformed? How

---

*If you would like to contribute to The Merrick Scholarship Fund, please see further information on page 188.

conscious am I of the changing rhythms of my own nature? In what ways do I hear my Life Steward asking me to deepen my response to my Inner Beloved?

Nature's Creative Expressions

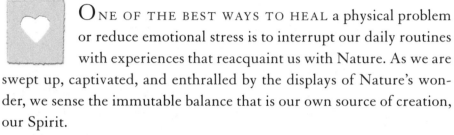 ONE OF THE BEST WAYS TO HEAL a physical problem or reduce emotional stress is to interrupt our daily routines with experiences that reacquaint us with Nature. As we are swept up, captivated, and enthralled by the displays of Nature's wonder, we sense the immutable balance that is our own source of creation, our Spirit.

The difference between normal recreation and experiencing Nature's creative expressions is that in seeking Nature for our own delight, we pay attention to the rejuvenation it inspires us to feel inside. We enter Nature's creative arena in order to recognize our union with it and to be regenerated.

Everything about Nature is impressive, from the bumblebees that aren't supposed to be able to fly but do, to the intricacies of flowers, the wonders of giant redwoods, and the brilliance of the sun glinting off a streambed filled with glistening stones. Everywhere we look we see that Nature is our greatest teacher. Engaging Nature means engaging our roots, which tie deeply into our heritage and allow us to appreciate our Earth home.

Imagine renting a canoe or kayak and going out for a paddle. We quickly settle into a different inner rhythm. Our arms move in harmony with the current, and we forget our worries and become part of the life around us—an intimate part. When we use chalk, watercolors, or oil paints to express the beauty of our gardens, hills, or snow banks, we flow into the images as we create them. What we depict in images has a greater impact on us than mere words.

Our lives become richer when we allow our senses to be stimulated by the images, sights, and sounds of the natural world. In experiencing Nature's creativity, we open our own vibrant inspiration. Our Life Steward energy is trying to get us to be creative, to participate in Nature's playground. We're in it for the fun of it—to calm our nerves, to awaken our delight in life, and to get out of our heads and into our bodies.

All of our creative efforts involve Nature in one way or another. When people say that they are uncomfortable in Nature, they are saying they have lost the fit with their own most basic source of creative expression. We have become city dwellers and business people. But first we were cave dwellers and hunter-gatherers. The Earth and the natural world are imprinted in the core of our being.

Finding inner balance comes from returning to the images of Nature and moving in harmony with life around us, not remaining locked away in constructions of concrete and cinder block. It is in our blood, our genes, to be Life Stewards—stewards and caretakers of the land around us and within us.

When we play music, walk in Nature, garden, hike, or sit quietly in majestic places, we redesign our lives more powerfully than we can through all the thinking and planning and articulating of great and lofty plans. When we find what we love and share it with others we love, our futures find us. When we move out of our inner harmonies by trying too hard, planning too much, wanting too badly, we drop the ball of momentum in our lives.

Activity without the need for achievement or control is the real nourishment. When we do something creative, we're reawakening the rhythms of our lives that are essential to us.

■ Creating Your Own Nature Space

A Nature space is any place—large or small, wild or planned, in your office, in your home, greenhouse, or back yard—that takes you into Nature's splendid mystery.

Spend ten minutes before work admiring or tending your indoor plants in your living room, greenhouse, or porch. Whether you have one plant or twenty-five doesn't matter.

Create window boxes or gardens that can be your Nature spaces, where you attend to yourself by attending to Nature.

Enjoy Nature's wild spaces by sharing a few moments on the way to work admiring and enjoying the sun shimmering through a stand of white pines, a freshly turned farmer's field, or a turtle crossing the road. On your way to work, find and pause for a few moments to breathe deeply, relax, enjoy, extend yourself into the Nature space around you and find renewal there.

If you find yourself too busy to take time in the morning or evening to develop a Nature space, take five minutes before or after lunch to look around your office, or the place where you spend most of your day, and see where Nature spaces appear. Is it in the picture of the Grand Canyon on your wall calendar, or in the bouquet of flowers on your table? Is Nature in the water in your glass, or is the music you hear a takeoff on Nature's sounds? Is Nature in the crackers and cheese on your plate, or in the ant crawling across the carpet? Find Nature around you, and enjoy the moment.

IN SUMMARY

Life Steward's Gifts

CONSIDER THESE SPECIAL GIFTS to us from our inner Life Stewards. Try incorporating one new thought into your life each week.

My inner Life Steward allows me to become more intimate with my own nature in order to better know and accept others.

◆ My Life Steward encourages me to expect the best each day, even though I know change will shift what is best.

◆ My Life Steward shows me how awareness of a single blade of grass can replenish whatever is depleted in me.

◆ My Life Steward guides me toward overwriting my current negative life script with the one from my inner hand that knows only everlasting balance.

◆ My Life Steward believes in right relationships to all life and helps me know when to say "yes" to myself and when to say "not now" to others.

◆ My Life Steward sees my link to all living things and encourages me to honor my place in the community of all life.

◆ My Life Steward allows me to see that everything I love including my own life is temporary, and so it is important to make opportunities to be a real friend to others.

◆ My Life Steward teaches me appreciation for the diverse nature
of everything, so that I lose my fear of honoring my own.

As you review the drawing of your Intimacy Bowl, consider these statements about the benefits you can derive from the practice:

My Intimacy Bowl governs my quality of Divine Intimacy.

*My Intimacy Bowl allows me to balance my past with the dreams for my
future by learning from the natural world.*

*My Intimacy Bowl governs the health of my reproductive system and my
excretory system (including the breasts, uterus, ovaries in females and the
testes, penis, and prostate in males, and the kidneys, bladder, and skin).*

*My Intimacy Bowl represents the actual energy center of my Second
Chakra, which is located in the pelvic area of my body.*

*Creative expression is the most useful healing practice for awakening the
feeling of intimate connection with my Inner Beloved.*

THE MERRICK SCHOLARSHIP FUND

Please send your check or money order to:
The Stillpoint School of Advanced Energy Healing
The Merrick Scholarship Fund
PO Box 640
Walpole, NH 03608

For more information contact us at:
Phone: 603-756-9281 ext. 106 or 800-847-4014
E-mail: stillpoint@stillpoint.org

Or visit our webside at: www.stillpoint.org or www.wisdombowls.com

---

Healing is taking away the pain—
sometimes physically, usually emotionally, and often spiritually.

———————————

CAmeron Sesto

ABUNDANCE

The Question

If God is the answer, the Source of all life,
then what is the question that hangs in your heart,
directing you inward toward greater abundance?
If God is All-Knowing, the One who's in charge,
then who are you...do you know...do you care?
Are you God in disguise in these clothes East or West?
Are you Earthling, Martian, or Star-Seed-descended?
What purpose is yours for this Earthly existence?
What's your purpose...?
Ah, now that IS THE QUESTION you've intended to ask.
Your purpose is clear, according to Grace.
It's about loving and sharing and doing things that grow goodness.
That sounds much too simple, too easy to think
that stars in the heavens hang in their place,
awaiting your answer to this basic truth.
Will you finally agree to love what you see
without judgment or anger or need to be right,
in delight and rapture to accept God's directive
to live in abundance and fullness of life?
I now can say "Yes"
to my purpose on Earth...
to live with the knowing
that only love counts!

— Meredith Young-Sowers

CHAPTER EIGHT

ABUNDANCE

An open bank account allows money to flow in.
An open heart allows money to flow out.

WE STOOD SIDE BY SIDE like sisters, looking out the window at the stately white-columned mansion on the property adjacent to Stillpoint. The gracious antebellum structure, situated on a grassy knoll overlooking rolling fields, had been sadly neglected and needed a great deal of repair. Now it was up for sale. I'd often thought the old place would be a magnificent headquarters for Stillpoint, but buying it seemed out of the question financially, considering what we'd have to invest to restore it.

Jennifer startled me when she said, as if reading my mind, "We could buy that for Stillpoint!" I looked at her, assuming she was kidding, but she was deadly serious. "How could we afford it?" I asked. "Manifesting money is never a problem," she replied. "It comes to you when the time is right and the work is worthy." It was a surprising answer from a woman whose relationship with money seemed problematic. She had made a handsome profit in real estate, and she had lived with an extremely wealthy man, but she was never able to attract the funds she wanted for actualizing her dreams.

Jennifer came into our lives as a result of a synchronicity linked to a trip to India that Errol and I took to visit Sathya Sai Baba, the Indian holy man, at his ashram or religious retreat in Puttaparthi, a small town in southern India. We stayed for two weeks, although this was not an easy place for Westerners to visit—the conditions, the language, and the customs made it difficult for us to feel at ease, but all the hardships we underwent paled in the brilliance of our personal interview with this renowned spiritual teacher.

Our group of ten Westerners, along with two Indian couples, was granted an audience with Sai Baba on our fourth day at the ashram. Interviews are prized because there is no way to request personal time with this spiritual teacher. The experience is simply a gift. If you're fortunate, he tells you about your life and guides you to the next step on your spiritual journey. At the end of our interview, Sai Baba told me that he would help me with my life and my work. He said, "In three months"— and then he made a motion with his hand that indicated all would fly.

After we returned home, and three months to the day after the interview with Sai Baba, a woman from Australia called to find out about Stillpoint's next workshop. Discovering that it was to start in two weeks, she reserved a space and showed up at the designated time. Jennifer found Stillpoint in quite an extraordinary way. She was browsing through a bookstore in her native Sydney, Australia, looking for a set of guidance cards. She found what she wanted, only to discover that in her haste to purchase them, she had picked up the wrong set of cards. The checkout clerk, apologizing profusely, went to retrieve the correct set for her. But Jennifer, noticing that the set already in her hands was written by the author of *Agartha: A Journey to the Stars*, which had been extremely meaningful to her, told the clerk, "I'll take the set of *Angelic Messenger Cards* instead. Clearly, I'm supposed to have this one."

When I met Jennifer, I was struck by her warmth and engaging smile. Although she radiated confidence, there was something about her that told me she knew what it was like to be poor. It was during a break at the Stillpoint workshop in which I mentioned Sai Baba's name that she told me she had studied his teachings for a long time. Recounting how she found her way to Stillpoint, she commented, "I don't believe in coincidences; things happen for a reason." I wondered what the reason might be that had brought her into my life. Could her arrival be the event that Sai Baba had predicted would occur in three months' time? Intrigued with the mystery, and believing that she was a harbinger of good things to come, I invited her to come home with us for a visit before returning to Australia.

When I took her upstairs to the guest room, she stood in the doorway and said, "Oh yes, I knew this room would look just like this, and I imagined that I'd be staying in it for a while." I wondered how she knew that. Over the next several days, Jennifer entranced us with stories of her travels around the world. We listened spellbound to her accounts of trying to persuade government officials in Fiji to grant her a building permit for a large healing center. She felt guided to start this center but had been unable to move it forward despite several years of effort. She was about to give up, she said.

I found it interesting to watch Jennifer. She sometimes gave the impression of a daffy blond, but there was a part of her personality that told me that playing dumb was the way she got what she wanted in the world. She struck me as a smart and savvy woman. I wondered why she was afraid to use her inner authority and be honest with people.

I couldn't help thinking, "I mustn't underestimate this woman." Yet, for the most part, I was intrigued and delighted to visit with someone who was so much fun, so interested in my work, and so willing to talk for hours about expanding the Stillpoint work into the world. It had been a long time since I'd felt that kind of surge of creative energy around planning the future of Stillpoint.

From Jennifer's reminiscences about her experiences of the last ten years, I learned that she had made similar plans with other well-known authors and successful small-company owners, plans that had blown up with disastrous consequences. According to Jennifer, the other person was always the one at fault, and she was the one who had been duped. As I listened to her stories, I heard a loud and clear message inside of me: "Meredith, pay attention! This could be your scenario." I didn't want to hear it. I had faith that God had sent this wonderful new friend and ally to me to help me birth the next stages of my work as a healer and spiritual teacher. I wasn't interested in dissenting views, even my own.

We went ahead with plans to work together. One day, in the course of a casual conversation, an amazing idea was birthed. Jennifer asked me, "What would you do next if you could do anything in the world?" Out of my mouth came the words, "I want to start a school." I had no idea where that idea came from, but I knew immediately that the school was going to be a reality. I fell in love with the idea instantly. In my heart I knew that the time was right to create a program to teach the healing and spirituality work I had been practicing for the last seventeen years. Jennifer told me she wanted to learn to do my work and to help me to teach it. We discussed starting a foundation to help Stillpoint engage in service work in the United States. I felt that she still wanted to start the Fiji project, although she denied it.

Our plans were loosely and lovingly developed. We put nothing in writing and agreed to nothing specifically, but we generated lots of great ideas. We were doing God's work, so everything was bound to work out fine, I believed. Our plan was for Jennifer to go back to Sydney to rent out her home. She would also contact four young people with whom she had previously worked, who, she assured me, would be huge assets to the school. They would arrive at various times during the summer, and I agreed that everyone could stay with us, in the apartment and first floor of our newly constructed Stillpoint Institute building. They would work at the Institute and help out around the property in exchange for room and board, until we could afford to pay them for their work. We would develop a wonderful school program, and Jennifer would be the School's associate director.

After Jennifer left for Australia, I had time to think more clearly about our plans. On reflection, in jumping into a plan to start a school and a foundation, I didn't know Jennifer well enough to trust either her allegiance to Stillpoint or her business savvy. From what she had told me, I knew that her track record in business was poor. I decided that it would be better to start only the School, and to keep it a part of the Stillpoint Institute that Errol and I ran jointly. But now I was stuck, because Jennifer had gone home to rent her house in order to return to the States and start working with me in starting both the School and the Foundation.

I had a terrible feeling of foreboding. I wrote Jennifer by e-mail that I no longer wanted to tie the newly-proposed School to the Foundation that she and I had planned, and that I instead wanted to keep the School linked with the Institute. What I really meant to say was that I wanted to keep my financial future tied squarely to my husband rather than to Jennifer. But that's not exactly what I wrote to her. I told her everything would be fine, and that she was not to worry.

As it turned out, both Jennifer and I had hidden agendas. These agendas blinded us to the truth of both our own and each other's motivations. Jennifer wanted to establish a base in the United States from which she could launch a search for wealthy Americans to fund her various projects, including the one in Fiji. I believe that she wanted to help me with the School, but she had no idea of the work that I would be teaching and had assumed that it would be something that nourished her. My hidden agenda was to create an organization under my leadership that would help me avoid the power struggles with my husband over how my work and efforts should be sent out into the world.

As I pondered the predicament I'd gotten myself, my family, and the Institute into, I realized that what I had done was to substitute one alliance and form of control for another: Jennifer's for Errol's. Why, when I was the one with the successful career, was I giving her the authority to draw me into her agenda? For the first time, I saw that I'd allowed myself to be seduced by my need for someone's seeming devotion to helping me further the development of my work. I'd failed to listen to my own inner warnings and had been suckered by Jennifer's flattery and loving attention.

When Jennifer returned from Australia, she acted as if we were still following our original agreement about working together and completely ignored my letter that spelled out an altered scenario. Jennifer felt that she could talk me into going back to our original plan. When she realized that wasn't going to happen, she lost interest in the School, which wasn't her passion after all. Her interests lay in starting a foundation that Stillpoint would fund. The young people Jennifer invited proved to be a disaster, harboring their own hidden agenda of working with Jennifer on her foundation. They had no interest in helping me develop the School.

By this time, Errol was so furious with me and with them that he could hardly speak, and I didn't blame him. We had thought the four young people were coming to help us in the Institute in exchange for their room and board, but all they did was to sit on the freshly-mowed lawn eating picnic lunches, talking, or sun bathing, while Errol worked in the hot sun, weeding and making the gardens beautiful. Their unwillingness to help in any way, despite our providing for all their needs, seemed a blatant display of selfishness.

We met their needs in every way possible. They had the run of the two main floors of our new office building, which included a brand-new kitchen installed for their benefit. We provided them with cooking utensils, bought their food—nothing but the best organic produce, as they requested—and supplied the bedding, sheets, blankets—everything we could think of to make their stay at Stillpoint comfortable. In short, we had become their full-service, exclusive country resort.

In an attempt to rescue some semblance of a relationship, I suggested that Jennifer send the four young people home and that she and I try to establish the School, as we had originally planned. She asked me to sit with her and the others and talk with them. I did, but I couldn't believe my ears when the young people told me, in no uncertain terms, what vision had brought them to Stillpoint. They planned to create a worldwide foundation for developing projects, primarily in Fiji and the Far East, and, they said, they might consider incorporating the Stillpoint Institute and School into their plans as one of their projects.

Jennifer looked as if someone had punched her in the stomach. She had obviously encouraged them to believe they were starting a global foundation. I didn't know if they had even discussed the School as an option. I sat speechless, with Jennifer silent as a stone across the table. If she had any genuine attraction to my work, or if her numerous proclamations of commitment to the School were true, this would have been the time for her to set the record straight. Instead, she lowered her eyes to the floor. I was forced to conclude that she had made her choice. I felt a strange combination of guilt and anger that she had disregarded what I said and invited the young people to come to Stillpoint under false premises.

No future relationship was possible now. I asked the most strident of the young people, an Englishwoman, "What, then, is the exchange you offer for the use of our home and all our facilities so that you can pursue your funding interests here in the United States?" She looked directly at me and said, "There isn't one!"

I felt as if I'd been delivered from the belly of the whale. Had this been the plan all along, to use Stillpoint for Jennifer's private agenda? Or was Jennifer the victim of her own confusion over telling the entire truth about her intentions? I would never know. I was so furious that I walked out of the meeting, concerned that I might say something I would regret. Completely humiliated at being so naïve and gullible, I decided to tell them the next morning that they would have to leave.

That night I had a dream. In the dream, Sai Baba told me, "You are now spiritually strong enough to hold a higher intention. I want you to *extend yourself* to your visitors." Dreams of Sai Baba are always teaching dreams. There is nothing vague or abstract about his lessons, and this message was clear and direct. When I woke up, I was shocked. "Extend yourself" meant to me that I was to leave no stone unturned to make the visitors' lives as happy as possible. I felt it meant that I was to offer them every comfort and help, even though I knew that there was to be nothing in it for my husband, for Stillpoint, or for me. I couldn't fathom why Sai Baba would tell me to do this, but in my heart, my desire to do the right thing spiritually won out over doing what felt more satisfying at a personality level. It was clear that we were being used, but something else was in the wind. I knew I needed to stay with it to get to the full picture.

The tension in the office became palpable as members of the Australian group wandered around, talking about what they might do, or huddled in meetings while the rest of us tried to focus on the School and the Institute's work. The living space they occupied was a disaster scene that became worse when Jennifer went off on trips in search of new living and funding arrangements. I gave the group until November to find a place and move out, which meant they had four more months to remain at Stillpoint. When Jennifer was away, the young people settled into evenings of fun, sometimes with too much drinking. This was another piece of the picture that had been misrepresented. Jennifer told me the young people would be wonderful role models for my impressionable and struggling teenage daughter!

Despite my dismay, I held to Baba's directive. I even said to Errol, when he was ready to throw them out on their ears, "I know this is our spiritual lesson. It doesn't matter what they are or are not. Their character is not the issue here. There is a gift in this for us, and it is to understand our agendas around money." These agendas, I knew with absolute certainty, were building blocks to the future we wanted for ourselves and Stillpoint.

Errol thought I was deluded. I understood his terrible frustration and told him, "If you are too upset to stay while they are here, go away for a few months until it's time for them to leave, then come home. I don't intend to fail this spiritual test." Errol decided to remain and somehow managed to stay out of their way until they left.

For all my certainty that I was doing the "spiritually correct" thing, there were times when I thought I needed my head examined. "What is this really about?" I'd ask myself, over and over. On one level we were being taken advantage of, but on another, I believed that God was at work here doing something important—but what? Clearly, he had sent Jennifer to me, but why? Had it been for her sake? For mine? Or for all of ours? What was I to learn? I'd thought I was headed for the pot of gold; instead, I found myself holding a bucket of useless fool's gold.

Jennifer never did find another base of operations in the United States. She jumped frantically from one organization to another, trying to endear herself to each group in the same way she had done with me. The two young women went on to Malaysia to work with street children; one man had left earlier, and the remaining man went back to Australia to try winning an American green card in Australia's annual immigration lottery. By November first, they had all left the United States except for Jennifer. She had made an arrangement with one of my publishing friends in New York City to stay at her apartment in the hope of writing a book about the principles of abundance. I found this a mind-twister! Eventually, I heard she left for Australia.

Jennifer and I never had a wrap-up conversation to set things straight, a talk that could have helped us let go of the pain from the previous year's experiences. She seemed totally undone by what had happened. Perhaps this experience would be a good thing, if it taught her that honesty and full disclosure were essential to working effectively with people. For my part, lack of clarity and self-honesty were issues I would need to look at. I'd done a great deal of assuming and had paid too little attention to what was going on with my rational left brain. Jennifer and I had lost the initial magic we had together, but I knew that in some way we had served the purpose God intended, and our experience together was complete.

What was the purpose that Sai Baba, a holy emissary of God's Love, had postulated for the dream to "extend myself"? And what could have been the purpose of an episode that seemed to generate only unhappiness for all concerned? In the months that followed, I began to understand the incredible gift I had been given, not in material goods but in something infinitely more important.

As a result of the experience with the Australians, I gained two qualities that I needed as the Director of the Stillpoint Institute and School. The first quality was discernment: the clarity to see what people needed, how I could help them, and whether I was in a position to offer that help. The second quality was authority: for the first time, I had been able to hold my own authority with my husband, Errol, to stay centered on what I believed was God's goal and mission for us, and to hold steady in that belief. That experience birthed in me a new strength and confidence that allowed me to step fully into my power as a business woman and a leader. It has helped me generate abundance for Stillpoint in many ways.

Perhaps this experience was a convoluted way to learn such fundamental leadership skills. But how else would I have learned them? Would I even have recognized that I was lacking in those qualities? Probably not, is my honest answer. I am not suggesting that others might learn to be leaders by walking over hot coals, but it worked for me.

Subsequently, reflecting on the experience, I wrote what I call my Personal Contract on Abundance. It summarizes my understanding of spiritual abundance as a path for spiritual development and personal success.

■ *My Personal Contract on Abundance*

♦ Guidance is intended to alert me to an opportunity for abundance, but it is not a guarantee.

♦ I am a Life Steward of God's resources, and I have a right to use them, grow them, and share them.

♦ I am responsible always for the well-being of others, using the same enduring love and tenacity that I exhibit for my own family, because I am kin with all life.

♦ I am responsible for dismantling my hidden agendas of personal greed, self-interest, judgment, and fear, which block God's intention of abundance for me.

♦ I can trust God's word that what He/She offers is truly being manifested. The speed at which this manifestation takes place depends on my own actions and attitudes about sharing with an open heart.

♦ Although I do not understand how The Creator is working in my life, that lack doesn't change the fact that He/She is.

♦ I have the self-confidence necessary to proceed toward abundance, knowing that I must use my heart, my mind, and all my previous experiences to determine the most appropriate ways to use my energy, time, and money.

♦ When I enjoy the abundance that is already in my life, I open each day to a greater flow of abundance in my life.

I had wanted God to hand me abundance in the form of immediate expansion of my work. But the magnetism that attracts others to our work and words has everything to do with the "teaching" and little to do with "the teacher." God could give me confidence in my own abilities as a teacher only by helping me realize the power of the "teaching" about abundance. My grasp of "abundance" itself, with all its personal pitfalls, was the gift that allowed me to generate abundance from my own inner light.

I realized that others, no matter the specifics of their personalities, are also my "kin." The teaching I can share now is to stay steady and use love as a means of encouraging others to step fully into their Divinity. God hadn't judged Jennifer, and he hadn't judged me. He did, however, expect that we would be able to drop the secret agendas we harbored that sabotaged our efforts at success. He was saying that love isn't just accepting; it is clear, insightful, respectful appreciation of the capability of others. When a clear intention of the ability to follow through with a plan is lacking, we should be obliging even when we can't oblige.

Stillpoint has unfolded in many wonderful ways since that experience with Jennifer. The Stillpoint Institute and School are now one entity under my direction, and Errol has launched a wonderful vehicle for his own loving energy, The Stillpoint Foundation. He is now happy to have people come to stay for short periods of time as they help us grow the various organizations, or just for personal spiritual renewal. As a result, we've both been deeply changed. I've learned not to judge what I don't understand but to stay steady and find the blessing in the challenge. I've accepted that others who play the roles of those who trip me up, make me look foolish, or cost me my job or some future gain are God in disguise, helping me open my heart to the abundance of His Love.

Abundant Servant Friends

Abundant Servants have power that comes from caring about others and finding enjoyment in sharing. Abundant Servants may see their mission as directed by God, or they may be strongly motivated, successful business or political leaders who realize that the world needs every person to be a contributor. The Abundant Servant might as easily say "It's just good business" as to say "It's God's will."

Abundant Servants help us see the beauty in life that comes from having our own chance to thrive. Abundant Servant friends direct our attention to the challenged and disadvantaged, whom we would like to believe don't need our support. They quietly but firmly direct time, energy, resources, and money—theirs and ours—toward providing those in need with adequate money, medical attention, decent housing, and fair compensation for meaningful work, all in the name of making life better. Our friends who are Abundant Servants are those who work in, or set up, charitable trusts to fund far-sighted programs serving the needs of the Global Family, "Because it's the thing to do and we can and should do it. It just makes sense" is the emerging thinking of many of today's Abundant Servants. They realize that in order for the global community to survive and prosper, the planet needs every citizen's mind and heart.

Abundant Servants may be obvious selfless servants of God, like Mother Theresa, or former President Jimmy Carter, who is identified with Habitat for Humanity. But they can also be the corporate heads of multinational corporations, like Bill Gates of Microsoft fame who, with his wife and their foundation, funnel millions of dollars for children's health care to various parts of the world. Having a good mind and using one's business acumen are as much The Creator's gifts as reading a holy book and blessing people's lives and families. It's all the same energy guiding us into greater planetary wellness and more equitable distribution of wealth.

Abundant Servants feel blessed to have earned, or to have been born with, resources that others don't have. They do not, however, consider it their birthright to have what others do not. If they've "drawn" an easy life this time around, it is their time to use their abilities to help others so that when they experience a lifetime in which they have great needs, others will serve them.

In God's eyes, we must all seem like charity cases because of our blindness to the value and opportunity to share the resources that are gifted to us. Yet hope lives in The Creator's heart because we are provided with constant opportunities to use the power of Love to enhance the lives of all members of the Global Family.

Our Inner Abundant Servants

Today the message of our Abundant Servants is informing us how to manifest abundance for our sakes and that of the Global Family. Abundance is anything that feeds our souls. This leaves lots of room for the myriad ways we enjoy life and the people around us. Yet, in spite of America being the wealthiest country in the world and offering its citizens more of the conveniences that create leisure time, we are among the world's most stressed people. We know the reasons this is true: we simply have more to do each day than time allows. We find ourselves re-prioritizing daily lists that are already top-heavy with top-level priorities. We have precious little time for fun. And we have little discretionary time left for service to non-family members, even though most people believe in what we call charity.

Our world is changing, and with it our need to re-examine our priorities so that we have time for the more pressing items on our schedules. We make time for the things that really matter to us. We have always been a generous-hearted nation, and we do consider that we are "our brother's keeper." But today, we need to shift our thinking from "charity," what we do *for* others, to "service," what we do *with* others. The greatest travesty isn't saying "I can't help now;" it's saying "I won't care."

The Dalai Lama, the spiritual and cultural leader of Tibet, spoke eloquently to our need for a change in attitude toward abundance when he asked people around the world to consider what he sensed would be the most significant question of the new millennium: "How can we decrease the disparity between the rich and the poor?"

■ *Sharing Comes from Caring*

In one of my classes, when I asked students—adults in their best earning years—what they considered "service," many gave me examples of the old, once-a-year obligation to the poor that we usually think of as "charity." The world and Spirit expects more of us today. We can't honor all the requests we receive each week, but the idea that we need to participate in the global challenge of sharing wealth is a choice. It is a chance to reconsider our attitudes and beliefs about personal wealth and, by our actions and activities, put them into practice.

As I consider "charity" versus "service," I realize that there are several striking differences between the two:

♦ **Service** is what we do *with* others; **charity** is what we do *for* others.

♦ **Service** is working with someone who *has* less; **charity** is working with someone whom we believe *is* less.

♦ **Service** produces self-worth and inner value; **charity** furthers the dole and eliminates hope and self-respect.

♦ **Service** produces opportunities for dialogue about difficult issues; **charity** contributes to grave inequities.

♦ **Service** eliminates differences; **charity** promotes them.

♦ **Service** helps heal the world's wounds; **charity** leads to rampant terrorism.

Implicit in caring about others is the realization that we have no option but to solve the crisis of the global disparity of resources and wealth. We are asked to consider not only what time we have available, and our attitude about service, but also our attitude toward money and power. It isn't just global warming that should concern us but the heating up of issues that distinguish the "haves" from the "have-nots."

How do we get past our cultural, religious, ethnic, and racial differences to see that we are all the same? The way we learn to care is by having someone care about us. If no one cared that we were hungry, without a decent job, under-educated for today's job market, or with too little money to buy nice clothes for our children, then whatever we managed to scrape together we would be unwilling to share.

Our local Drop-In Center, which serves the poorest parts of our community, published a series of articles to inform the community about the needs and attitudes of those who live "on the edge." The message was this: When you've been without care, you've had no role model to teach you how to care about others. The Director relayed an account of a young man in one program who found a bag of doughnuts. He sat in a room with ten other young people and ate the doughnuts, one after the other, without a thought of sharing them. Sharing comes from being cared for. As we practice caring for our families and friends in our communities, we actually begin to change future generations of the Global Family. Changing one young person today changes his or her children and their children.

Even when we're told, "Eat your dinner because children in China are starving," we may hear something different from what was intended. Instead of hearing, "Be appreciative that you have food," we hear, "Take care of your goods and money so you'll never become one of those people who go without." One way to reshape our attitudes toward service and away from charity is to count how many times a day someone serves us. We drop a pencil and a friend picks it up. We're too tired to cook, so our spouses suggest we go out. We're a little short on the rent, so our parents or children kick in. A friend at work needs time off, so we re-arrange our schedules to cover her shift. We are constantly serving others, and they are serving us.

Letting service become the way we share, sometimes for a desperate need and sometimes for a trivial one, in whatever way we express our caring, we are moving our lives into the abundance column. It isn't how much we give; it is realizing that caring is the way we find satisfaction and feel genuinely abundant.

Wealth as a Sign of Spiritual Maturity

In the Hindu culture, people's wealth signifies that the Gods have blessed them. We assume being blessed in this way means unparalleled opulence with no obligations. But acquiring wealth is filled with pitfalls, both in gaining wealth and losing it. Along with wealth comes an obligation, that of sharing. God smiles on those who smile on others.

Spiritually, before we entered our present lives, we may have chosen to learn about the issues of wealth. If so, we will have a preoccupation with money—making it, losing it, and sharing it. Financial disasters such as bankruptcies, divorces, or deaths in our families may signify a potential readiness to handle money differently.

Rather than feeling hopeless, we are wise to realize that we are given the opportunity to acquire personal wealth when we deepen our appreciation of how wealth—emotional, spiritual, and tangible dollars—is intended to be used to spread good in the world rather than just for our personal indulgence.

When I talk about wealth in my workshops, I draw two big squares on a flip chart, and label one "A" and the other "B." I draw a large X through the middle of both boxes to represent the amount of money that we need each month to live comfortably. Then I double the size of the box labeled "B," and label the new space "C." This new space is the same size or greater than the original box. "C" represents the discretionary money we have to share with others. I tell workshop participants that when they earn more money than their needs, the additional dollars are available to them for serving the Global Family.

We may look down on others for having wealth because we assume that all their money is devoted to personal extravagance. That merely makes us jealous. But when we view wealth differently, aware of our obligation to participate fully in the Global Family, we can find deep joy in the idea of being able to make life better for others. Sometimes the way to serve someone else is with the tangible means to give him or her a foothold in life. We can talk about spirituality, but when you're hungry, have no home or the means to get one, and feel tired and sad in every bone of your body, what is needed are tangible demonstrations of love: groceries, a home, a means of earning a decent living.

But sharing isn't just for the disadvantaged. The opportunity to share our resources presents other ways for us to serve: providing childcare, healthcare coverage, or retirement packages for our employees. As we look at the people around us, we see the importance of treating others as if they are part of our families, because they are!

In order to be abundant we need to feel abundant. In order to have wealth, we need to feel wealthy, deserving of wealth, and comfortable with the idea of it. If we've never had any discretionary dollars to spend, doing this is no easy task. The idea of oneself as "wealthy" is laced with many hidden messages: "People will think we're better than they are" or "What will the neighbors think of us?" or "Everyone will be after us for something." Even more difficult are the messages that have been inculcated from our religious and spiritual heritages that tell us money is the root of all evil. It isn't money that's bad; money is energy that can be used for good or for ill. When money becomes our God, it fails to contribute to personal happiness or planetary usefulness. Without doubt, wealth can be corrupting, but it doesn't need to be that way as we ride the wave into the global future.

Decreasing the disparity between the rich and the poor doesn't require us to sink to the level of poverty; rather, it asks us to raise others to the level of abundance. The difference is that with the latter, we are putting our energy into helping people to learn to fish rather than just giving them fish.

Making Deposits in the Global Family Bank Account

One day, as I was thinking about abundance in terms of spiritual wealth and how we can benefit from an "I can share" attitude, I began to think about the idea of "karma." Karma refers to the positive and negative consequences that come to us through successive lifetimes as a result of our thoughts and actions. Positive thoughts and actions produce good karma, and negative thoughts and actions produce bad karma. I imagined this scenario: What if we call karma the Global Family Bank Account, or GFBA? What if our angels deposit a coin and a prayer into the general fund under our names for our every cooperative, loving, caring, and helpful thought, feeling, and action, and they take one away for every attitude and action that hurts others or contributes to jealousy and strife?

As we live our lives, we can imagine that we are depositing and withdrawing according to our positive and negative thoughts, feelings, and actions. The more coins and prayers we amass through good deeds, the greater our sense of personal security, because we know that we have a substantial level of spiritual wealth to draw from when times are hard. We can use our coins and prayers to produce abundance in whatever manner we choose.

We can even double our coins when we need to, by borrowing against the common fund, the amount depending on what we have in our accounts. If we have earned thirty coins and prayers, then we can get thirty more and have a total of sixty coins and prayers. We can redeem the coins to get out of difficult financial situations or to manage our retirement funds so that we accrue better than average gains. We could trade our coins and prayers for insight into the reason there was so little love in our families or how to find the lovers we've always yearned for. We may decide to draw on our prayer supply when a son is in a serious auto accident or a wife has a suspicious tumor that we want to keep from becoming cancerous.

If we are living and acting in ways that leave us in a continual deficit situation, then we may be living on the spiritual edge—but how will we know? We'll know because life is a terrible struggle, and we never seem to get any breaks. We'll know because we feel depressed and unhappy and have great trouble maintaining our sense of equanimity. We lose our coins and prayers as quickly as we amass them, because we aren't aware that we are supposed to help find solutions not just to our own personal problems but to global ones.

We may be lucky and possess a lot of coins from a previous life, so even if we're selfish and uncaring in this one, we manage to get to the end without much difficulty. But then, of course, we may begin the next life in poverty.

If this scenario of the Global Family Bank Account were true, and we were losing someone we loved deeply and were praying frantically for help, would Heaven take pity on us and bail us out, even though we had few coins or prayers to our credit? Our angels might like to see the kind of prayers we've offered previously on behalf of others in trouble, and decide, "Oh, well, their track record's getting better, so why not help them just this once?"

The prayers in our accounts might be useful when we seek Heaven's help for impoverished people. Our coins, along with those of other people, would add to the value of the GFBA, allowing it to obtain loans for projects to help the Global Family, projects like healing the holes in the ozone layer, reducing global warming, decreasing toxic pollutants in the air, cleaning up nuclear wastes, or finding a cure for cancer. Our personal accounts would remain in our names, but assets could be pooled for planetary healing.

I tried to imagine what my tally sheet would look like. I considered one hour of one day, and I imagined what kind of balance I'd have in my spiritual bank account. I realized how much grace has come to me, undeserved, as a gift. God in His or Her mercy responds to all our calls for help and assistance, showing us a way out even if we don't deserve it. Maybe, just maybe, we're supposed to do the same thing for folks around us.

My Mom's Healing Journey

Shortly after I began to sense the Voice of Love, I called my mom and asked her if she was sitting down, because I had something rather unusual to tell her. I told her about the experiences I was having, and I relayed my ambivalence and uncertainly about what to do with this amazing connection.

Mothers are the most important source of approval in our lives. My mother was thoughtful and encouraging without being pushy. She told me that this "special relationship" sounded important and intriguing, and she was certain I'd find the way to proceed.

Several weeks later, while I was visiting her and my step-dad in their lakeside home in upstate New York, she told me that she had scheduled surgery to relieve a bad case of carpal tunnel syndrome. She had severe pain in both wrists, especially the right. Later, I read that carpal tunnel syndrome comes from pressure on the median nerve, which carries messages between the hand and the brain. The carpal tunnel itself is a narrow opening in the wrist, made up of eight bones that form three sides of the tunnel and the transverse carpal ligament, a band of tissue that forms the fourth side.

Almost as an afterthought, as I set the table that evening, she asked me if there was anything that the Voice of Love might suggest for her healing. Taken aback, I stammered that I wasn't sure, but that I'd think about it. I realized that my fear in asking about her healing came from knowing I was being called to the test. What if the Voice of Love's suggestions were wrong, or what if they didn't work at all? What if she thought I was an imposter and had made up the entire experience? I put myself through several days of absolute misery before deciding that I could ask and see what might happen.

The Voice of Love gave me a special healing visualization to perform with my mother and told me all would be well. I wrote down the instructions, later naming it The Dark Star/White Star Healing Visualization.

I was to use the visualization several times a day for five minutes per session, and I was to teach my mom to do the same. We didn't need to perform the visualization at the same time. And it wasn't a problem that I was driving home the next day and would be several hundred miles away from her. I was told to concentrate on the "white star" and to allow healing to happen.

■ *The Dark Star/White Star Healing Visualization*

♦ Picture yourself seated across from your mirror image.

♦ Point to the place on your body where there is pain and, closing your eyes, imagine a six-pointed star of a dark color placed directly over the pain.

♦ Tell yourself silently that you're drawing to this star all problems and contributing factors, both known and unknown to you, from this life or any other, that are related to the disease/pain you're healing.

♦ Wait a moment or two for the negative energy to be drawn to the dark star.

♦ Imagine in your mind's eye a pure white star of the same six points, and place this healing star directly on top of the dark star so that their points are as closely matched as possible.

♦ Tell yourself silently that you acknowledge that your White Star represents the power of God's healing love, or the Power of Divine Love, or just the Power of Love. Continue with, "The Power of Love is the strongest form of medicine that exists, and it dissolves any fear or pain in its path." You may at first have trouble aligning the two stars. Symbolically, this tells you that you've given your illness/problem more power than you've given to Love to heal you. As you practice, you'll be able to create closer alignment between the two stars.

♦ Focus your entire inner attention on the White Star for three or four minutes.

♦ ♦ ♦

For three weeks, my mother and I both worked on her healing. Every time I engaged in the practice, I noticed that the dark star appeared weaker, less intense in color, and seemed to be losing its texture. The white star by comparison became increasingly luminous. I felt as if I were watching the transmutation of energy. The energy from the dark star, representing my mother's fears and struggles, was being diminished before my eyes and transformed by the white star that was the power of God's love taking charge. Each day the white star became more and more luminous, and the dark star began to shrink and crumple up like a dried leaf. I realized I was watching her pain dismantle, transforming it to strengthen her belief in the Power of Love to heal. Three weeks to the day from beginning this practice, she called me and said, ecstatically, "The pain is completely gone." In my visualization that morning, there was no longer any dark star, just the brilliant white star. What a testament to the healing power of love! She cancelled the surgery, which was no longer needed. That healing happened twenty-two years ago, and she has been pain-free ever since.

I've continued to use this powerful healing visualization with clients, and I teach it to my students, who also have had amazing results with it. The Voice of Love's healing practices always deal with the power of love juxtaposed to a problem or struggle—whatever energy needs to be shifted or transformed.

A few years ago, my mom and I performed the Mending Your Bowl practice around her need to continue to strengthen her bones and skeletal structure. Our skeletons are governed by the quality of energy that flows through our Abundance Bowls.

When Mom and I settled down to engage in the practice, I asked her to pretend that I wasn't her daughter but just someone who wanted to assist her in whatever way was needed. We turned the lights down, and she found a comfortable chair across from me. I asked her to talk to me about abundance in her life.

Mom said, "I've never felt that I was abundant. I never felt loved or supported during the entire time I was growing up. My dad remarried, and his new wife had two children of her own, and though it may sound melodramatic, I was the Cinderella. I was convinced that I was going to get in trouble, no matter how hard I tried to stay out of it. I used to get a whipping for every small transgression. I know my daddy loved me, but he was influenced by my stepmother, and she and I had absolutely no relationship." I told Mom that at an energy level, her skeletal system was in charge of protecting and supporting her as she grew in her ability to share abundance.

I explained that by abundance, I meant emotional, spiritual, and tangible wealth that filled her with a sense of her own authority and was free to flow into the world through various channels of sharing with others. I asked her how she felt she shared her abundance with others. She talked at length about feeling that she was trying to do God's work by visiting nursing homes and shut-ins several times a week, meditating, and praying—in effect, trying to prove to God that she was worthy. She told me that she was trying to make up for all the years that she had been an agnostic.

"How do you share abundance with yourself?" I asked.

"I eat well," she said. "I go for walks every day, and I try my best to deserve God's Love."

"Yes," I said, "those are ways of sharing abundance with yourself in tangible ways. How are you sharing with yourself, emotionally?"

For several moments she said nothing. Finally, in a subdued voice, she said, "I'm not sure I'll ever get rid of the nagging feeling that I'm really not good enough to measure up to what God expects of me."

I suggested that she quiet herself and imagine her Abundance Bowl. "This bowl holds your belief about service to others," I said. "The flow of abundance is also meant to bring you happiness. Sharing means just that: keeping some of the good feelings and good things for yourself and offering some to others."

The Abundance bowl she pictured was a shiny metallic bowl with steep sides dropping to a small base. I asked her about any broken or cracked places. She announced in a very matter-of-fact way that the small bottom was actually a hole. "So there is no bottom to your abundance bowl?" I asked, to be sure I had the image in my mind that she was describing.

"That's right."

"And what does this lack of a bottom, lack of support, remind you of?"

In a sad little whisper she said, "When I was a little girl, probably five or six, I had a teacher who hated me. I wasn't pretty, had thick glasses, and was probably difficult because I was so unhappy at home. One day in class, just being silly, I tied one end of my hankie to my glasses. My teacher, Miss Tyson, called me to the front of the class and told me that since I was so conscious of my looks, perhaps I should stand in front of the class all afternoon so that everyone could see how beautiful I was. I'll never forget that experience till the day I die." I was silent myself, overcome with the pain of a child's feelings handled in such a mean-spirited way.

We continued, and I asked her whom she needed to have a conversation with, spirit-to-spirit, to find out what blessing was hers from this challenge. She said, "I want to talk to my stepmother." Clearly, the teacher, Miss Tyson, represented the unsupportive mother image that she also felt in her stepmother.

The dialogue with her stepmother was fierce at first, as Mom listed experience after experience that had destroyed her self-confidence to such a level that she was terrified of her shadow. Then, when she was ready, I asked her to move to her heart and ask, from that true place of lasting love, what her stepmother had to say. She said, "My stepmother says she's sorry for being such a terrible mother. She didn't know how to handle me, and she knew that my father adored me, so she was jealous of his love for me. She regretted that we'd never had a relationship. She wants to know if I can forgive her."

"And can you?" I asked.

"I don't know. I am so filled with misery over it, but I'll try."

"And what is the gift to you?" I continued.

"That my father really did love me—that I was worth loving. As I think about it, I guess I feel sorry for my step-mom. She didn't have much of a life. Maybe I wouldn't have done much better under the same circumstances."

I noticed that my mother's need to prove to God that she was worthy seemed to be based on her need to prove to her father that she was worth loving. I asked my mother how she would mend her bowl. She said that she would put a cork in the bottom of the bowl. That way she could take the cork out to clear away any old painful memories that came up, and she could put the cork in to hold her new energy of sharing with herself first, before giving everything away in order to measure up to God's expectations. Leaning over to take her in my arms, I said, "I think you've more than measured up to God's expectations."

As I thought about my mother's carpal tunnel healing, I realized that we were talking about the skeletal system, the tiny bones in her wrist, and the nervous system, the median nerve that connected her hand to her brain. Our nerves are governed by the flow of energy in our Wisdom Bowls that reflects our kinship with The Creator. My mother's wrist pain came from being afraid that she wasn't "kin" with God and from feeling unsafe in His care, thus mirroring her fear that she wasn't good enough to be loved by her earthly father. Her way of compensating for this perceived inadequacy was to give abundantly to others without absorbing the goodness generated by her efforts to nourish her own heart. Perhaps her healing was her confirmation that God saw her intention, understood her life with all its fears and pains, and was walking with her, as He/She does with each of us.

Sketching Our Abundance Bowls

Now you're ready to draw your Abundance Bowl. The Abundance Bowl is located near the base of the spine and is related to the First Chakra or energy center. It governs your skeletal system and seeks to protect, support, and help you serve the needs of others and yourself.

This bowl governs your spiritual, emotional, and tangible wealth, your attitudes about service to others and about sharing what you have.

Spiritual wealth is accepting that you and the Beloved are made of the same Love energy. Emotional wealth is having the discernment to know when you can help others, how you can serve them, and what your own hidden agendas are in order to see and act with greater clarity and integrity. Tangible wealth is available to you as you act on your commitment to participate in helping to heal members of the Global Family.

As you think about your relationship with wealth, ask yourself these questions: How was I brought up to feel about money and service? What have I learned about giving to others? How do I share with myself? Am I comfortable with sharing and, if not, why not? What do I think will happen if I have a lot...or a little? Do I consider myself a wealthy person? What feelings come up when I think about being a wealthy person? Have I considered earning more than I need to spend on myself?

Acting with Kindness

ACTING WITH KINDNESS BEGINS with being kind to ourselves. So often we've learned that unless we give it all to others, we are selfish and uncaring. Recently, I experienced an example of the power of acting with kindness when I discovered the benefit of sharing.

A dear friend sent me a small bouquet of spring flowers for my birthday. They were brilliantly-colored tulips that arrived at a time when there were few blooms in the garden. They lit up my office, and I was delighted. Then a call from a long-time friend brought me to a difficult decision point. This older woman had just come home from extensive cancer surgery. Over the years, she had taken care of our cats and dogs and in the process loved and cared for me in special ways by polishing the silver, ironing, fixing and mending so that I'd have less to do. I loved her great jokes and spunky spirit. I told her I'd come by to see her later that afternoon.

I looked at the tulips on my desk, and my spirit said, "How lovely; give them to her." But my personality said, "Oh no, these are mine; they are my birthday present." For the entire day I stewed about what to do. I could have bought another bunch of flowers, but I realized from my resistance that I had something important to learn from my dilemma. As I thought about what to do and why I couldn't easily give up the flowers, I suddenly realized I didn't need to give them up, I needed only to share them—share the delight and the beauty and the birthday cheer. I divided the flowers and, with a peaceful heart, I arrived at her doorstep to deliver the gift. It felt just right.

Acting with kindness and sharing whatever is at hand opens the heart and allows us to participate in building abundance. The more energy of sharing we have around us, the more that can come to us. When stagnation sets in, whether in our thinking, our spiritual practices, or our bodies, we are in need of new energy. Acting with kindness brings fresh energy into our lives, and we experience renewal.

■ *Practice for Honoring Ourselves as We Honor Others*

The motivation to share is the spark that sets the desire for service burning in our hearts. After becoming motivated to help, we are prepared to offer our time, talent, and resources to assist in filling the needs of others. But then comes the difficult part of sharing with kindness: making room for the opinions and needs of other people. It is easy to be right or wrong. It is much more difficult to acknowledge others as equals and to discuss our needs, fears, and divisive issues with the courage to know that, together, we can find a workable solution no matter the problem. It takes time and patience. It takes walking away and coming back. It requires re-adjustment in the thinking that's been handed down to us from our parents and grandparents. This process of listening without judgment asks that, instead of always playing to our differences, we learn to cooperate in order to find common ground. Is there an alternative to solving the problems in our cities, in our families—in the world? No, there is no alternative but to seek to honor what is unique about each of us and about our diverse cultures.

We all have similar spiritual needs. When we attend to our needs, they give us a way to envision our world differently. Here is a starting point for honoring human diversity. I call it the Spiritual Bill of Rights, and I hope you will talk about it with your friends and families.

■ *A Spiritual Bill of Rights for All People*

♦ **Unity**—we will live together as one family.

♦ **Perception**—we will see clearly the true feelings, fears, and needs that rest beneath our assumptions, judgments, and determinations of right and wrong.

♦ **Intention**—we will seek to identify, understand, and share our real questions and concerns.

♦ **Passion**—we will use love to nourish ourselves and others.

♦ **Trust**—we will have confidence in our efforts.

♦ **Balance**—we will seek the center between opposing pressures and opinions.

♦ **Manifestation**—we will use our efforts to bring benefit to all.

We have a future to design, but are we up to the task? Accomplishing the design will take all of us. No one is without value, and no idea is a bad idea. All can be used for the common good. But we can't learn in a vacuum. We need to reach out and learn how other people think and what they need, but that requires meeting people who are different from us.

We are all heroes and heroines. We shouldn't assume that all the wise people have already lived and died. Look around and see who is sitting next to you. Today, make up your mind to talk to someone with a different point of view and, rather than doing the talking, try to listen. Or, if you tend not to share your opinions, decide that today is the day to state what you think. Read something that puts a different spin on a situation you care passionately about, and try to hear and appreciate the arguments even if you believe them wrong.

We are the future; what each of us thinks and believes is a matter of survival and planetary thriving. Everything rests in our hands.

IN SUMMARY

The Abundant Servant's Gifts

CONSIDER THESE SPECIAL GIFTS available to us from our inner
Abundant Servants. Which ones speak to you? Ask your own inner
Abundant Servant to show you how you can benefit from these gifts.

My inner Abundant Servant manifests ample resources for my life.

- My Abundant Servant allows me the experience of "having"
  and "not having," so that I may understand that the difference between the two is in my perception.

- My Abundant Servant gives me a full and abundant heart, so
  that my service becomes my normal way of guiding my days.

- My Abundant Servant believes that I'm capable of listening
  to my true deservedness, never being frightened by setbacks
  and knowing they are always temporary.

- My Abundant Servant has the capacity for serving the needs
  of the less fortunate, not on one or two days a year but as an
  attitude of daily sharing.

- My Abundant Servant helps me be less stingy with the good
  feelings I allow myself to hold in my heart.

♦ My Abundant Servant shows me that the more I expand my
views to include the concerns of others, the more "manna" I
have to spread around to alleviate my own concerns.

♦ My Abundant Servant guides me to love myself as part of the
Divine Plan, for in this simple way I discover the power of
kindness.

As you review the drawing of your Abundance Bowl, consider these
statements about benefits you can derive from the exercise:

My Abundance Bowl governs my quality of Divine Abundance.

*My Abundance Bowl teaches me to share with myself so that I may share
with others, in order to produce abundance in the forms
of spiritual, emotional, and tangible wealth.*

My Abundance Bowl governs the health of my skeletal system.

*My Abundance Bowl represents the actual energy center of my First
Chakra, which is located in proximity to the base of my spine.*

*Service to others is the most helpful healing practice for strengthening my
appreciation of the power of sharing with myself and with others.*

Abundance is anything that nourishes your soul.

CAmeron Sesto

HEALING
REFLECTIONS

Find the Gold

Restless in your first attempt
to find your way toward Heaven's gate
where gold awaits, if truth be told, and dreams are met
with life reborn.
You are enticed to seek The Path,
yet restless in this second chance
at making peace with efforts lost.
Like wound-down hands on Grandpa's clock,
your time on Earth has ceased to mark
the purposes for which you've come.
Yet time today becomes your friend,
and energy renewed as painted hues creates you new,
and day's events confirm your change.
Preparations not undone
invite you to your choice of roles:
to set things straight and make them right,
to find the way and meet the mark,
to find the gold and make it yours
to serve the whole,
and do your part!

— Meredith Young-Sowers

CHAPTER NINE

HEALING REFLECTIONS

IT WAS AFTER NINE O'CLOCK in the evening when the phone rang. I don't usually answer late phone calls. I am a very early riser, and I go to bed early, but this call was one I felt I should pick up. A woman's frantic voice told me, with her words tumbling over each other, that her one-year-old daughter was in Intensive Care and was losing her battle for life.

I didn't know Anna, but she was a friend of someone who had worked with me. That person had given Anna my unlisted home phone number. Anna told me she was preparing for her daughter's first birthday party when she saw that Sadie was having trouble breathing. What at first seemed like a minor problem quickly escalated into a major medical emergency, and Anna felt a terror she had never experienced before.

She picked up her daughter, and her husband drove them to the emergency room of a nearby hospital. It was a busy day, and the nurses asked them to wait. Looking at her baby's face, Anna knew that if they waited, the girl's life would slip away. After screaming at the nurse that her baby was dying, the staff finally looked at the child, saw the truth, and rushed the little girl into Intensive Care.

Anna learned that Sadie had a viral infection that had settled on the left side of her heart, the pumping side, and her heart was losing its ability to pump blood and oxygen through her body. The doctors told her and her husband that to save the child, the only choice was a heart-lung transplant. Realizing the risks of such an operation, and knowing that a donor might not be located in time, Anna felt beside herself with worry. She was living her worst nightmare: one minute preparing for her child's birthday, the next minute possibly facing her funeral.

Anna pleaded with me to help: "What can you do for Sadie?" she asked. I told Anna that I would help her in whatever way I could and to give me the child's full name and the family's home address so that I could check out Sadie's condition intuitively. When I did, I could see that the child was hanging on the edge of life, and that the left side of her heart was very weak. But I believed that the child's spirit had not decided whether to stay or to leave.

Anna knew very little about energy healing, but she had an intuitive sense that she could help her baby in ways other than opting for surgery. For her, surgery was a final option, not the first. She told the doctors that she wasn't ready to sign the papers yet.

I told Anna that I felt the next forty-eight hours would be critical for Sadie's healing. I continued, "I think the child's soul has not yet decided whether it will stay or leave, but we can help—or, more specifically, you can help. The heart problem is on the left side, the side that deals with one's love for a partner or, in a child's case, for one's primary caregiver. Your relationship with Sadie is the one that is most important and has the most power for her and for you."

"You and I are going to do two things right away," I told her. "First, I'm going to teach you a simple practice called Loving Touch that will help you and your daughter to generate, amplify, and focus the power of God's Love, which she needs for healing her heart. Second, we're both going to put Sadie on every prayer list we know about and ask everyone we know to pray for her."

Anna seemed quieter and slightly reassured. Of course, she wanted to hear me tell her that Sadie was going to live. I was as kind as I could be, but I was also honest. I reiterated that the next forty-eight hours would be crucial. I explained about Loving Touch and the way it helps to focus the energy of Divine Love so that it can be used in specific ways. I instructed her to do the following:

Place your hands on your child's chest—either front or back, it makes no difference.

Say a short prayer, and imagine your hands filling with warmth, with light, or with love.

As you hold one hand over Sadie's heart center, her Love Bowl, move your other hand in gentle strokes anywhere you feel drawn to move. In doing this, (I told Anna) you're filling your child's body with Divine Love.

I advised Anna to perform this Loving Touch practice on herself as well, in order to find the calmness that would reassure Sadie. I told her that she was now a powerful vehicle for her daughter's healing, and she needed to try staying as calm and clear as she could be. "You will know what to do, and you can do much more than you imagine to help your daughter regain her health. Just do your best."

Anna hung up the phone. I knew how important it was for Anna to realize that she could do something significant for her daughter's healing. No matter what happened, this had been a good beginning with Anna. I told her to call me the following afternoon, when we would again "check in" on Sadie.

When Anna called back, she said, "There hasn't been any change in her physical condition, but I did the Loving Touch many times. She seemed to like it, and I felt much calmer." After I intuitively checked on Sadie's health, I told Anna that I believed the child had decided to stay, and if this were true, she would begin to heal. I told Anna to keep up the Loving Touch practice and the prayers, and that I would continue to work on the child from my home. I assured her that I didn't need to be in the room with Sadie for her to receive the benefit of my attention.

Anna called me many times during the next weeks. Slowly, Sadie began to heal. No one at the hospital could explain it. Her echocardiogram, a test that measures the strength of the heart muscle as it pumps blood out into the body, was still abnormal, showing a weak heart. By all the medical signs, the child should have been listless and pale and in serious—even life-threatening—danger. Yet Sadie was seen jumping up and down in her crib, looking like the peak of health, with roses in her cheeks and a big smile on her face. The staff at the large teaching hospital where Sadie had been transferred started calling her "the miracle baby." It was apparent that Sadie's heart was strengthening because of a stream of loving energy coming into her from The Creator's Love through her soul. It was a miracle, the miracle of Grace.

Anna and I became close friends through the many months of Sadie's healing. Sadie finally went home from the hospital—something we thought might never happen. Anna and her husband were deeply changed by the experience, recognizing the grace that had been given to their daughter. They knew that this child would grow up to care deeply about others and to help others in ways she had been helped.

Anna started to learn more about spiritual healing and to realize that her instinctive pursuit of an alternative means of healing had made the difference in Sadie's life.

Several times a year, Anna sends me pictures of Sadie and her baby brother. The little girl, now seven years old, is the most beautiful little angel I've ever seen.

This story is one of my favorites because it is such a striking example of the healing power of Divine Love. Healing came about both through the mother's actions and through the devotion of an entire support network of many people working in unison for the child's recovery. Prayers are energy, and the energy of loving intent filled the child's body with Divine Healing Light.

Another important factor that contributed to Sadie's healing was her mother's deep love for her daughter. Anna was willing, both emotionally and spiritually, to try something new. Even though she was terrified that she'd lose her daughter, she was able to settle down and get to work despite her lack of certainty about whether Sadie was going to be able to stay in her physical body. This spiritual openness allowed The Creator to work through her, like sunshine pouring through a partly-opened door. Anna wasn't a religious person, but she was a warm and loving woman. Asking for God's help in a calm and loving way draws Divine Love to us just as if we were dialing a friend's phone number. Prayer, even those expressed under our breath and on the run, draws us to those who can help us heal ourselves and others.

When a parent is unable to save a child's life, that doesn't mean God isn't listening or is unwilling to help, or that the parents have failed. It simply means that God has another piece of information that we lack. He/She ultimately has the full picture, while we have only a partial understanding. Sometimes God responds to our requests by saying, "No, I have other plans," for reasons we cannot understand. Guidance in any form is not a guarantee but an opportunity.

Physical, Emotional, and Spiritual Healing

Healing comes in many forms. We seek relief from physical pain when our bodies hurt, from emotional pain when we're depressed, sad, and out of love with ourselves, and from spiritual pain when we're out of love with God or believe He/She is out of love with us.

In *Wisdom Bowls*, I've shared stories of clients, friends, and my own family that speak to the many different ways we heal. Our lives revolve around the growth of love in our hearts. The more deeply and unselfishly we love, the happier we are as human beings. The body is the vehicle through which our souls function in the physical world. The physical body is not destined to live forever. Inevitably, it wears out, no matter what care we give it. It is meant to be recycled, since that is the way the soul learns and advances from life to life. Just as we don't mistake the wrapper on a candy bar for the chocolate inside, we don't want to mistake our physical bodies for our souls, the generators of the power of love. The soul is the essential part of our being; it doesn't feel pain or discomfort in the brief time we live on Earth.

Our bodies don't choose to be in pain, either. They constantly re-adjust, correcting the damage done by the foods and beverages we eat and drink, the drugs we use, the polluted water we imbibe, the dirty air we breathe, and our lack of exercise. Our bodies are living, feeling fields of energy that flow in harmony with our thoughts, beliefs, and attitudes about every aspect of our lives. Our bodies are "conscious" essences rather than machines, and our inner chatter imprints our fears and wor-ries on them. "I'm so stupid. Why can't I do anything right?"

"That's a dumb idea," we say without thinking.

"She's incompetent. Why don't they fire her?"

"He doesn't understand anything." We are oblivious to this negative self-talk that continues in our heads all day long.

Each negative judgment of ourselves or others sits in our energy fields. When we feel unhappy, out of control, or victimized by life, we iron those negative attitudes and beliefs into our tissues. Eventually, our energy flow is slowed down, producing the physical imbalances we know as disease.

We can see how the body has reacted to years of negative comments by observing the flows of energy through the seven main energy bowls. As on a radar screen, we can pick up intuitively what the body is "hear-ing," and we can do it in time to change the destructive messages, which, if continued, could produce disease.

We are each wired as a fully-integrated living system, body, mind, and spirit. In order to facilitate healing changes we need information from all three levels of ourselves.

■ *Physical Healing*

Physical healing is the restoration of functional health in the body, which is what we commonly think of as healing. In reality, it is the last in a series of energy shifts that make it possible for the body to heal. The first step is connecting with our essence, our spiritual selves. Next, we begin to shift the old ways of thinking and feeling associated with our pain. When new emotional patterns are well established, the stage is set for us to heal physically.

Pain alerts us to a problem so that we can take action to eliminate it. If we have pain from a splinter, we probably won't spend much time considering the emotional and spiritual implications behind it. But if we're diagnosed with a life-threatening illness, we will spend a lot of time trying to understand why we got sick and what we can do about it on all three levels of healing.

Acute pain is pain that is sharp in the moment, but once the source of the pain is removed, the body is pain-free. Appendicitis is associated with acute pain. When the inflamed appendix is removed, our pain disappears. Chronic pain is a more difficult type of pain to handle because it wears away at our good intentions and our assumption that we're going to be all right and have a normal life.

Acute pain may be the result of a series of emotional upheavals or long-standing beliefs that settle in a certain area or organ, like the appendix. Chronic pain can represent long-standing beliefs or attitudes held not only by us but also by our parents, grandparents, or even an earlier generation. Many times, people are healing from years and even generations of negative thinking.

We know that we have physical predispositions toward certain diseases such as heart disease and breast cancer, but the link that creates disease in successive generations may be more emotional than physical or genetic. The emotional patterns that were flawed in earlier generations may be the same ones we've learned as children. Breast cancer demands that we nourish ourselves by giving time and attention to our needs—physically, emotionally, and spiritually. It also requires us to understand the impact of major losses, to grieve our losses, and to find the blessing—the part of our authentic selves that is ready to shine in a new way. As we honor the process of healing at all levels, we move out of harm's way, reprieved from dreaded illnesses that hang over our heads through successive generations. When we shift the distribution of energy in our energy bowls, we change the energy balance in our bodies and become healthier and happier.

■ *Emotional Healing*

Emotional healing helps us release painful experiences, disappointments, and sorrows in our lives—all the ways we've been undone rather than empowered by events in our lives. When we experience more suffering than joy, more worry than contentment, we're probably in need of emotional healing. This type of healing used to be the sole province of a minister, rabbi, priest, or psychiatrist. Today, a vast array of energy-healing therapies is available to us, as well as myriad trained counselors and practitioners skilled in helping people release their old pains and repair old wounds.

We didn't accumulate our painful attitudes and beliefs overnight, and we don't transform them overnight. The process of healing and developing a positive attitude is just that, a process. It's exciting and beneficial, and sometimes it takes our full attention, but at other times we coast along, reaping the benefits of the work we've already done. The enormous opportunity and gift we give ourselves is to find out how we're put together and what part our thinking and feeling play in our overall well-being. Finding out about ourselves and giving ourselves permission to delve into our inner lives is the place to start.

Whether we're versed in emotional and spiritual exploration or not, whether our careers involve helping people or not, we are human and have a human need to talk about our emotional dilemmas. Talking to others helps us find our direction, especially when we talk to a sensitive friend or to a professional who has the emotional and spiritual makeup that fits with ours. We have many people to choose from, but for our healing, it's extremely important to exercise our inner authority by choosing friends and counselors who respect our feelings and opinions.

A valuable and accurate way to understand the emotional debris that experience dumps in our energy fields, blocking the free flow of energy in our bodies, is to sketch the bowls for each Chakra. Our drawings tell us how burdened our energy fields are, what old experiences have limited our lives, who we blame, and what we can do to change this picture. As we perform the Mending Your Bowl practice, we learn what we can do to release the emotional toxicities that slow down our energy flows.

We are the ultimate experts on ourselves. While medical professionals can order important tests and procedures that indicate our level of functional health, we are the ones who must take in what is offered and make it our own. We are the experts on our lives because we have a lifelong perspective. We have known ourselves since the cradle, and we are aware of experiences and feelings that we've never shared with anyone. Emotionally, healing is deciding that we can trust our choices, realizing that we all make mistakes and sometimes fail at what we've tried. For many of us, trusting ourselves is a radical departure, but it's a vital step in emotional healing and personal empowerment.

■ *Spiritual Healing*

The most natural and least-understood aspect of healing is spiritual or sacred healing. With physical and emotional healing, we experience pain and know we need to take action. We look for a direct connection between the problem we're experiencing and the remedy, treatment, or therapy. Spiritual pain, however, is neither obvious nor short-term. There is no direct link between our feelings of disconnection from the Source and an answer or solution that offers relief. Relief from this pain comes moment-by-moment and day-by-day, as we choose to explore the Great Mystery. The search itself is our healing.

Because we are spiritual creatures, we come into this life with a yearning to know God. We enter and are abruptly detached from the obvious connection to spirit that is our lifeline. We have no explanation for this, except to learn, through trial and error, what brings us lasting joy and satisfaction. We may spend many years looking for relief from our inner uneasiness with God or our lack of satisfaction in religion. We may want a more personal relationship with The Creator, or we may want a relationship that is based in the magnificence of the natural world or in connection to the Global Family.

In our spiritual quest, we're drawn this way and that, looking for a belief system that feels right to us. This process of searching is the actual healing experience. From the moment we ask our first question about the quality of life, we're on a Sacred Path. Gradually, we move from assuming that spiritual healing means arriving at a destination to accepting that it is the sacred process of questioning, learning, reacting, absorbing, and accepting our evolving beliefs and faith. We move from wanting to think our way into a spiritual belief system to allowing the sacred process to infuse us with the spiritual qualities of our experiences. Sacred healing comes from wanting to know what you're doing on the Earth, how best to use your time, and the obligations and pleasures of sharing with others. Sacred questions lead to sacred answers. The process of sacred healing is available to each of us.

Healing at a spiritual level is learning to love. The more we love, the less self-conscious and afraid we are of failing. The more we love, the happier and more satisfied we become with our efforts each day. The more we love, the more connected we are with our inner lives and the lives of others. The more we love, the better we know that God is the essence that generates the goodness we reap so much benefit from, and that loving is the name and the face of The Almighty.

The Momentum of Healing

One of the most difficult ideas to accept is that we are all one—all kin at an energy level, and we are continually influencing and being influenced by every manner of life. I describe this oneness factor of interconnection to my students by relating it to the telephone. We can pick up our phones and dial a number to reach anyone we know. This is similar to what a trained intuitive healer does to "dial up the energy" of a person, using the person's full name and address. The one caveat is that an intuitive healer must be invited to do an evaluation before proceeding.

I used this process when I suggested to Sadie's mother that I would "check out" her daughter's health. The more experience you have as an intuitive healer, the quicker you can make this connection. This is also the way prayer works. If the communication between you and another person is charged with love, healing thoughts, and favorable intentions, not only will the person on the receiving end be helped, but so will the sender. As the Voice of Love taught me after my daughter Melanie's healing, "Whenever you lay your hands on another person lovingly, in actuality or in thought, a healing occurs on the appropriate level."

The converse is true as well. When you're thinking angry and judgmental thoughts about someone, that person is affected by these negative vibrations, and so are you. If we send peace and healing thoughts for understanding and acceptance, these "vibrations" are felt on a conscious level by people who are receptive, and they are felt unconsciously by people who are preoccupied with other thoughts.

Larry Dossey, M.D., the well-known physician and author, speaks to this idea of energy connectivity in his book, *Reinventing Medicine*. In it, he cites research in which people as well as inanimate matter are shown to be influenced significantly by the thoughts and feelings of others. The understanding that all life is interconnected is the basis of Era III Medicine, a new medical model now emerging in the West.

Healing has more to do with what we don't see than what we do. Feelings, beliefs, attitudes toward ourselves and others, and belief in a Higher Power are all-important contributing factors in our healing. There is no single way to heal, no "one size fits all" remedy. We read about a healing remedy or regimen that works for one person, so we rush to buy the product, and we're disappointed when it doesn't work for us.

Whatever we select as our personal healing or empowerment program needs to fit our likes and dislikes, our points of power, vulnerabilities, fears, and struggles. Dr. Bernie Siegel, one of the medical pioneers of mind/body/spirit healing, has commented on what makes the difference between a person who heals and those who don't. In his book, *Love, Medicine and Miracles*, he calls people who heal from a life-threatening illness "exceptional patients." They hear their diagnosis, but they don't surrender to the illness. Illness is an imbalance, and balance is always possible.

When people ask me whether they are going to heal from a health problem, I tell them, "Make today as meaningful and as filled with love as possible. If today is good, it's likely that, not only will you have a tomorrow, it will be just as healing. Today is what we have to work with; it's the only thing we have. Healing isn't for the future, it's for today, this moment, and what we do with it."

■ *Healing from the Inside Out*

We get sick from the outside in, but we heal from the inside out. Getting sick, depressed, or falling out of joy happens because of the way we respond to people and events in our lives. Unhappiness in our lives causes imbalances in our bodies. We heal from the soul level out by changing our attitudes and beliefs, then changing in our physical bodies, and finally changing in relationship to people and circumstances around us.

We think that medicine in a pill can heal the body. It can influence the molecular workings of the body and possibly relieve pain in the short term, but it is of limited value in changing our unbalanced and mis-aligned thinking and feeling.

For lasting healing to occur, we must be at peace in our lives. When we think that we're unhappy in a relationship but that being alone would be worse, or a hated job is needed for the benefits, we're kidding our-selves. Our bodies and souls care nothing about perks; they care only about peace of mind. Our bodies require nourishment to perform their tasks of keeping us healthy. It's not our bodies that should go to the doc-tor's office when something's wrong, it's our minds, because that is where most imbalances start.

The Quantum Leap to Health

Health is a dynamic, continually-shifting state of well-being. We don't "get healthy" physically, emotionally, and spiritually, and stay in this good place forever. Each morning we wake up brand new, with a new outlook, new opportunities, new ideas, and new resources. We need not carry over the problems of yesterday into today. What wasn't resolved yesterday could fall into place today.

Healing requires us to pay attention and adjust to the shifting condi-tions in our environment. We are all healing every day of our lives. Healing doesn't necessarily mean we're recovering from being sick, it means we're adapting, finding a better sense of balance in response to the outer world. By following our intuition, we can work on our relation-ships one day while concentrating on something else on another day—for example, our diets, or our exercise programs. The body lets us know when we've got a problem by causing us to feel pain. Our minds tell us we need to pay attention when we feel stressed. Our emotions tell us to "listen up" when we're fearful, and our spirits get our attention when we feel unloved.

When we get sick, especially with a serious illness, it's tempting to think we've caused our own illness. Don't believe it. We are works in progress. When our bodies are struggling, they are telling us to reevaluate our priorities, to look more closely at our feelings, and—most significantly—to ask for the grace of Divine Love that is always available to us. Sometimes, because of the complexity of our lives, we forget to breathe in the joy and abundance that is there for us.

We can, at any time, make the choice to be happy, even when our bodies are showing us they are sick. When we get sick, we may feel that we're being punished for past mistakes, or that we're taking on an illness in order to save our children from pain or a mishap. Everything I've learned about healing and the powerful flow of healing love that moves through us tells me that we are forgiven over and over again. We must forgive ourselves and realize that we are not serving God or our lives by wasting them living in the past.

Guilt about the past, and shame over behaving in a way that is contrary to who we are, give us room to grow our spirit with new behavior and more worthy ways to love. It is always time to review the past, but sometimes we need to get on with life and stop fighting our old emotions and pains. Moving forward with good, honest intentions for ourselves and others always produces positive results.

One negative thought does not damage our bodies. We have the choice to "keep" a thought or "dismiss" it. We all have initial reactions to people and situations that are judgmental. We can choose to accept the thought and swallow it, so that it appears in our energy fields, or we can dismiss it, not taking it in. It is the repeated, negative emotional patterns that cause us problems because we've been leaning on these angers, miseries, and dis-empowered beliefs for years.

■ *Ignition in Healing Comes from Universal Electricity*

God reaches His or Her hand out to us in a gesture of help and healing. But for healing to take place, we must reach out to touch God's hand, too. While this is a beautiful thought, we may wonder what it means for our healing and empowerment. Just how can we touch God's hand?

There is a healing arc connecting our souls, our bodies, and our minds. This healing arc, which is symbolically like a rainbow, connects our spirits with our physical bodies and our thinking with our feeling mechanisms. Because we are made of energy, we are able both to receive and to transmit the energy of Divine Love. When we focus the universal flow of Divine Love toward helping others heal, using practices like Loving Touch, we can see healing happen, sometimes in miraculous ways. When we open our hearts to loving more fully, we ignite the arc of healing.

In order to create the right energy environment for manifesting a healing arc, we need to generate harmonious movement in our energy fields. The more positive movement we create at a physical, intellectual/emotional, spiritual, and life-style level, the greater the likelihood of experiencing "quantum healing." Positive movement results from taking an active part in our healing, adjusting our thinking, healing past pains, eating and living more consciously, and experiencing our authentic selves. These actions create positive energy flows within the body's energy field.

When enough energy has been generated, our entire selves settle into a dynamic inner rhythm. When that inner rhythm reaches a peak level, it crosses a threshold, and we are "ignited" for total healing. This personal threshold is unique to each of us and is spiritual in nature, based on past karma and many other specifics of our spiritual destiny that only The Creator knows.

Ignition is a spiritual "rush" that sets up "healing" by filling every corner of our bodies with the energy of Divine Love. Enlightenment and total healing are the same, although while enlightenment can be momentary, healing is meant to be lasting. The ignition of the arc of healing is what is called a miracle healing.

■ *Ways We Heal*

Healing occurs in three ways: immediately, over an extended period of time, and when we cross the veil to spirit.

Immediate healing is what we think of as miraculous cures that result from encounters with living saints, touching holy relics, or by Divine Grace in answer to our prayers. It is spontaneous and instantaneous.

Healing over an extended period of time is the recovery that is most familiar to us. We heal over time because it takes time to make the many adjustments necessary for our bodies to be restored to health. Total health requires personal and life-style changes that take time, not only time to be put in place but also time to become established as habitual behavior. When we have no time for quiet contemplation or meditation, feel rushed and numb with tiredness yet continue to work at our desks, and we resist addressing the painful issues that rub us and our partners, we need time and guidance that help us to get geared up for total healing.

Healing requires us to take charge of our lives and become responsible in new ways: as spirits that desire to grow in love. For us to achieve lasting physical healing, all the parts of our lives must come together in an inner rhythm of love.

Several of the stories in *Wisdom Bowls* deal with people who have healed but died, which is the third level of healing. How is it possible to heal but die? Extended healing often takes us past the boundaries of our physical lifetimes because the body can't always make the necessary changes in time to remain in physical life. Remember, we begin to heal at the spiritual level first; then we must find the courage and tenacity to change the way we look at our life experiences; and finally, we begin to cast off the emotional and physical toxicities resulting from years of poor health and self-defeating thought patterns that have triggered the onset of the illness. By the time some people find themselves ready for physical healing, the illness may be a runaway condition that has gone too far for it to be healed in this life.

A person dying of cancer can experience healing, as we've seen in both Johanna's and Joan's lives, but in their cases, the physical body was unable to make all the changes necessary for keeping them alive. Although we all want to remain alive, our deaths don't mean that healing has failed. Healing continues across the line of physical life and death, once a person begins to take action spiritually, emotionally, and physically. In Joan's case, the three black horsemen who frightened her in physical life became her teachers after death, helping her overcome her fear of the unknown. The veil that separates life and death is apparent to us only in life. The spirit continues to expand and learn to love right through the death experience, without a pause in the action. Spiritual growth is continual, on and on forever.

The Power of Practice

Of all the many ideas and stories we've shared in *Wisdom Bowls*, one of the most important parts of each chapter is the practice. Each practice is designed for the optimum functioning of the Chakra or energy bowl discussed. Let's look more closely at these practices and what they mean for your health, spiritual growth, and well-being.

■ *Prayer*

Praying is a form of healing because it connects our inner light with the brilliance of the Divine Light. It is a pause in our daily busy-ness in order to receive Grace. We may pray for spiritual insight, the ability to love better, or to be persistent in our intention to share. We pray for emotional stability, asking to remain steady in light of challenges that we fear will sweep us under, to resist temptations or addictive relationships that we know aren't good for us. We pray for physical health and rejuvenation for our bodies, for lives that are purposeful and contribute to the greater good. We can pray for the resources to calm our worries and provide for those we love and others in need.

We pray because we are meant to continually touch the source of our Light. In so doing, we are replenished. Praying is talking to God, while meditating is listening.

■ Meditation

Meditation is the time-honored means of furthering spiritual growth. Meditation is difficult because we have over-active minds that want us to listen to them. Our minds play the role of the "parent" in our trilogy of child, parent, and adult. Our authentic selves are the adults, able to mediate between the child (our emotional needs) and the parent (our ever-vigilant thinking). When our "child" is telling us that we would rather sit on the couch and drink coffee than meditate, our "parent" chimes in with how little we're accomplishing and that we could find a better way to use our time. But meditation does strengthen our "adult" through perseverance. When we make the decision to meditate for a few minutes to a half hour daily, we develop spiritual discipline—the ability to direct our spirits to take charge of our minds. Spiritual discipline is what we call on to keep us from phoning the friend or lover whom we know is poison for us, or from reaching for the bag of cookies we crave because we're depressed, or from pouring the third glass of wine to drown our loneliness. The ability to choose how we will direct our thinking and our attention is one of the major benefits of choosing to meditate.

Meditating isn't a decision we make every morning. It's a practice. We show up whether we're tired or sick, rushed or unhappy. We show up and learn we have within us something that we can trust that is available when we need positive reinforcement.

There are many ways to meditate. But all of them center around quieting our thinking to allow us to focus our attention, intention, and loving energy on a single item, phrase, or spot. It doesn't matter if our minds wander; we can continue to bring them back to center, to the still point. We are learning to be fully present in the moment, by not thinking about what happened yesterday or what's coming up tomorrow. The point of meditation is to create inner balance because it reminds us that this is also the point of life.

■ Breath Awareness

Breathing is so natural that we forget its ability to calm and center us. Normal breathing brings oxygen to our blood and our cells while removing cellular debris and carbon dioxide. Breathing more deeply has the additional benefit of calming our minds as we exchange worry and stress for peacefulness and joy. When we remember to take several deep breaths throughout the day, while putting our hands over our heart centers, we see our daily tasks in better perspective.

Breath awareness can be used either as part of a meditation practice, while enjoying a Nature Space experience, or by itself as punctuation throughout the day, to remind us of what we're really trying to accomplish: overcoming fear and coming home to our authentic selves.

■ Loving Touch ™

Loving Touch is powerful medicine. It's the medicine of love that can be used under every circumstance and by every one of us for ourselves and the others we love. I've talked about Loving Touch in two stories in this book, my experience with my daughter Melanie and Anna's experience with her daughter Sadie. These stories demonstrate the miraculous healing power of Divine Love. Loving Touch requires nothing more than our intention to love. We can place our hands on someone, or put our hands on a picture of a person or place in the world that needs our loving attention. We can use Loving Touch with someone who needs love but wouldn't be comfortable being touched, by imagining that we're performing Loving Touch on them, and it will have similar benefits. Loving Touch is a spiritual aspirin—an action prayer—meant to stir love in someone's heart as well as in our own.

When working on friends or clients with Loving Touch, have them place their own hands, palms down, across their heart centers. Place your hands over theirs. This preserves people's privacy and also adds their intention to the healing experience.

■ *Movement with Intention*

Movement with Intention applies not only to jogging, walking, yoga, or a trip to the gym; it can be applied to any conscious movement at work or at home. The idea is to bring our personal intention to feel and act with genuine empowerment in every activity that requires us to get up and move, even for just a few steps. When at home, as we walk up the steps to put the laundry away or make the beds, we can do so with the intention that we're bringing happiness to others and thus to ourselves. Simple duties train our minds to find the benefit of doing everyday things that make our lives with others more enjoyable. When we walk into a board meeting, we can walk in with the intention that we'll be steady, powerful, and appreciative of others' efforts. When the baby cries or an older parent needs help, we can practice movement with intention as we walk with them up and down the living room or around a courtyard, feeling our power as compassion. Every time we move, we do so with the intention of holding power that is perfect for the situation in which we find ourselves at this present moment.

■ *Creative Expression*

Creative expression means giving ourselves the opportunity to experience our own designs without the limitations of other people's opinions and restraints. Rarely do we take the time to do something just for ourselves, with total abandon and with no constraints on our way of doing it. No rules or regulations need apply, and there is no one to please, including our inner critics. The point is to liberate our spirits with free-flowing energy that arises from doing something that steadies and calms us.

Creative expression as self-expression brings unlimited joy and fulfillment to our lives. For a short time, we lift the restrictions we're living under, restrictions that we've forgotten. We abandon the "right way" or the "correct way" to do something and just enjoy the process of giving ourselves totally to the experience.

Acts of creative expression can include anything that opens us up to see and enjoy things differently. Creating a Nature Space might mean putting several special leaves together with a pinecone and putting them on a desk or windowsill. Or it can be simply enjoying the way the wind whips through the trees and imagining that we're flying a kite higher and higher. Drawing or painting, composing music, singing, writing, or dancing according to our own special rhythm—no holds are barred.

Self-expression means shifting from mentally expressing what we think to emotionally and spiritually expressing what we feel, an experience that brings us into rhythm with our unique inner vitality. We need opportunities in life to escape the confinements of everyday chores and to fly free. When we give ourselves the opportunity to create, we feel less stressed, breathe more fully, think more positively, and generally find greater motivation to pursue our dreams.

■ Selfless Service to Others

Service to others means that we are willing to share. It doesn't mean that we have to be saints or entirely selfless people. It means we have a part of us that isn't solely self-focused; we can peek out over the edge of our full lives to care about others. Service is an opportunity to grow our capacity to love. And because love is the energy of life, the more we love, the stronger, healthier, and happier we are. Loving others doesn't mean they will love us. Sharing with others doesn't mean they will share with us. We're sharing because it's important to us. There is no explanation for the charge we feel when we share with others. We have to try it to believe how wonderful it makes us feel. Sharing small things can make a difference to someone. Sharing doesn't mean depleting your resources; quite the contrary. Sharing creates abundance to meet your needs, with resources left over to assist others.

Sharing with others is like owning a goose that lays golden eggs. The golden eggs are the little things we do to make life better around us. The goose, the source of love and joy, is our own heart and its ability to generate Grace.

■ *Keeping the Energy Moving*

Create a plan that shows how you will manage to do each of the daily seven practices. Plan around your usual schedule so you can determine how, what, and when you will perform each practice. Otherwise, days can fly past, and even with the best intentions you may never get to the practices that can change your life in the ways you most desire. While we're all short on time, we do find the time for what we prioritize as essential to our health and to our mental and spiritual well-being. By combining some practices, you can easily cover them all in a day.

What counts isn't the length of time we spend doing a practice but the quality of the time spent. When you hold an intention to be successful, the practices can become a way of life. The benefits will be visible right away in feeling centered, renewed, and in touch with our inner, sacred selves. If we're recovering from an illness, we'll see significant progress in our healing.

The results will be proportional to our willingness to show up. Slow and steady is the pace we want, rather than sprinting with new commitments that are impossible to keep. The only reason we're performing the practices is that they serve our health and happiness. Our lives may feel out of control, but the ways we choose to spend our time are up to us.

Recovering Our Authentic Selves

"You already are authentic; the challenge is to feel that you are." The room was quiet. Fifty men and women sat in front of me, waiting for the much-anticipated beginning of the year-long training in Intuitive Perception and Energy Diagnosis at the Stillpoint School of Advanced Energy Healing.

As I looked around the room, I thought of conversations I'd had with many of them. In front of me were men and women who were healers, accountants, physicians, nurses, therapists, social workers, carpenters, artists, interior decorators, investment bankers, and moms and dads. What we shared was a yearning to heal our lives. My students came to School to learn how to become intuitive healers but also wanting to understand themselves and their lives better. We all wanted to renew ourselves and make peace with our failings, fears, and negative attitudes, to find the sacred within us, and to locate a spiritual community with whom to share experiences on the journey. We needed to understand the nature of our relationship with The Creator, both as the energy of the Universe and as a personal friend and mentor to whom we could turn for guidance, comfort, and unconditional love. When these men and women started the year, like most of us, they felt inauthentic and burdened by fears and anxieties. By year's end, they saw the truth—that they were genuine reflections of God's love, and many of their fears had dissolved.

All of our success in the world and our progress on a spiritual path comes from learning to maximize the insights we receive from our authentic selves. Sensing a divine guiding hand is the way we look past our old emotional blocks, even though they come from real problems that we've actually experienced. We learn that our lives aren't made up of what we know through our intellect but of the love and compassion we experience in our hearts.

Working with people over the last twenty years has taught me a great deal about myself and others, including how we can accept ourselves and the circumstances of our lives. Acceptance gives us power and courage to stay steady and strong instead of shifting the blame to others and losing the will to make our own choices. Often, we don't understand why things happen in our lives. But we don't need to understand *why* if we consider *what*; what will I do now? Or: how can I respond to this scenario?

Life is a difficult journey. There is no way to change how our lives are put together. We know that we are born, we live, and we die. We know that we can't control these elements and that some of us are unhappy more than we are content. If we can't change the framework of our lives, how can we live out our years, getting the most from them? My answer is: by seeing our experiences as gateways to greater understanding and compassion.

The cracks in our Wisdom Bowls teach us about our courage and grace as much as our suffering and betrayals. When we remember only the misery and the pain, we stay locked in the past. But the reason we feel upset is not what we think it is. By finding the meaning of our negative experiences, we discover the ways we truly are authentic, thus freeing ourselves from the pains and sorrows of the past.

The End Becomes Our New Beginning

Coming to the end of *Wisdom Bowls* brings us to a new beginning. Nothing is set in stone. We know that many possibilities lie before us. No illness is absolutely terminal, no relationship is irrevocably doomed, no loss is forever, and no suffering needs to shroud our futures. We are The

Creator's charges—His/Her hands and feet here on Earth to experience and enjoy the sacred seeds of love He/She has planted in our hearts.

For me, this book has been a rebirth of greater confidence and commitment to the work of spreading love in the world. I hope it is a rebirth for you as well, as you face new possibilities for your life with renewed energy and determination. We have everything we need in order to live full, successful lives, assured that we are kin with all the life on Earth. Our circle of caring is large, embracing all people and all nations. Every creature and habitat is part of our web of life, and every effort we make to strengthen it, no matter how small, changes our future for the better.

The Earth and her children depend on each of us to be wise, to have vision, to speak in joy, to extend love and compassion, to own our power, to accept our true natures, and to allow others to share our bounty. If our capable hands and steady hearts shift ever so slightly in the direction of loving, we move the planet in an entirely new direction from where it has been in the past. If we each lean just a little toward love and understanding, what might our lives look like? What might our children grow up to believe? What suffering that we've borne through the years would we heal? Our futures rest in our ability to love each other enough to overcome our differences and reach out to one another in peace and understanding. Peace in our hearts will create peace on the planet. Fear is not in charge of our destiny; we, as our authentic selves, are the creators of the future we will pass along to those who walk in our footsteps.

The Voice of Love

And the Voice of Love arrived with a key.
What key is this? you ask in delight,
expecting great gifts for which you've prayed.
This key is special—given to those who ask the right questions:
how to be kinder to those who can't see,
how to be stronger with those who can't walk,
how to be happy for those who find no delight in each passing day.
"You see," said the angel, "most people
forget where to look to see God's Light,
or how to walk with kindness and care,
leaving soft footprints in morning's fresh dew.
This key is magic, guaranteed to work,
bringing you the greatest treasure of all: awakened love in every heart!
Use it with friends near and far,
ones who are brown and black, white, yellow, and red,
ones who fly and crawl and walk here and there.
Use it well, and with faith abiding,
all life will respond as never before.
I'll be back…
but make haste for now, no time to tarry.
Use your key in each human heart,
and as you do, you'll find the truth
that only through Grace and joy abiding
does life go on and Love prevail.

— Meredith Young-Sowers

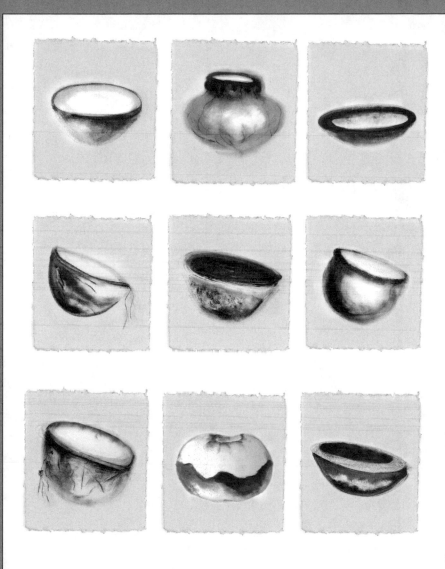

MENDING YOUR BOWL

MENDING YOUR BOWL—
HEALING YOUR LIFE

A Step-by-Step Process

1 **CREATE A PICTURE** *of an imaginary bowl in your mind. Each bowl represents one of the seven aspects of your authentic self:* Wisdom, Vision, Joy, Love, Power, Intimacy, *or* Abundance. *You'll be instructed later as to which bowl to draw and when.*

Your bowl will have its own specific texture, color or combination of colors, and a definite shape. It can be made of, for example, wood, plaster, porcelain, crystal, gold, silver, cloth, paper, or metal. You are the creator in this process, and there is no right or wrong way to imagine your bowl. However you picture this bowl will have special meaning for you. You'll notice how clearly you can view your bowl, and whether the bowl is resting on a table or other surface.

You'll want to take note of the particulars of your bowl without trying to change them. Use the first images that come to you. These images need not be the same every time you perform this practice even for the same bowl.

2 **DISCOVER THE CRACKS,** *broken places, chips, or holes in your bowl.* **MAKE THE CONNECTION** *to the experiences or relationships that are the source of your suffering.*

You will find that you may already have sketched in one or more imperfections without realizing what you were drawing. If not, look again at your bowl and find where the broken places show up. Draw them so you're clearly aware of them. Other types of imperfections may emerge or be evident in the shape of your bowl.

Allow the image of your bowl to accurately reflect your situation. You're not trying to create a perfect bowl but to develop a clear understanding by letting the bowl "speak to you." Is it closed at the top, so that energy can't enter? Is your bowl too flat, so that energy can't stay in your bowl? Notice the color of your bowl. Dark, heavy colors may suggest dark, heavy feelings while pastels often suggest more positive ones. Are the sides of your bowl sloping or uneven in a way that suggest that the energy would have difficulty moving into and then out of this bowl? Be aware of how clearly you can see the bowl. Is there a fog around the bowl, for example, that makes viewing the bowl difficult? Is the bowl turned upside down or on its side? Observe where your bowl is sitting. Is it resting squarely on the surface, or is it wobbly?

Do not force your memories about past events. Instead, allow the experience that is the core event to come into your consciousness. You'll know when you find a relationship or event that seems significant. Use whatever experience feels right to you, whether or not you immediately see the connection to your healing desired positive changes. Your own true self knows what it is showing you to heal. You may find yourself working with a familiar issue, or you may be surprised at the nature of the sorrow that presents itself because you weren't aware how deeply you felt about this seemingly trivial event or exchange. Work with what comes to you most easily.

3 SPEAK THE TRUTH ABOUT YOUR LOSS, THE GRIEF *it has caused you, and the person you hold most directly responsible. Imagine him or her seated across from you.*

You have drawn your bowl and found the imperfections. You have identified the sorrow that accompanies the crack(s), hole(s), or imbalance(s). Now you are ready to heal your sorrow by engaging in a spirit-to-spirit dialogue with the person who played a key role in your suffering.

Special Help in Identifying Your Loss

LOSS: IDENTIFY WHAT YOU'VE LOST AND WHAT YOU NEEDED.

Have you, for example, lost a father or father figure or a mother or mother figure? Have you lost an opportunity for success? Have you been blamed for something that has haunted you and prevented you from getting on with your life?

What have I lost?

Write about the situation that is causing you pain and what you feel has been taken away from you or that you've lost. The issue might be your health, if you are seeking ways to heal a physical problem, or a loss of trust that you attribute to one or both of your parents or to one of your children. Perhaps the painful issue in your life is that you never found your passion, got your work off the ground, or developed a close personal relationship with God. Whatever is causing you pain qualifies. The point is that you want to get to the buried causes of your suffering that are still pulling your strings so you can see them and face them down, at last. You are ready to discover more about your authentic nature and to overcome the fear that is holding you back from knowing greater happiness and success in your life.

Whom do I blame and why?

Be clear about whom you blame. It doesn't matter that you've told yourself you shouldn't blame this person because he or she didn't know any better, didn't realize he or she had hurt you, or even that you were yourself at fault. Override the rationalization that you told yourself, and be real with your feelings. What you honestly feel is what is conveyed to your body and influences your health and the quality of your communications and interactions with others.

Tell the truth about what you feel. This is your feeling about the situation, so don't try to explain it away. Be real. When you face the feelings, you will dissipate their hold on you.

How upset, angry, resentful, filled with rage, or filled with remorse am I?

Let yourself experience the range of emotional reactions to your painful situation. Get in touch with the deep feelings that you hold. Write down below the full measure of your feelings.

_____

_____

_____

_____

_____

_____

_____

_____

Special Help in Learning to Grieve

GRIEF: IMAGINE THE PERSON YOU HOLD MOST DIRECTLY RESPONSIBLE FOR YOUR SORROW TO BE SEATED ACROSS FROM YOU.

This person may be alive or in spirit—it makes no difference. Tell him or her how you feel without holding back or dismissing the feelings you have. Allow yourself to acknowledge the tremendous loss, pain, or anger you feel. Do not judge your feelings or rationalize them away. Be honest with what you feel. *Choose a time and place to engage in this dialogue when you are alone in your room and feel free to make noise, cry, or shout.*

Some of us have little experience with grieving, either because we are afraid to express the depths of our sorrow or because we're not sure what feelings are appropriate to the situation. Of course, the answer is that all feelings are appropriate. If you have limited experience with grieving, you might want to consider how you feel about grieving before undertaking the Mending Your Bowl practice. Once you determine that it is okay for you to grieve in any way that is authentic for you, you will get more from the practice.

How do you grieve?

When you grieve, which of the following do you give yourself permission to do? (With those that you don't give yourself permission to feel, note why they are not okay for you.)

- ◆ Cry
- ◆ Get angry with the person you blame
- ◆ Get angry with yourself
- ◆ Take time off from work to do something for yourself
- ◆ Take time over a few months to be with your feelings of sadness
- ◆ Share your sadness with others
- ◆ Ask for support, comfort, love, and help from others
- ◆ Take your concerns and feelings into your quiet times for understanding
- ◆ Pray about the pain
- ◆ Take the pain seriously, knowing it is more of a guidepost than a statement of unworthiness

♦ Be kind to yourself when you feel you should get past the pain but seem unable to do so

♦ Try to see how the pain is guiding you to view life differently

Write about your way of grieving the pain of a deeply felt sorrow. When you have answered the questions (above) as honestly and thoughtfully as you can, go on to the next set of questions that reflect your "growing edges" of change.

Why am I afraid to acknowledge or let go of these feelings?

♦ What do I want to heal or successfully change right now in my life?

♦ What will need to be different about my life, once this change is successfully made?

♦ As I begin this change process, what relationship(s) will be affected most directly? Why?

♦ What do I anticipate to be the result of my working with this person around this issue?

♦ What can sabotage my effort to change in this specific way?

♦ Am I prepared to deal with the fallout from seeking to change and heal? Explain.

♦ What does life look like to me beyond this critical crossroad?

4 UNCOVER YOUR GRACE, *asking for loving feedback from that person's authentic self,* and FIND THE BLESSING IN THE CHALLENGE *by identifying the part of your authentic self that you are healing.*

Special Help in Identifying Grace and Your Blessing

GRACE: ALLOW YOURSELF TO LISTEN FROM YOUR HEART
TO THE OTHER PERSON'S HEART, TO HEAR THE WORDS AND THOUGHTS
THAT CAN MAKE YOU AND THE OTHER PERSON WHOLE.

What is the blessing in this challenge?

Imagine the person you blame sitting across from you.

From your real emotions, tell the person you imagine sitting across from you what you really feel. Be completely honest. Spare nothing. If it helps, place something—a photograph or a garment belonging to the person—in the chair you imagine him or her sitting in while talking with you.

Put your hand over your heart and find your own quiet center, the place of your authentic self.

From this place, ask the other person (in your mind or out loud) what he or she can tell you from his or her own sacred heart space.

Listen, don't judge, and write down what you hear.

Recognize that this spirit-to-spirit dialogue is a sacred process. The person you are conversing with, spirit to spirit, can only share love and forgiveness with you from his or her authentic self. The personality self is not present. Pause, breathe, and go deeper until you find the love that is there for you.

Identify the blessing you found in this challenge.

You will hear words of love and forgiveness. By putting your hand over your own heart, you will find the part of your authentic nature that was suppressed until now. Accept that brilliant jewel, that aspect of your true self that has emerged and made itself known to you. Remember, your authentic self has many facets, and they are all aspects of Divine Love. Your authentic self:

◆ Make wise choices.

◆ Shows you the vision for your life and helps you create it.

◆ Offers you joy in your closest relationships.

◆ Opens your heart to love and compassion for yourself and others.

◆ Grooms you to wield true power through your work/effort in the world.

◆ Provides you a genuine picture of yourself that allows you to choose a lasting and enduring partnership and friendships.

◆ Gives you the heart to create abundance for yourself as you serve others.

By doing this practice, you may find the part of yourself that you had disowned but are now willing to let shine in your life. You may have felt heavily criticized as a child, and that has remained your challenge. Your blessing may be the decision to feel worthy of trusting yourself, making your own choices, and looking inside rather than to other people for approval.

Another example of a challenge is having always felt invisible to others, passed over, and never taken seriously. The blessing could be welcoming home your willingness to approve of yourself even when you make mistakes, knowing that the only way to live is through learning.

What are the qualities of my own authentic self that I now accept and will use and express each day? **Write these down in bold letters.**

5 MEND YOUR BOWL, *transforming the cracks and flaws in your bowl into brilliant emblems of your courage, inner power, and healing.*

You will be ready now to mend the imperfections in the bowl image you created previously. There is no one right way to mend your bowl. You may want to fill cracks or holes with gold to help you feel the victor over old wounds. You may want to erase the cracks leaving only faint lifelines, reminding yourself that future nourishment can come from past pain. You may want to re-shape a pottery bowl, file down the sharp, jagged edges from a crystal bowl, or sew more material to the lip of a fabric bowl so it has a strong enough rim to hold ample energy. It doesn't matter what you do as long as you mend your bowl in a way that feels right to you.

6 HEAL YOUR LIFE, *every time the familiar pain returns, remembering to reaffirm the aspect of your genuine and authentic self that you've found and invited home to your heart.*

As you complete this healing process, realize you may have to perform some version of these six steps over and over again, often for the same issue. Be patient; you lived with this pain for many years, and you'll need time and effort to move in your new direction. But know that this process of Mending Your Bowl and Healing Your Life creates a genuine and lasting healing, because instead of remembering the sorrow every time the old pattern is triggered, now you can remember what you learned about its cause and the part of yourself that you have reaffirmed.

Every time you return to one of your bowl images in your prayers, meditations, or quiet times, affirm your mended bowl and the blessing that you've accepted and now welcome home. The more you reinforce the healing instead of the original pain, the more smoothly your healing will proceed.

Each imperfection in your bowl shows you that life is a series of struggles that either destroy your joy and zest for living or awaken a deeper understanding, a more compassionate heart, a stronger sense of conviction, and a truer desire to serve the needs of others. Each sorrow, rather than being a mark of failure, represents a tribute to your success. You will slowly, over many years—for this is a lifetime journey—put the pieces of your true self together and see who you are: nothing short of an Embodiment of Love. All manner of joy and success follow such a discovery.

ACKNOWLEDGMENTS

WISDOM BOWLS REPRESENTS A JOURNEY of more than twenty years. Many, many men and women have shared their healing journeys with me, both as friends and as clients. I'm grateful for their confidence and insights, which have shaped my understanding and appreciation of the quality of the human spirit and the courage to heal.

I value many special people for their contribution to *Wisdom Bowls*:

Caroline Myss, long-time friend and sister, for her outrageous sense of humor and tender heart in writing the Introduction and offering her loving support.

Luise Light, editor extraordinaire, whose tenacity and dedication, not to mention her brilliance, has brought this book to life. Her insight and support have given *Wisdom Bowls* the masterly touches that it needed. I thank her from the bottom of my heart.

Dorothy Seymour Mills, a long-time friend and sister author, who has stood by me over the years as my trusted editor, and who, twenty years ago, began to teach me how to write.

Eileen Woolbert, my wonderful personal assistant and friend, whose quiet quality of spirit, tireless efforts, and ability added essential components to our editorial team. Her "eye" for the right shot also resulted in the glorious image of the bowl on the cover.

Patti Lucia, whose warmth and friendship over the years has meant a great deal. Her willingness to help in a million ways lets Stillpoint touch many people's lives. She even gave the last chapter a hearty "thumbs up."

Kathryn Sky-Peck, whose artistry, skillful design, and loving heart crafted a book that is lovely beyond words.

Cameron Sesto, whose beautiful, original charcoal drawings are the inspiration for others to sketch their own wisdom bowls.

Patricia Garvey, Associate Director of the Stillpoint School, whose amazing enthusiasm and love helped me through the times when I wasn't sure I'd ever get to the finish line.

All my students and graduates of the Stillpoint School who teach me each day.

Peg O'Donnell, whose friendship and support, both in presenting this book to our sales team and leading the charge for its sale into bookstores, is beyond anything I ever expected. I'm deeply grateful.

My wonderful family, especially my husband Errol, whose loving support has been an essential component in making this book a reality.

Finally, *Wisdom Bowls* belongs to the inspiration, courage, and dedication of God's love in my heart and mind, day after day, as I sat to write this book. Both the Voice of Love that I've heard since the beginning and my beloved Sai Baba, who has shown me my life, together give this work the power and heart it needs to make a difference in the world.

INDEX

Meredith Young-Sowers

Co-founder of Stillpoint Publishing Company, director of The Stillpoint Institute, and founder/director of the Stillpoint School of Advanced Energy Healing, Meredith Young-Sowers has been teaching, counseling, and performing deep, intuitive healing work for more than two decades. A pioneer in the development of "energy diagnosis" methods, she lectures, offers workshops, and gives teleclasses to audiences around the world. Her work is a new path to healing that brings greater love, joy, and peace to people's lives. Considered a significant breakthrough in the emerging field of energy medicine, her work centers on seven spiritual qualities that can be sensed in the body and amplified to aid healing and restore balance to body, mind, and spirit, using techniques and principles taught at the Stillpoint School.

She is the author of several best-selling books, including *Agartha* and the *Angelic Messenger Cards.* An alumna and a recipient of a distinguished graduate award from Centenary College for Women, Meredith holds both a Master's and a Doctor of Divinity degree from Universal Brotherhood University. Meredith and her husband live in rural New Hampshire.

For more information about Meredith, go to *www.stillpoint.org* or *www.wisdombowls.com.*

Cameron Sesto, Artist

Cameron Sesto, artist, author, and teacher, illuminates the spiritual nature of the mundane world through her drawings and paintings. Sesto's interest in meditation and visual expression evolved over the last 14 years as a result of teaching workshops called "Drawing into Creative Wholeness." Her book, *One End Open,* is a compilation of paintings and prose/poetry developed using the process she teaches. Sample pages of the book, paintings, and prints can be seen on her web site: *www.cameronart.com*. Cameron and her artist husband live near the ocean in Massachusetts.

The Stillpoint Institute
22 Stillpoint Lane, PO Box 640
Dept. WB
Walpole, New Hampshire 03608

The Stillpoint Institute
22 Stillpoint Lane, PO Box 640
Dept. WB
Walpole, New Hampshire 03608

Meredith Young-Sowers
Invites You to Create Wellness in Your Life!

Learn how to heal everyday health problems
with simple practices that re-program Mind, Body, and Spirit.

Mail this card and we will send you **FREE**:
A highly valuable, bi-monthly e-newsletter* from Meredith, entitled:
Wisdom Bowls: The Emotional and Spiritual Issues Behind Common Illnesses.

E-mail Address* *(required)* _____

Name _____

Address _____

City _____ State _____ Zip _____

Telephone (day) _____ (evening) _____

For more information about Meredith Young-Sowers and the work of The Stillpoint Institute,
visit: www.stillpoint.org or www.wisdombowls.com   Or call 1-603-756-9281

Meredith Young-Sowers
Invites You to Create Wellness in Your Life!

Learn how to heal everyday health problems
with simple practices that re-program Mind, Body, and Spirit.

Mail this card and we will send you **FREE**:
A highly valuable, bi-monthly e-newsletter* from Meredith, entitled:
Wisdom Bowls: The Emotional and Spiritual Issues Behind Common Illnesses.

E-mail Address* *(required)* _____

Name _____

Address _____

City _____ State _____ Zip _____

Telephone (day) _____ (evening) _____

For more information about Meredith Young-Sowers and the work of The Stillpoint Institute,
visit: www.stillpoint.org or www.wisdombowls.com   Or call 1-603-756-9281